The Federal Social Dollar
in Its Own Back Yard

Contributors

Mark Arnold

Julius Duscha

Mary Lynn Kotz

Nick Kotz

Sar A. Levitan

Eugene L. Meyer

Barbara Raskin

David Swanston

Walterene Swanston

Eric Wentworth

The Federal Social Dollar
in Its Own Back Yard

Edited by
Sar A. Levitan

Center for Manpower Policy Studies
The George Washington University

THE BUREAU OF NATIONAL AFFAIRS, INC., WASHINGTON, D.C.

Illustrations by Robin Ulmer
Original maps by Joseph P. Mastrangelo
Charts by *The Hatchet*

This volume was prepared under a
grant from the Ford Foundation.

Printed in the United States of America
Library of Congress Catalog Card Number: 72-92352
International Standard Book Number: 0-87179-182-X

PREFACE

The rising costs of government—a central issue in the most recent national election—are receiving increasing attention. Mounting outlays, and the growing tax burden they occasion, have been widely condemned for infringing on individual liberties.

There is, however, another side to government expenditures, for these taxes are collected from some citizens to benefit themselves and others. Yet the benefits of government operation have received remarkably little attention. It is the squeaking wheel that gets the oil: those who pay taxes and do most of the complaining get the attention, while little is heard, except the usual demand for more, from those who benefit.

Conceptually, it should be possible to measure the costs of any government program and to compare them with the benefits derived. In practice, such measurements are nearly unattainable. The taxpayer is often not a beneficiary, and a calculus has not yet been devised to compare the costs to a millionaire taxpayer with the benefits that accrue from these taxes to a destitute mother on relief.

This volume attempts to appraise the impact of federal social outlays made to states and localities. Rejecting the goal of precise measurement of cost and benefits, the study has the more modest objective of drawing an impressionistic evaluation of federal social expenditures in a single locality, especially in terms of those who benefit from the program. Instead of relying upon rigid academic approaches, which frequently become obscurantist, the editor invited nine experienced journalists (including a husband-wife team who worked as one) to appraise the impact of the federal expenditures in Washington, D. C., in the area of their expertise. All have written widely on the subjects which are discussed in this volume, but most had emphasized national programs; in this case they focused their investigative talents on a single area.

The selection of Washington requires explanation. No claim is made that the District of Columbia is "typical"—which major city is? Nevertheless, the District has several unique properties. Congress doubles as the District's city council and state legislature and must approve the District's budget because the city lacks self-government. The federal government contributes roughly one sixth of the District's expenditures by a direct payment unavailable to other cities. As the nation's capital, Washington often serves as a "model city" in which federal grant-in-aid programs are demonstrated. With its concentration of federal employment and its massive influx of tourists, the District is also unique in its employment and business patterns. For all these reasons, Washington, D. C., is hardly comparable to other states and localities.

Nevertheless, it has significant advantages as a case study for assessing the impact of federal funding of social programs. The 1968 riots demonstrated to the nation that its capital was more than a governmental seat and an historical center: The burning buildings and mass chaos made it painfully clear that the District is a large central city with all the urban ills associated with size and population density. The District shares the pressing problems of other large cities: poverty, inadequate health care, transportation difficulties, unemployment, hunger, decaying housing, a deteriorating educational system, and high crime rates. Some problems, such as education and crime, are more severe in Washington than in other large cities. But whatever their relative severity, all of them put demands on the District's limited resources. Washington, even more than other central cities, has experienced a rapid suburbanization of middle-class and white families and a growth of the black and less affluent population. In 1960, 55 percent of the residents were nonwhite; by 1970 the proportion had increased to 72 percent. This is a higher ratio than for any other major city in the nation, but it represents a trend which many are reluctantly following. The desertion of the District by affluent white families leaves behind a citizenry which requires even more urban services but is less able to contribute to its own maintenance. Caught in this pinch of rising demands and a slowly increasing tax base, the District government has severe financial difficulties. Even the direct payment from the federal government has proved to be inadequate. Like other central cities, D. C. has turned to the grant-in-aid programs for relief. To receive them, it is required to follow the same guidelines and controls as other areas and is subject to at least the same oversight. Thus, despite its unique characteristics, Washington has the same general problems as other large cities; and it relies increasingly on federal grants-in-aid to alleviate its ills.

The city's singularities, however, make it a good basis for studying the impact of federal dollars at the local level. Congressional review of the budget generates a wealth of information about the District that is unavailable in other areas. Much of the rhetoric and confusion that obscure and distort program performance in other areas is not present in the District because of the close congressional scrutiny. The fact that District officials are close to the seat of power and deal on a day-to-day basis with their "aldermen" in the congressional appropriations subcommittees assures that the city participates actively in almost all federal programs. It is also selected as a testing ground or model for many federal efforts and has been more carefully studied than other areas. Finally, the city has no layer cake of state, county, and city governments; and its politics are low key. Though politics are becoming more important as the District gains greater self-determination, the focus of the city's leadership, which is appointed rather than elected, can be longer range since elections do not intrude.

For these reasons the District provides a good model for investigating the impact of federal grants-in-aid. As long as its unique characteristics are kept in mind, much can be learned from experience in the federal government's own backyard.

It should not be at all surprising that the observers did not arrive at a consensus about the impact of the federal social dollar in Washington. Some of the efforts are hindered by inadequate knowledge about their implementation or because techniques have not been designed to cope with the problems that prompted the programs. Other programs suffer from inadequate resources. Experiments designed to revamp elementary education have floundered because of a lack of clear goals and the difficulty of selling the program to the community. In contrast, aid to higher education suffers because the Administration and Congress have not committed adequate funds to meet the aspirations for higher education of Washington youths and young adults. Manpower programs have helped some enrollees, but many others have received little more than stipends. A case could be made that the greatly expanded funds to improve the health care of the poor have been dissipated, but experimentation with health delivery systems may bring greater returns in the future. Welfare payments remain low, but an increasing proportion of the population qualifies for assistance. As long as vast numbers continue to receive near-poverty wages, it is unreasonable to expect that society would provide welfare assistance which is more generous than potential earnings. The issue obviously is not work *or* welfare, but how to combine work and welfare in our society. The expanded food-stamp program helps the poor buy food, but it is not at all clear that the recipients would not be better off if they were to receive an equal amount in cash. Criticism of the Great Society's antipoverty programs has been rampant, but a closer examination of its legacy shows that the community organizations funded by the antipoverty efforts have strengthened the democratic institutions in the District of Columbia. Finally, the housing program adds a new dimension to the difficulties faced by social programs. Unlike health and education, housing programs face no technological obstacles in the delivery of shelter for the poor. Nonetheless, of the eight social programs examined in this volume, housing and urban renewal has met with the least success. The obstacle here is not a lack of technological development but the difficulty of getting people to live together. The result is that the shelter provided for the poor is more costly than that used by more affluent families, but the facilities remain dismally inadequate.

One might reach the quick judgment that the vast amounts expended on public services have not paid off. It is necessary, however, to bear in mind that the problems which gave rise to the newly expanded social programs have persisted over many generations. And it is too much to expect that the recent expansion of federal funding would quickly correct deep-rooted problems.

This volume has benefited from David Marwick's critical review and his many valuable suggestions to the contributors. Barbara Pease kept track of the contributions in their several draft stages and was responsible for putting the volume between two hard covers. Robert Taggart helped prepare the overview chapter. I am indebted to them and to the contributors for their patience and willingness to indulge the editor.

This volume was prepared under a grant from The Ford Foundation to The George Washington University's Center for Manpower Policy Studies. In accordance with the Foundation's practice, complete responsibility for the preparation of the volume has been left to the editor and the contributors.

SAR A. LEVITAN

Independence Day, 1972

LIST OF CONTRIBUTORS

MARK ARNOLD is congressional correspondent for *The National Observer.*

JULIUS DUSCHA, director of the Washington Journalism Center, is author of *Taxpayers' Hayride: The Farm Problem From the New Deal to the Billy Sol Estes Case* (Little Brown, 1964) and *Arms, Money, and Politics* (Ives Washburn—David McKay, 1965).

MARY LYNN KOTZ is a freelance writer and is preparing a book on the White House.

NICK KOTZ, a national correspondent for *The Washington Post,* is author of *Let Them Eat Promises: The Policies of Hunger in America* (Prentice Hall, 1969; Doubleday Anchor Books, 1971).

SAR A. LEVITAN is research professor of Economics and director of the Center for Manpower Policy Studies of The George Washington University.

EUGENE L. MEYER is a reporter for *The Washington Post.*

BARBARA RASKIN has contributed articles to many periodicals. Her first novel will be published in January by Bantam Books.

DAVID SWANSTON, a former newspaperman, established and directs the public information service for the Public Broadcasting System.

WALTERENE SWANSTON, a former television and newspaper reporter, is now a freelance writer.

ERIC WENTWORTH is an education writer for *The Washington Post.*

CONTENTS

TABLES

CHARTS

The Federal Social Dollar
in Its Own Back Yard

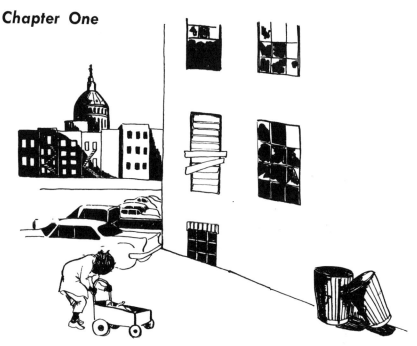

Chapter One

THE ART OF GIVING AWAY
FEDERAL DOLLARS

by Sar A. Levitan

EXPANDING FEDERAL LARGESSE TO STATE AND
LOCAL GOVERNMENTS

The massive social legislation of the 1960s accelerated the trend towards more centralized government. Though the growth of state and local expenditures more than matched that at the national level over the last decade, an ever-increasing share was provided by grants-in-aid from the federal government. In 1960, $6.8 billion was distributed by the federal government, and this accounted for 13.5 percent of state and local general revenues. Federal contributions to state and local governments accelerated as a result of Great Society legislation, and the increases continued under the Nixon Administration (Chart 1). By fiscal 1972 such assistance had expanded to $39 billion and accounted for more than a fourth of all state and local revenue. The Emergency Employment Act

CHART 1: FEDERAL AID ACCOUNTS FOR NEARLY ONE THIRD OF STATE AND
          LOCAL GOVERNMENT EXPENDITURES

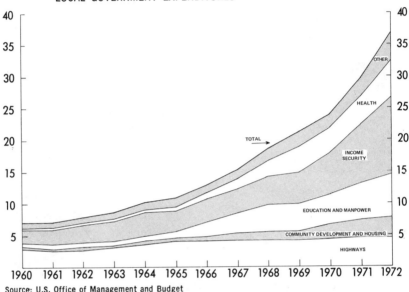

Source: U.S. Office of Management and Budget

of 1971 was the latest major addition to grants-in-aid, adding
more than $1 billion to the total on a "temporary" two-year basis;
but proposals soon abounded to extend this legislation. President
Nixon urged Congress to raise the federal contribution by another
$5.3 billion a year upon enactment of his revenue-sharing plan.

Grants-in-aid finance a vast array of state and local services.
Public assistance and other income maintenance programs (not
including government pensions and payments made to veterans)
account for roughly a fourth of grants-in-aid; and federal outlays
for welfare assistance would have expanded by another $5 billion or
more if Congress had adopted President Nixon's welfare reform
plan. Stimulated by the Great Society's social programs, grants-in-
aid in the community development, housing, education, manpower,
and health fields increased from $2.3 billion in 1965 to $15.7
billion in 1972.

Within these broad categories, there are hundreds of separate
programs. Food is provided under direct distribution programs for
institutions, schools, and individuals; under the special food-service

program for children; under the child breakfast, milk, and lunch programs in the schools; and under the food-stamp program. Manpower services are provided under more than 20 major programs, some of which are operated directly by the federal government while others are funded through grants-in-aid to states or communities and private institutions. And there are an almost equal number offering housing assistance to low-income families from a number of separate programmatic spigots.

Eligibility criteria, application procedures, and administrative controls vary greatly even among programs in the same area of activity. Some grants are made directly to states, others to counties and cities, and still others to individual and nongovernmental groups. Some leave a great deal of decision-making authority in the hands of the grant recipients, while others demand strict attention to detailed guidelines. Whatever oversight and control is exercised, the federal presence is always felt to some degree; and the states and localities must heed national intents and priorities in using grant-in-aid funds.

The impact of this diverse array of programs is difficult to assess. So many different services are provided, so many different activities are involved, and so many different programmatic systems are used that generalizations are difficult. Aggregate program statistics are usually gathered to assure that federal mandates are being met in the broadest terms; but there is little basis for measuring impact at the local level where the programs serve the people and where, in the end, they must succeed or fail.

It is equally difficult to assess the impact of the whole grant-in-aid approach. Obviously, states and localities are hard pressed for funds to deliver services demanded by citizens; and the federal government has stepped in to fill needs. But the costs of concentrating power in the hands of the feds have never been adequately assessed.

An assessment of this local impact is vitally needed. The dramatic growth of federal grants-in-aid has to some degree shifted the balance of governmental power away from the state and local level. Increasingly, the mayors and governors are looking to the federal government for a solution to their financial problems. This is especially true in the large cities caught in the pinch of increasing demands for governmental services and deteriorating sources of local revenue. But federal assistance brings some degree of federal control, and the decision-making power of the mayors and governors has been and is being eroded.

In recent years there has been increasing public concern about this centralization of authority. Proponents of decentralization argue that the federal government cannot effectively adjust its efforts to varying local needs, that the grants-in-aid are burdened with red tape, and that the people have little control over the governmental programs that so vitally affect them. Contending that states and communities cannot raise the revenues needed to meet rising demands, advocates of decentralization seek to increase federal contributions but to minimize federal presence in the administration of the programs. The Nixon Administration's sweeping revenue-sharing plan was to distribute $11 billion of present categorical grants-in-aid in block grants for manpower, economic development, education, transportation, and law enforcement, and an extra $5 billion with no restrictions to be used in any way mayors and governors felt most effective. The program actually enacted in late 1972 provided $5.3 billion in 1972, and a total of $30.1 billion over five years: two thirds to localities for public safety, environmental protection, transportation, health, libraries, recreation, and social services, and one third to states with no strings attached.

There is a great deal of opposition to these proposals. Advocates of centralized decision-making and categorical programs argue that state and local governments lack the expertise to administer complex social programs, that they need oversight to insure against local actions contrary to national goals, and that spending power should not be separated from revenue raising. Generally, they feel that federal dollars will be misallocated unless strings are attached.

Debate over revenue sharing, decentralization, and community control—in other words, over the proper balance among federal, state, and local governments—is likely to be one of the most acute political issues of the coming years. And if it is to be resolved on other than purely ideological grounds, much more must be learned about the impact of the whole range of federal-aid programs at the local level. Instead of focusing solely on aggregate program performance, it is desirable to shift emphasis to the local level, measuring the combined effects of the various grants-in-aid on specific areas and on the beneficiaries of the programs. What goods and services are provided by the federal dollars? How have money flows influenced and changed local behavior? Are they well designed to meet local needs? Can their impact be improved through decentralization? Are the programs reaching the intended target population, and what has been the impact of the programs on individuals? It is only through careful case studies at the state and local level that we can answer such questions. And it is only by answering these questions that we can determine the effectiveness of the programs and the proper balance among the city, state, and national governments.

FEDERAL AID TO THE FEDERAL CITY

The Washington budget has nearly quadrupled over the past decade (Chart 2). In 1963 operating income, including grants-in-aid and direct payments from the federal government, totaled $273 million. It rose to $434 million by 1967 and more than doubled in the next five years, surpassing the billion dollar mark in 1972. Inflation accounted for only a tenth of the more than tripling during the preceding seven-year period, while the population actually declined. The changes occurred in the services offered by the government and possibly in the added overhead that goes with growing government. Most of the funds for this expansion have come from local revenues, but the federal contribution has grown in importance. Where direct federal payments amounted to 11 percent of operating income in 1963, they rose to 17 percent in 1972. In addition, federal grants rose from 8 percent of the budget in 1963 to 21 percent in 1972.

Because it is the nation's capital and because the federal government is its major employer and tax-exempt property owner, the District of Columbia receives direct appropriations from Congress to supplement its revenues. These funds are allocated, along with local revenues, to the operating and capital expenses of the city, as outlined in the annual budget, which must be approved by Congress. In fiscal 1972 the federal payment amounted to $173 million, supplementing the $625 million raised by the District for operating expenses and the $102 million appropriated for capital outlays to be borrowed from the Treasury.

CHART 2: FEDERAL SUPPORT ACCOUNTS FOR AN INCREASING SHARE OF THE DISTRICT BUDGET

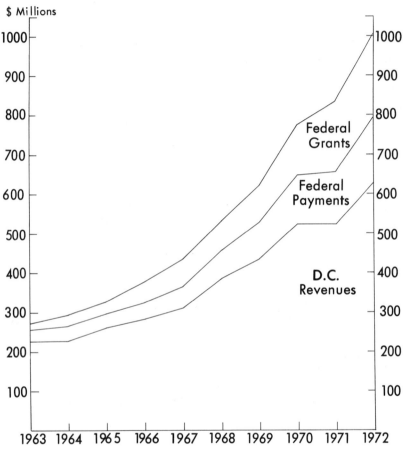

Source: D.C. Budget and Program Analysis Division

The direct federal subsidy can be viewed as a payment in lieu of property taxes. Some 55 percent of the land area of the District is exempt from local taxes; four fifths of this is federal property in choice locations. In fiscal 1972, $127 million was raised in realty taxes. If the federal land had been taxed at the same rate, the added revenue would have been $112 million. Considering the responsibilities which devolve upon the government of the District because of its status as the nation's capital—for instance, policing and cleaning up after parades welcoming foreign dignitaries and after political demonstrations—the direct federal payment is not pure largesse.

More important in absolute size as supplements to local resources are the grants-in-aid received by the District under national programs which are available to other states and cities. These amounted to an estimated $211 million in fiscal 1972, and the total is growing rapidly. In 1954 there was only about $3 million in such grants; by 1965 there was $31 million; and $247 million is projected for 1973.

The District's grants-in-aid provide for a wide range of activities, and they go to a number of separate local agencies. Altogether the District receives grants from more than 300 different federal programs. In some cases, such as the Neighborhood Youth Corps, projects in different agencies are funded from a general kitty; more often, however, application must be made separately for each grant. There is no central clearinghouse which applies for and monitors grants from the feds. Rather, each functional bureaucracy at the city level has direct ties with its parallel bureaucracy at the federal level. In most cases there is little coordination among these separate grant efforts or control exercised by the mayor or city council. In the budget process, attention is given to the amount of grants where matching funds are required, but little oversight is exercised over the disposition of the funds.

The largest program is public assistance, under which the District received $57 million in fiscal 1972. Medicaid, which received $22 million, and welfare have been the most rapidly growing grant programs. Housing and urban renewal received $37 million in federal grants. Elementary and secondary schools received $28 millon in federal grants, and the three District colleges received $10 million. Rapidly expanding grants-in-aid are also provided for crime prevention and control, corrections, community health care, manpower development, narcotics treatment, and environmental needs.

To gain perspective on the impact of these grants-in-aid on the District budget, it is useful to compare the grant amounts with budget totals (Table 1). The grant-in-aid usually exerts the most leverage where it constitutes a large share of total funds, since the efforts are likely to be subject to federal guidelines and controls.

Education and Training

The overwhelming majority of public-school funds are provided out of the District budget; but grants-in-aid for education, especially under the Elementary and Secondary Education Act of 1965, are becoming increasingly important. Federal grants now fund nearly one quarter of the District public-school operating budget, including many of the educational "extras," aid for disadvantaged students, and Head Start. The federal government also contributes unearmarked funds to the District's schools, as it does to hundreds of other communities, under the Impact Aid program, which assists school districts with large numbers of parents working or living on federal property.

Table 1

FEDERAL GRANTS TO THE DISTRICT FOR
SOCIAL PROGRAMS, 1972

	D.C. Budget Allocation	*Federal Grants to the District*
	(in millions)	
Elementary and Secondary Education	$141.7	$28.2
Higher Education	29.8	10.2
Manpower	a	11.6
Welfare	82.5	62.3
Food	.7	3.6
Health Care	99.7	40.8
Community Organization	b	b
Housing and Urban Renewal	b	36.9

ᵃ D.C. matching funds typically provided by in-kind contributions.
ᵇ Less than $500,000.

Note: These data do not necessarily coincide with those used elsewhere in this volume because of differences in who does the counting, what is being counted, and how expenditures are categorized.

Source: THE BUDGET OF THE UNITED STATES GOVERNMENT: DISTRICT OF COLUMBIA, FISCAL YEAR 1973 (Washington: U.S. Government Printing Office, 1972).

Seven years after the enactment of the Elementary and Secondary Education Act, it is difficult to find evidence that the federal dollars have improved the education of disadvantaged Washington children. These antipoverty dollars have been spent not only for poor children but for a deteriorating school system including many nonpoor, which neither local funds nor federal grants have been able to shore up.

Demonstration funds to help mobilize the community to improve the quality of education in the District have helped to create jobs for school administrators, teachers, and community workers but apparently have had little effect on the quality of education in the demonstration area.

It is becoming apparent that more than additional funds is required in order to improve the quality of education in the District's public schools. The name of the system itself may be a misnomer. A public educational system assumes that the students are drawn from all strata of society. This no longer holds true for the District schools because children attending the schools increasingly come from poor families. Few middle-class white families with children have remained in Washington, and those who have done so are joined by the growing black middle class in sending their children to private schools.

While the effectiveness of additional funds in improving Washington's elementary and secondary education system is unclear, few would disagree that the major problem facing higher education in the District is lack of funds. Whether society needs as many college-trained persons as there are persons who are eager to obtain an advanced sheepskin remains debatable. But it is quite clear that the institutions of higher learning in Washington, private as well as public, do not have adequate resources to satisfy the yearning of District residents for higher education despite the $10.2 million annual contribution of the federal government to District post-secondary public educational institutions. Until 1968, the District of Columbia Teachers College was the only institution of higher learning that was part of the Washington educational system. Howard University was supported by federal funds. And although about a fifth of the Washington high school graduates continued their education at Howard, it was predominantly a national, if not an international, black university. When Congress decided in 1969 after long debate to fund a Federal City College, it underestimated the aspirations of Washington youth and young adults for higher education. An initial enrollment of only 2,500 was planned for, but more than twice that number actually applied, and the college has suffered from a shortage of funds ever since. Congress did not appropriate even the necessary funds for brick and mortar to build classrooms for the new college, forcing the school to make do with classes in old buildings scattered throughout the city.

The line of demarcation between private and public colleges has been increasingly obliterated in recent years. Federal funds during the 1950s and 1960s accounted for a rising share of outlays by private institutions of higher learning. Many federal spigots were shut off during the early 1970s, however, and private universities in the District felt the pinch as did most other institutions throughout the country. Indeed, it is highly doubtful whether the District's private universities could have survived without federal aid; they certainly would have had to retrench, if not to close their doors. The two private medical schools in the city claimed that they faced imminent collapse if additional federal aid were not forthcoming in 1971 and again during the following year. The George Washington University calculated that 16 percent of its operating funds during academic year 1972 came from federal funds, and its ambitious construction program was financed largely from the same source.

More significant is the federal dollar in helping to equalize educational opportunities. In academic year 1971 the federal government contributed some $600 million in loans and grants to students, mostly from poor and near-poor families, to enable the students to pursue their higher education. In addition, the federal government spent about three times as much to subsidize the education of veterans. Washington's institutions of higher learning got about $3.4 million out of $600 million expended nationally to provide grants to poor students, to pay poor students for work performed, or to subsidize 3-percent-interest loans to college students. But available funds were far from adequate to meet the aspirations of needy students. Each of the private and public colleges and universities in the District reported that many students from low-income homes applying for assistance had to be turned away because of lack of funds.

A great many of Washington's citizenry have not mastered the basic education needed to function effectively in present-day American society, nor have they acquired other skills to compete effectively in the job market. To help the unskilled and the deficiently educated, the federal government has funded a series of manpower programs, most of which either provide stipends to participants while they are undergoing a course or training or place the clients on jobs and provide services that help these individuals to function in the labor market. Most of these programs are relatively new and have developed during the past decade, and the federal $29 million for these programs accounted for the bulk of manpower funds, with local contributions providing only a tenth of total outlays, and these in kind rather than in cold cash.

The District is unique in that its manpower programs are operated directly under federal auspices rather than by state or local agencies. There is, however, little difference in the scope of programs that the federal government funds in Washington as compared with other major cities. And while the administrative structure may differ, the same manpower services are provided in Washington as in other cities.

In 1972 the federal government funded 11 distinct and separate manpower programs. On the surface it would appear that such proliferation of programs serving essentially the same clientele is inefficient and possibly even wasteful. Closer scrutiny of these programs reveals that while there is some duplication, each of the programs may cater to a specially designated clientele—youth, welfare recipients, unemployed adults—and different approaches are used to address the varied problems faced by those who have difficulty in finding or holding jobs. As the manpower administrators have gained experience, the trend toward proliferation and categorization of programs is slowly giving place to more efficient operations and consolidation of efforts. After 10 years of experimentation, no appropriate criteria have been developed to assess the success of the manpower programs, but the need for these programs remains obvious. In a generally prosperous city with ample opportunities, one sixth of the population still lives in poverty and many poor adults never had an opportunity to get a basic education or to acquire needed skills. The manpower programs are supposed to offer these thousands of adults another chance to function effectively in modern society.

The Welfare System

The investment in training and job creation for the unskilled and deficiently educated has not had any discernible impact on the economic dependence of the Washington population. On the contrary, despite the rapid growth of manpower programs during the past decade, welfare outlays have increased even more rapidly. Almost a seventh of the District population was dependent upon public assistance for most of its income in 1972, and the federal government footed over half of the $105 million bill. The burgeoning welfare rolls have placed considerable stress upon the fiscal resources of the District, and the Congress has manifested a greater propensity to act as the city's alderman on welfare than on any other District activity.

Though the cost of living in Washington is higher than in most other cities, welfare payments in Washington have been kept close to the national average, but an increasing proportion of the District population has come to depend upon welfare. Concerned that ineligible persons would qualify for public assistance, Congress has insisted that the District maintain close surveillance over applicants and check carefully their eligibility, though the courts have cramped the congressional style by ruling that people on welfare have the right to be protected against welfare "snooping." Inadequate as welfare may be, a rising number of females responsible for the support of their families find that these payments offer a more reliable source of support than the earnings in the open labor market of unskilled women whose work is frequently interrupted by family responsibilities and the needs of their children. It is becoming increasingly clear in the District of Columbia, as well as in the rest of the United States, that the traditional dichotomy between work and welfare is no longer applicable, and the challenge is to design programs that will combine income from work and welfare to support the millions of working poor and low-income families.

In addition to contributing funds to the District of Columbia to provide cash income to the poor, the federal government provides grants to states and localities earmarked for the purchase of specific goods or services. Recent years have marked a rapid expansion of federal assistance for health care and food. In the health field, federal outlays, amounting to about $350 million in 1972, are mainly for hospital operations, Medicare (health insurance for persons 65 and over), and Medicaid (medical assistance to public assistance recipients and other medically indigent persons). In addition, the federal government has provided grants to the District of Columbia to experiment with delivery systems to improve the health care of the poor and near poor. Under the Great Society's antipoverty program, the federal government funded the establishment and operation of neighborhood health centers in poverty areas. Another noteworthy experiment in the District is the subsidization of preventive medical care for a thousand poor people, instead of aid only after illness strikes. Finally, the federal government has funded for more than a score of years the construction of hospital facilities, and some of the District public hospitals have been built under this program. The goal of Medicaid and the delivery of other health care services to the poor is to offer the poor opportunities to share in the achievements of modern medical technology. "Quality" medical care is still rarely delivered to the poor, but the federal grants have made it possible for the District to purchase medical care for the poor which they did not have before.

Federal subsidization of food programs dates back to the depression of the 1930s, and the program was widely expanded when congressional hearings in the District of Columbia and elsewhere exposed the persistence of malnutrition and hunger in the United States. The two major food programs that the federal government subsidizes are school lunches and food stamps, which allow the poor to purchase food at reduced prices. The 1971 federal outlay in the District amounted to $20 million. The school-lunch program extends to all school children, but children from poor homes get their meals either free or at a reduced rate. Insensitive to the needs of the poor, the District was slow in obtaining free or subsidized meals for poor children, and federal bureaucratic regulations made participation by schools in poverty areas difficult because of diverse restrictions. However, the school system eventually succumbed to pressures by parents and others concerned with improving the nutrition of poor children. The subsidization of food purchased by poor families has also expanded rapidly in the early 1970s and is now available to most poor people in the District.

The food stamps have become an integral part of the welfare system, and any overhauling of the present public-assistance system will have to take into account the value of subsidized food to the poor.

Community Organization and Facilities

The support of federal housing for the poor also dates back to the New Deal. Of all the major social programs, the federally subsidized housing programs and the closely related urban-renewal efforts have the least to show for the dollars spent. The problem is not how to build dwellings but where to build. Spreading public housing throughout the metropolitan area is necessary to avoid concentration of "projects" and the high costs of building downtown. But racial factors compound economic differences when this strategy requires subsidizing poor blacks and Spanish-speaking people to move into middle-class white or black neighborhoods.

By any reasonable standards, it would appear that the District's urban-renewal program, which has cost nearly $200 million since World War II, has been a failure for the poor. It has been "successful" in clearing most of the slum areas in southwest Washington but at the cost of ignoring the needs of the poor. The cleared slums made land available to the affluent where the poor once lived. Four years after the destruction and burning following the assassination of Dr. Martin Luther King, Jr., little has been done to reclaim the destroyed areas. The few housing units that have been built for low-income families have been completed at a prohibitive cost. At the same time, over 700 of the 11,000 public-housing units built over the years were vacant in 1972. The conclusion seems to be inescapable that urban renewal and attempts to provide housing for Washington's poor have met with little success.

The argument has been made that programs for the poor are frequently failures because the poor do not have the political clout to secure their rights under the law. At least, this has been the underlying philosophy of the Great Society's antipoverty efforts, and the Economic Opportunity Act of 1964 provided for the participation of representatives of the poor in the planning as well as the administration of programs on their behalf. The most highly publicized tool for implementing this strategy was the Community

Action Program, which funded agencies in every major city in the country and in many rural areas. These agencies were to serve as vehicles not only for delivering services to the poor but also for experimentation in reaching the poor, motivating them for self help, organizing them to participate in shaping the programs and institutions that affect their lives, and, hopefully, helping them out of poverty. In Washington, this antipoverty superagency has been the United Planning Organization. It has received grants from the Office of Economic Opportunity and other federal agencies. The projects it has funded, at a cost to the federal treasury of $26 million in 1971, include preschool and remedial education, employment and job training, birth control, consumer education, recreation, legal aid, new systems for delivering health services to the poor, and neighborhood centers aimed at providing a large array of services.

The neighborhood centers are an outgrowth of the concept of decentralizing services and making them more responsive to poor people. The orientation of these centers has varied widely from preoccupation with changing community leadership to strict devotion to the delivery of traditional welfare-type services.

The principle of participation by the poor in programs on their behalf became a cardinal point of the Great Society's welfare and social legislation. It has also been a focal point of controversy. While observers may differ as to whether UPO and other community organizations have improved the delivery of services to the residents in poverty areas, few would question the fact that these organizations have given the poor a better opportunity to participate in the running of institutions that affect their lives.

Two other areas which have attracted a great deal of attention, but which are not further explored in this volume, are crime and transportation. Despite the publicity given to the government's war on crime, federal aid to the police, courts, and corrections is small relative to District allocations. Though the federal funds coming largely under the Law Enforcement Assistance Act finance innovative projects which may be highly publicized, the bread and butter is provided from local monies.

The federal role in transportation is greater. Congress has tried to use its leverage to assure that its mandates are followed by the

District and by the neighboring jurisdictions that must be involved in metropolitan transportation efforts. Although various groups within and outside the city have opposed freeway construction, the federal government has used grants as a bludgeon to enforce its will. The bludgeon was the money provided by the federal government for the Washington metropolitan subway system. The Washington Metropolitan Area Transit Authority (WMATA) receives substantial assistance from the federal government—for instance, a guarantee on the loans it has obtained from the private sector. But more significantly, the District's share of the massive subway cost is provided through loans from the government—$41.6 million in 1970 and $38.3 million in 1972. Additionally, nearly two fifths of the estimated $3 billion cost of the subway will be provided by direct subsidies. This is not included as a grant-in-aid to the District since the independent WMATA will receive the funds. But this is the single largest public-works project in history, and neither the federal government's role nor the impact of the project on the District should be underestimated.

The Diverse Spigots

This broad-brush review suggests that the impact of grants-in-aid varies from program to program and from function to function. In some cases, such as urban renewal, manpower, and community develoment, the feds provide the major funding and direction, while in other efforts they only marginally subsidize ongoing activities or else finance supplemental services. Experimentation and innovation are also financed largely through grants which may have anywhere from a meager to a massive impact. And in some cases, such as community antipoverty organization and public housing, private or independent public agencies within the District receive federal monies which have a massive impact on the welfare of the city though these do not go through city hall. In turn, the degree of control exercised by the District government over such agencies varies widely.

Quite clearly, the federal dollar is distributed in various ways and serves numerous purposes. There is no neat conceptual umbrella which includes the whole lot since the influx of federal monies is complex and uncoordinated. The direct federal payment that supplements local revenues in lieu of taxes is unique to the District, and little of general interest can be learned by studying the allocation and application of these funds. Federal loans for capital expenditures are also unique because in large measure they are merely a substitute for borrowing by the city, which is prohibited by an act of Congress. Grants provided directly to the city government are of major interest because the District participates in these activities much like other states and localities, and its experience can yield significant lessons. Additionally, however, a number of separate grants must be considered: food-stamp subsidies are not made directly to the city but nonetheless help feed its residents and supplement welfare payments; public-housing subsidies are made directly to the semi-autonomous National Capital Housing Authority; federal contributions for the community anti-poverty organization are made to the United Planning Organization and other agencies without passing through city hall; and manpower funds are administered directly by the feds but serve the city's employees and unemployed workers. Howard University receives the bulk of its support from the federal government, but the District government has no authority over the disbursement of the funds, though possibly a fifth of its college-bound high school graduates end up at Howard. Though these forms of federal assistance do not fit neatly as part of the federal state and local grants-in-aid, they have a major impact on the welfare of the District's residents; and experience with them is also transferable to other areas.

COMPARISONS WITH OTHER CITIES

A comparison of the District's grants-in-aid with the experience of other large cities is useful to help assess the impact of the financial assistance offered. All indications suggest that the District receives a disproportionate share of aid relative to the severity of the problems to which aid is directed or for which it is considered. A breakdown of federal aid by major functional category indicates that on a per-capita basis the District received more than three times as much assistance as other areas and almost twice as much when the direct annual federal payment is not counted (Table 2).

Table 2

FEDERAL ASSISTANCE PER CAPITA, 1970

| | Federal Grants Per Capita | |
	District	National Average
Public Assistance	$ 25.40	$ 36.36
Health	22.39	5.09
Education	97.31	14.74
Miscellaneous Welfare	120.01	24.62
Highways and All Other	99.07	34.38
TOTAL	$364.18	$115.20

Note: This tabulation includes grants made directly to institutions that by-pass the D.C. government.

Source: U.S. Bureau of the Census, STATISTICAL ABSTRACT OF THE UNITED STATES, 1971.

Comparing the District of Columbia with other large cities, however, would probably yield much less of a differential. An increasing share of grant-in-aid funds are now being channeled into the large urban areas because of the rapid growth of their welfare populations and because of the proliferation of urban-oriented social programs over the last decade. Washington, D. C., along with other cities of comparable size, probably receives a higher per-capita share of grants-in-aid than rural areas, small towns, and medium-size cities.

Participation in federal grants-in-aid varies markedly from city to city and from program to program; but the District gets a healthy share under most grant-in-aid programs and a generous share in areas such as education where the federal government provides support in lieu of state aid. In only a few large cities like San Francisco and Boston do per-capita grant dollars approach the total received by Washington.

One attempt to compare the "quality of life" in the District with that of the central cities of 17 other large metropolitan areas was carried out by Michael J. Flax, of the Washington-based Urban Institute, who compared conditions in these 18 cities using a variety of indicators and found that the District was worse off than most other large cities in terms of health and crime, but better off in terms of poverty, unemployment, and mental health. Over-all, based on the indicators presented by the Urban Institute study, it would seem that Washington is "typical" of large central cities (Table 3).

Table 3

RANKING OF WASHINGTON, D.C., AMONG 18 CENTRAL CITIES

Quality Category	Indicator	D.C. Rank
Unemployment	Proportion of labor force unemployed	5th
Poverty	Proportion of low-income households	Tied for lowest
Health	Infant mortality rates	13th
Mental health	Reported suicide rates	5th
Public order	Reported robbery rates	Highest

Source: Michael J. Flax, A STUDY OF COMPARATIVE URBAN INDICATORS (Washington: The Urban Institute, 1972), p. 123.

LESSONS FROM THE DISTRICT'S EXPERIENCE

Many lessons can be learned from the District's experience with grants-in-aid. Despite the city's uniqueness, and in some cases be-cause of it, the impact of the federal dollar can be measured more easily than in other areas, and insights can be gained which are applicable to most large cities. This will provide at least some ten-tative conclusions about the effectiveness of the grant-in-aid ap-proach in alleviating local problems, suggesting whether the cen-tralized federal system that has evolved over the past decades can function effectively or whether it needs to be changed dramatically to allow more local participation and control.

If such general conclusions are to be reached, the whole gamut of grants-in-aid, both to the District government and to independent institutions and groups serving the city, must be carefully and in-dividually examined. A number of very difficult questions must be asked and answered:

• First, what contribution do federal funds make toward solving the particular local problems to which they are addressed? Are the results measurable?

• Second, has the Great Society's legacy of massive social legislation had any noticeable impact upon the quality of life in our cities? Have these new programs had any discernible impact upon clients? How has the Nixon Administration changed the programs initiated by earlier administrations?

• Third, how are federal grants integrated with local efforts? Do they provide complementary services, experimentation and demonstration, marginal subsidies for ongoing activities, or services which would not otherwise have been provided?

• Fourth, how do these monies change the actions and allocations of the city? Do they merely replace local efforts or do they have substantial leverage to alter the direction of such efforts?

• Fifth, what strings are attached to the grants-in-aid? How much oversight and control is exercised by federal agencies? How much confusion results?

• Sixth, is the D. C. experience transferable to other areas, or do the city's singular characteristics limit the scope of the lessons?

• Finally, what are the future directions of each of these programs? Have they contributed to continuing change? Will they expand and improve, leading to a greater contribution in the future?

If these questions can be answered about the wide range of programs operating in the District, much can be learned about the effectiveness of the grant-in-aid approach and about the urban problems to which grant-in-aid programs are directed.

No claim is made that this volume provides precise answers to the questions raised. Indeed, it is highly doubtful whether the impact of the federal expenditures can be measured. But it is hoped that the following analyses of federal contributions to eight major areas of District activity not only will provide insights for the assessment of federal grants-in-aid, but also will point the way to more effective strategies for the distribution of federal social dollars.

Chapter Two

PUBLIC SCHOOLS

by Mark R. Arnold

On the table in Marie Perry's office is a small graceful statue of Sisyphus, arms outstretched, struggling to push a huge stone uphill. According to the legend, the stone always rolled downhill as he neared the top with it. The odds were overwhelming against Sisyphus, and so they often seem to Mrs. Perry too.

Mrs. Perry is principal of the ninth poorest school in Washington, D. C.: Cleveland Elementary, in the heart of the riot-torn Shaw Urban Renewal Area. It's a three-story brick structure, 55 years old, surrounded by chain-link fences eight feet high. Its windows are barred, its doors reinforced. Outside, unshaven, sad-eyed men huddle against the cold in the shadow of abandoned buildings, sipping from bottles wrapped in brown paper bags. Within a block is a storefront building with a sign, "Pride, Inc.'s Urban Rodent Control Project." Also the Safari A-Go-Go bar and grill, the boarded-up Howard Theater, and enough trash and rubble strewn in back yards and on sidewalks to keep local sanitation workers busy for days.

The fence, the bars, the locks keep children from this world for part of each day. And for that part of the day, Mrs. Perry and her teachers have put together a program of instruction and enrichment that even some suburban schools might envy. Because Cleveland is a Title I school, each classroom is outfitted with a record player and a film-strip projector. There are community aides to help teachers, and pupil personnel workers to attend to home and health problems, plus visiting speech therapists, psychologists, and reading diagnosticians. There are also occasional trips to the National Gallery, the Kennedy Center, or to a local black arts production at nearby Howard University.

The problem is that just as the school fills up each morning, it must empty out each afternoon, sending the children back to the neighborhood the school seeks to rescue them from. "You wonder if anything we can do will be enough," Mrs. Perry says grimly. "And sometimes, you try not to wonder. After the 1968 riots, you know, when Martin Luther King died, we saw some of our former students, even the girls, looting stores, and their mothers were in there helping them."

Title I gives Mrs. Perry roughly $250 a year worth of extra services for what the Elementary and Secondary Education Act of 1965 describes as "meeting the special educational needs of educationally deprived children." Eighty-five percent of the 316 children at Cleveland fit that description, and Mrs. Perry thinks $250 is a pitifully small amount of extra money to spend on them.

In fact, however, Title I's problems in the District of Columbia go deeper than lack of funds. From the time the first $5.4 million was received in 1965, with little or no advanced planning, the program has been characterized by poor planning, sloppy management, superficial evaluation and—until recently—-precious little concern with results.

With a budget of $7 million in fiscal 1972, Title I is the largest and most politically potent of more than 40 separate federal programs in the District's schools. Together these programs channel in excess of $30 million into the schools, or nearly one quarter of the school system's operating budget.

In no other city or state does the federal contribution play so important a part in local school finances. Nationally, according to the National Education Association, the federal share of local school costs has fluctuated from a high of 9 percent in 1967-68 to a low of 7 percent in 1971-72. Thus, potentially at least, federal dollars in the District of Columbia have three times the educational impact as elsewhere in the country.

What effect does the federal dollar in fact have in the schools? Does it plug holes in the local educational dike? Or does it force local administrators to put resources where they don't need them? Does it reinforce or subvert local priorities? Are there ways it could be better put to use?

These are important questions to answer, and the answers are better sought in Washington than elsewhere for a number of reasons having to do with the composition of the local school population and the very uniqueness of the city's relationship with the federal government.

THE PROBLEMS OF THE SCHOOLS

It is a little remembered—but highly significant—fact that Washington's black school population made up slightly more than 50 percent of total enrollment in 1950—four years before the Supreme Court declared the local dual school system (and those everywhere else) unconstitutional. Eighteen years later, with 95 percent of the enrollment nonwhite, Washington's schools are the forerunner of a dozen or more big-city school systems likely to become predominantly nonwhite in the next decade (Chart 3).

The problems of Washington's schools, however, derive less from color than from class, for the schools are increasingly devoid of middle-class students, white or black. With an estimated one quarter or more of the city's 145,000 school children living below the poverty line, the local schools provide an important test of whether today's urban school systems, built around the values and norms of the middle class, are flexible enough to adapt to the needs of today's disenfranchised minorities.

No one who examines the D.C. schools can be sanguine about the prospects. There are, to be sure, some improvements to be

CHART 3: THE DISTRICT'S PUBLIC SCHOOLS ARE INCREASINGLY BLACK

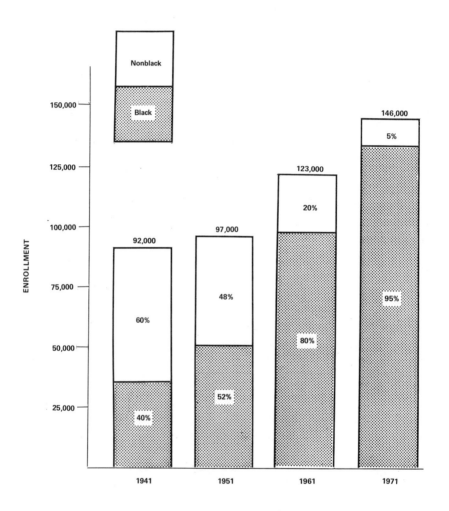

Source: D.C. Board of Education

noted. A higher proportion of District high school graduates are
going on to college than did 10 years ago. Improvements in vocational education appear to have cut the dropout rate, if only slightly. Per-pupil expenditures, after several years of lag, have now in-

creased to the point that Washington ranks fifth among the 15
largest cities in outlays per student. It also ranks high in teacher
salaries, pupil-teacher ratios, and teacher-administrator ratios.[1]

Yet every objective measurement points to a slow and steady
deterioration in the performance level of students. The authoritative
Strayer study, ordered by Congress in 1948, demonstrates that the
deterioration set in long before the courts began to intervene in
local education. Concluded that study:

> The survey committee would suggest that there must be some factor
> other than instruction which may account in part for the downward
> trend of achievement in reading, numbers, language, and spelling
> as shown by these tests. It is perhaps the movement of a large num-
> ber of underprivileged children into the District from areas where
> public education is very inefficient in the development of the funda-
> mental tool skills.[2]

The most graphic illustration of the decline came at Dunbar
High School, Washington's traditional incubator for black talent.
Massachusetts Senator Edward W. Brooke, former Federal Housing chief Robert Weaver, and Army General Benjamin O. Davis
("the first Negro general") were all among graduates of the school,
which was named for the late black poet and novelist Paul
Laurence Dunbar.

In an excellent study of the "old" and the "new" Dunbar for
the *Washington Post,* reporter Lawrence Feinberg wrote:

> The old segregated Dunbar sent about 80 per cent of its gradudates
> on to college in the early 1950s—a higher proportion than any
> other high school, white or black, in the city. The 'integrated' Dun-
> bar—whose enrollment still is over 99 per cent Negro—became the
> high school in Washington with the smallest percentage going on to
> college.
>
> Outside the sandstone bannisters have crumbled from what once was
> an imposing front entrance. Inside, old traditions have crumbled as
> Dunbar is beset by the same intractable problems which beleaguer
> high schools in big-city slums throughout the country.[3]

---

[1] U.S. Department of Health, Education, and Welfare, National Center for Educational Statistics, Public Elementary and Secondary Schools, Fall 1970
(Washington: U.S. Government Printing Office, 1971).
[2] George D. Strayer, The Report of a Survey of the Public Schools of the
District of Columbia (Washington: U.S. Government Printing Office, 1949),
p. 464.
[3] *Years Bring Change to Dunbar High School,* The Washington Post, December 28, 1969.

In the 23 years since the Strayer report, much has been tried
—and little accomplished—to reverse that deterioration. Superintendent Hugh J. Scott's solution to learning disabilities centers
around his Academic Achievement Plan, a program of intensive
training in basic skills that stresses competition between classes
and schools. The program was introduced in September 1970, along
with semi-annual standardized tests administered to each child in
grades one through nine to measure its results. While it is too
early to draw conclusions about the success of the program, the
results of the first complete cycle of testing confirm that the longer
a child stays in school, the further behind national norms he
falls.

Nothing done in the first year seems to have made much difference. The September 1971 test results, for example, showed
that second graders in Washington schools lagged seven months
behind second graders nationally. The gap widened year by year.
Local ninth graders scored two years behind ninth graders nationally. These results help explain why more than a third of the
16-year-olds in the school system drop out before graduation, and
why absenteeism, by official estimates, ranges up to 21 percent in
the city's high schools.

"The D.C. school system is a classic example of an educational system failing to prepare its charges for life or even for productive employment," says former school-board member Julius
Hobson, the school system's most trenchant critic. Hobson's suits
against D.C. school administrators are cited by other critics as
bearing a large part of the responsibility for that failure.

Hobson's suits against D.C. school officials have played a central role in the evolution of the schools in recent years. In 1967,
Federal District Judge J. Skelly Wright, siding with Hobson in a
celebrated suit against Superintendent Carl Hansen, ruled that a
"track" system—with students separated into ability groupings—
operated to discriminate against disadvantaged children, particularly blacks. The judge ordered the school board to increase faculty
integration, bus students from crowded black schools to "under-
crowded" white, and make other changes to overcome discriminatory practices. The school board's decision not to appeal the
ruling forced Hansen's resignation.

In May 1971, a second Hobson suit culminated in a decision by

Judge Wright that found disparities in per-pupil expenditures, with schools in affluent white areas spending up to twice as much as schools in slum black areas. The judge ordered the school board to equalize expenditures within a 5-percent range between schools, using teacher transfers and other methods.

There's no question the two decisions hastened the exodus of many remaining middle-class families, white and black, from the D.C. schools. They sounded the death knell for the elitist system that had permitted certain schools to remain immune to the general decline in standards that followed the influx of poor black families in the postwar years.

In one sense, the decline of Washington's schools presents an unparalleled opportunity for imaginative use of federal funds. The death of elitism could mark the rise of an era of democratization in educational opportunity in the District. Federal money can either strengthen this thrust or thwart it. It can, for example, reinforce the traditional professional prerogatives or facilitate the introduction of new voices and new skills into the classrooms. It can bolster centralized control or encourage community participation and accountability.

In reality, the bulk of federal money in the District's schools has been used to prop up the system in traditional ways—to train more teachers and upgrade their skills, to swell the bureaucracy rather than streamline it, let alone build rival centers of power. At the same time, however, small but increasing amounts of money are being used to introduce paraprofessionals and technically proficient "community people" into the classrooms, provide career ladders for them to climb, and involve parents in the design and evaluation of programs in the schools.

FEDERAL FUNDS: WHERE THEY COME FROM, WHERE THEY GO

With this background, we shall take a look at the scope of federal school aid in the District of Columbia, then examine in closer detail two particular federal programs: Title I of the Elementary and Secondary Education Act (ESEA) of 1965 and the Anacostia Community School Project, a major demonstration experiment initiated by the U. S. Office of Education in 1968 and

phased out four years later because of shortcomings in performance.

The D. C. public schools were budgeted to receive $30.8 million
in federal funds in fiscal 1972. More than two thirds the total
came from the Department of Health, Education, and Welfare.
This aid was distributed through many mechanisms, with 25 of
the 43 programs emanating from the U.S. Office of Education,
and served a variety of purposes (Table 4).

Other funding sources were the Department of Agriculture, $2.6
million for food programs; the Labor Department, $3.3 million
for manpower programs; Housing and Urban Development, $1
million for support of students and education; and the Department
of Justice, $80,000 for burglar alarm systems in the schools.

Administratively, the programs fall into two categories:

• "State Plan" programs, such as Title I and Impact Aid, in
which money is distributed by state departments of education according to a formula set down by law. That is, under these programs a school district with so many children meeting certain criteria is entitled to so many federal dollars.

• "Grant Application" or "Discretionary" programs, such as the
Anacostia project or Follow-Through for disadvantaged preschool-
ers. These programs, which may or may not filter through state
departments of education, are selected for funding on the basis
of applications from local districts.

Despite the multiplicity of programs, five accounted for three
fifths of the federal outlays in fiscal 1972.

Title I, ESEA ($7.1 million) is the largest current federal
school effort locally with expenditures in the past seven years
totaling more than $40 million. Aimed at supplementing instruc-
tion and providing other needed services to the "educationally
deprived," Title I was expected in the 1971-72 school year to
serve 11,000 children in 47 elementary schools, 11 junior highs,
and 8 nonpublic (parochial) schools.

Impact Aid ($5.9 million) provides general assistance to dis-
tricts with large numbers of school children whose parents work
on and/or live on nontaxable federal property. Impact Aid has
brought in excess of $40 million into the schools in the last eight
years. Roughly one quarter of the budget goes for school administration, and a like amount for instructional services. As the

only flexible federal money in the D.C. schools, it tends to be used to plug holes rather than as a part of a coherent educational strategy. Small amounts go to furnish the "local share" in matching

Table 4

FEDERAL PROGRAM GRANTS TO D.C. PUBLIC SCHOOLS, FISCAL 1972

Purpose	Cost (in millions)
Compensatory education for educationally disadvantaged children	$ 7.1
Acquisition of instructional materials	.3
Innovative educational programs	1.0
Anacostia school demonstration project	2.3
Strengthening administration and evaluation	.5
Improving vocational education	1.5
Enabling adults to overcome English language limitations	.4
Attracting and training teachers and teachers' aides	1.7
Aiding handicapped children	.6
Assisting neglected and delinquent children in institutions	.4
Providing food, with emphasis on needy children, and food-service equipment	2.6
Supporting the Harrison Community School	.3
Supporting early childhood education	1.6
Supporting school systems enrolling children whose parents live or work on a tax-exempt government facility	5.9
Providing basic education and training	2.2
Providing part-time employment for students from low-income families	.9
Paying students from low-income families to attend summer school	.6
Improving and disseminating techniques for teaching reading	.5
Integrating career development into all levels of instruction	.1
Providing alarm systems in schools to deter illegal entries; driver education; civil defense	.1
Job creation within the school system	.3
TOTAL	$30.8

Source: D. C. Public Schools

grant programs, to support food services, career development, and adult education programs for which regular funds are scarce.

Title IV, ESEA, Anacostia Demonstration Project ($2.3 million) is aimed at increasing community involvement and pupil performance in an area of Washington marked by poverty and unemployment. Underfinanced from its earliest days, the program involved 11 schools serving 13,000 students and a staff of 205, of whom 149 were paraprofessionals working with children in classrooms or in community organizations. It was scheduled to be phased out in August 1972.

Vocational Education Amendments of 1968 ($1.5 million) accounts for almost half the local budget for vocational education, supports teacher salaries and administrative expenses. Funds also go to programs for the handicapped and cooperative work projects with local employers.

Education Professions Development Act ($1.3 million) supports teacher training and staff development. It also permits persons with nonacademic skills (*e.g.,* auto repairmen, welders) to become certified instructors while teaching in the classroom. In addition, training in bilingual education and drug abuse prevention is supported with these funds.

Given the number and diversity of federal programs in the schools, generalizations are difficult to make. Some have unquestionably been highly successful, both from the point of view of filling real needs and of achieving their objectives. Highly acclaimed programs include a clothing distribution center financed by Title I and several Title III experiments, such as a "school without walls" for creative but hard-to-teach youngsters.

One measure of success is that a dozen or more programs begun with federal funds were later adopted as part of the regular budget. These include a school for pregnant high school girls, use of classroom educational aides, prekindergarten programs, a data-processing course, a planning and research unit in the central administration, use of nonteaching professionals, and the extended school day for community education.

Yet two of the largest programs, Title I and Impact Aid, have until recently been without coherent direction. Because local money was not involved, neither the board of education nor congressional overseers have devoted to these two potentially powerful programs the attention they deserve.

One problem is that traditionally the school board has considered the federal programs' budget separately from its regular operating budget—usually several months afterwards, in fact. Complains board member Bardyl Tirana:

> We never knew if the priorities we set were being met, or if they weren't, what we could do about it. We'd approve an operating budget, and then the Superintendent would come in later and say, "We need so many more people in the central administration to do what we've agreed to do under the operating budget," and he'd want to pay for them out of Impact Aid. You might end up with half your Impact Aid budget going for straight pure overhead. This year we have insisted on seeing a unified budget, operating plus federal programs, so we can make sure our priorities are met.

> The idea is to make federal aid part of our overall educational strategy. It's something that's never really been done here.

TITLE I—BUT CAN THEY READ?

Title I of the ESEA is easily the most ambitious federal program ever undertaken in the schools. Reversing the nation's long love affair with the gifted and the middle class, it seeks to redirect federal educational dollars to focus on those youngsters whose needs have been most neglected through the years: the poor and the slow learners.

The largest education effort today, it provides supplementary educational experiences and social services to 8 million students in low-income neighborhoods of 16,000 school districts across the nation. As of September 1971, $7.3 billion had been allocated to the states, D.C., and outlying areas since the program began in 1965.

For all its promise, however, Title I has been severely hobbled by poor management, diffuse goals, and lack of federal oversight. In its annual report to the President and Congress in 1971, the national advisory group established by ESEA to evaluate Title I summed up the program this way:

> The atmosphere of hope and expectation which surrounded the birth of Title I is now becoming one of wider frustration and even sporadic despair. . . . Title I has become another exercise in despair.

Its catalogue of complaints was a long one: more than half the teachers in Title I classes have no background or training in teaching the disadvantaged; funds are adequate to serve only a third of those eligible; public support for overcoming the educational disabilities of the poor is evaporating under the pressure of skyrocketing school costs.

In addition to monetary limitations and educational shortcomings, said the council, "the money has been too little and too thinly spread to accomplish the intent of the law." Finally, it pointed to a long list of administrative shortcomings that have gone uncorrected year after year.

In September 1971, U. S. Education Commissioner Sidney P. Marland, Jr., requested six states and the District of Columbia to repay more than $4.5 million in Title I funds that had been spent for unauthorized purposes. The District was informed the government would seek to recover over $1.6 million in misspent funds, all of it stemming from the first two years of the program.

The violations discovered by HEW auditors were fairly common ones: Three fourths of the total was for an "Environmental Improvement Project"—actually a building renovation program having no direct relation to the learning problems of the disadvantaged, the auditors said.

Such flagrant violations probably no longer exist. For one thing, federal guidelines are tighter. For another, the Federal Programs Department of the D.C. Schools, which operates as the supervisory "state agency" for the local schools, keeps closer tabs on the use of the money.

Nevertheless, Title I continues to operate at considerably less than its full potential in the District. Though individual teachers and principals attest to its worth, its overall effectiveness has never been measured. Furthermore, the program consistently has been undermined by political pressures, congressional appropriations delays, lack of coordination, and inadequate evaluation. The following are some examples of the problems:

Political pressures: Though educators agree Title I money must be concentrated to be effective, the number of participating schools has fluctuated wildly through the years—from a high of 95 schools in fiscal 1968 to a low of 34 in 1969, then up to 66 in fiscal 1972 —in response to pressures on the Board of Education. "This is a classic example," says Superintendent Scott, "of a program a mile wide and one inch deep."

Appropriations delays: Only once in six years, in 1970, have the schools had money at the start of the school year in September. In typical fashion, the appropriation for the fiscal year beginning in July 1971, carrying funds for expanded Title I programs, did not clear Congress until December 1971.

Lack of coordination: Until 1972, the customary way of apportioning Title I funds was by negotiation among administrators of various school divisions—Elementary, Secondary, Model Schools, and Pupil Personnel Services. Says local Title I coordinator Anne W. Pitts:

> The money would go to the divisions. They would have so much to work with and come up with the programs they wanted. The programs may have been sound in themselves, but they have never been coordinated.

Inadequate evaluation: For the first five years, Title I was described on the District's project applications as a dropout-prevention program. Thereafter it was redirected toward increasing achievement levels. As of February 1972, however, no effort had been made to gauge whether or not Title I schools had indeed lowered dropout rates or had achieved academic gains beyond what had occurred in non-Title I schools, though the raw data needed to make such determinations were readily available.

Says Martha Swaim, the Board of Education's chief watchdog of federal programs:

> Title I has had damn little impact on the children of Washington. It's put icing on the cake without changing the cake. When you put money money into poorly run schools and don't change the people who run them, you get schools that are poorly run with more money.

A teacher who has worked in both Title I and non-Title I schools expresses it another way:

> There are good schools in Washington and there are bad schools in Washington. The difference seems to lie chiefly in the principals. In the bad schools, Title I is probably wasted. In the good schools, it makes a difference. But it doesn't make enough of a difference to really change the lives of these kids.

This reporter's conclusion is that Title I money has been extended to too many schools, for too many uses, and with too little imagination to have had a significant impact.

A New Plan Aborted

For the first time, in 1972, the school administration was presented with a plan that might have concentrated Title I resources on a small enough number of children, with a specific enough objective, to have achieved appreciable gains. The "Total Learning Center" concept, designed by curriculum specialist Anne W. Pitts, sought to redirect Title I from a program of social services and enrichment to a strategy for achieving quantifiable reading and math goals among deprived third and seventh graders in Title I schools. Other classes—music, art, physical education—were to have been reoriented toward driving home reading and math lessons.

A highly successful summer program in 1971 had been built upon these very lines. Hence, the impetus to extend the program systemwide in the next school year.[4] What happened subsequently was a case study of bureaucratic subversion.

Under pressure from principals, the plan was enlarged to include Title I youngsters in grades one through three and seven through nine. Inevitably, the Board of Education expanded the list of participating schools. The whole procedure was delayed by the school department's failure to devise an equitable formula for selecting Title I schools by the opening of schools in September, the old formula having been deemed unacceptable by HEW in 1969.

By the time the revised procedures were approved by the Board of Education, it was December 15. It was three weeks later before any of the 150 extra teachers needed for the program were hired. Then almost immediately, Superintendent Scott decreed a freeze on hiring and new spending in the wake of disclosures that the

---

[4] The 1971 summer program was unique in that it included pre- and post-session standardized testing, and the results were immediately evaluated for 600 of the 2,500 participating youngsters. The tests showed an average 5.0-month gain in reading and 6.9-month gain in math in the eight elementary schools participating in the six-week intensive course. Students were chosen on the basis of referrals from teachers. Even assuming the program drew more highly motivated youngsters than the typical Title I classroom, the results were startling. Whether the program could yield comparable results if carried system-wide, however, is questionable. The summer school was marked by a 15-1 pupil-teacher ratio, control of each school by the "Total Learning Center" director, and a high enthusiasm level among students and staff. None of these conditions prevail in the year-round schools.

schools were headed toward a $5.5 million operating budget deficit. Though federal funds are managed separately from regular operating funds, the freeze also extended to all federal programs.[5]

The upshot was that a serious attempt to meet the special educational needs of disadvantaged Washington school children was put off once again, probably for at least a year.

How Title I Works

Most of the shortcomings of Title I throughout the country fall into one of three categories. Money has gone to

1) the wrong schools;
2) the right schools but the wrong children;
3) the right schools, right children, but the wrong uses.

To understand these distinctions, some background in the intricacies of Title I regulations is required.

Section 101 of Title I requires that funds be used for programs designed to meet the "special educational needs of educationally deprived children" in school attendance areas having "high concentrations of children from low-income families."

HEW regulations require that all attendance zones within a school district be ranked in order of concentration of children from low-income homes. Only those schools are eligible for Title I whose incidence of low-income children is greater than the average for all schools in the district. The procedure is for the district to serve the school with the heaviest concentration first and work its way down the list of eligibles. All of the eligibles may be served or only some of them, depending on how narrowly or how broadly the district wishes to spread the money. But it can't skip over schools—it can't serve the fifth poorest unless the first four have been served.

Note, too, that the law makes two "cuts" in choosing the student beneficiaries of Title I. One is economic, the other educational.

---

[5] The financial crisis into which the schools were plunged in January 1972 was the result of lax administrative procedures that cannot be dealt with in depth within the limitations of this study. It is clear, however, that the same lack of central control and accounting procedures that prompted Superintendent Scott to tell the city council he did not know how many people he had on his payroll obtains to the administration of federal programs, though to a lesser degree. The Department of Federal Programs is unable to determine how many persons are, at any one time, being supported with federal funds. Nor can it supply school-by-school expenditure totals for Title I.

The schools are chosen on the basis of a poverty index. But within the chosen schools, only those students can receive Title I services who are "educationally deprived." These students need not themselves be poor, and the noneducationally deprived—*i.e.*, the "achieving students"—cannot legally receive Title I benefits even if they are poor.

In the District, as elsewhere, these distinctions have caused and continue to cause no end of mischief.

Choosing the Schools

Administrators of many other school districts have misspent Title I money on nonpoor schools. In Washington, officials have consistently sought to focus it on the needy. But their criteria for deciding which needy schools to choose have long been a source of controversy.

The original 77 schools in 1966 were chosen on the basis of 1960 Census tract data on median income and other variables. The next year, a revised formula modified family income assumptions for areas with public housing. The new list should have included 13 new schools and deleted 13 old ones. What actually happened was something else. It was described by Acting Superintendent of Schools Benjamin J. Henley in a letter to the U. S. Office of Education in November 1969. Wrote Mr. Henley:

> After ranking the schools and retaining the same number of schools as were in the FY 66 list, there were an additional 13 elementary schools that qualified as Title I schools. A proposal for the inclusion of the 13 schools and the deletion of 13 other Title I schools was presented to the administration. However, due to political pressures, the 13 elementary schools were added to the list of Title I schools but none were deleted.

Accordingly, there were 90 Title I schools in 1967, and as a result of another revision, 95 in 1968. Figures furnished by the Department of Pupil Personnel Services show that the number of Title I students grew between 1966 and 1968 from 55,000 to almost 70,000. With roughly $5.5 million in Title I funds available, that meant an expenditure of roughly $80 a year per child in 1968, hardly enough to make a difference.

On the recommendation of then-Superintendent William R. Manning,[6] the number of schools was drastically reduced to 36 in 1969, then fell to 34 until 1972 when the number of schools was nearly doubled without an appreciable rise in funds. But the criteria for selection remained a bone of community contention.

The Title I area until 1972 consisted of schools in the Cardozo area just north of the central business district and the Shaw "urban renewal" area to the east. This meant the exclusion of needy schools in other areas of the city. Harris M. Taylor, Assistant Superintendent for Federal Programs, recalls discussions in 1968 about widening the Title I area to include some of the poorest schools in the depressed Anacostia area of the far Southeast. One problem, he noted, was that Title I schools were chosen on the "feeder" concept, *i.e.,* because Cardozo High School was included in Title I, it was logical to include junior highs and elementary schools that fed into it. To extend Title I to Anacostia would mean including many more schools than was economically feasible.

In addition, Mr. Taylor remarked in an interview: "The research people were concerned we only had $7 million for Title I in the whole city and Anacostia was scheduled to get $10 million of its own for a major demonstration project." Anacostia was left out of Title I.

In 1969, the school-selection process was roundly criticized in the first and only audit report HEW has made of Title I administration in Washington. It covered 1966 and 1967. Not only was the District not complying with regulations requiring that help be given to the poorest schools before the less poor were considered, said the auditors. In addition, even in terms of its own selection criteria, some money was going to ineligible schools. Said the report:

> Although records were not available to identify all expenditures of Title I grant funds by specific schools, we determined that at least $1,653,096 was spent . . . at 94 elementary public schools, and that, of this amount, *$264,714 was spent at 25 elementary schools which*

---

[6] William Manning became school superintendent in December 1967, following the resignation of Carl Hansen. Manning stepped down in August 1969. Benjamin Henley, long-time deputy superintendent, became acting superintendent upon Manning's resignation and ran the schools until the appointment of Hugh Scott in October 1970.

had less than the average incidence of children from low-income fami-lies. For instance, at least $145,188 was spent at a school that was not included in the 49 selected target schools. . . . [Emphasis added.]

Despite this finding, which went to Superintendent Manning in July 1969, it was two years before the School Department under-took to reexamine the criteria for school selection. By that time, a second HEW study—this one a state program review in June 1971 —had also found the District's selection procedures "not in accord-ance" with regulations. Said that report: "This failure to target Title I funds on those children who have the greatest needs for assistance . . . raises doubt as to the existence of a viable Title I pro-gram in the District of Columbia." HEW ordered the schools to come up with a new formula for school selection.

This the schools did, but the initial results of the labor were any-thing but satisfactory. During the summer of 1971, the School Department's Division of Planning, Research, and Evaluation re-ranked the city's schools on the basis of six proposed poverty factors, two of which the Board of Education questioned at length when the "rankers" presented their recommendations at a board meeting in October 1971. The two were "average assessed value of residential property" and "average improvement value of residential property."

Board member Mattie G. Taylor, running her finger down the list of rankings, noted that the four poorest schools in terms of welfare caseloads wouldn't qualify for Title I under the proposed new criteria. Their AFDC (Aid to Families with Dependent Chil-dren) points were offset by their proximity to high-priced office space and luxury apartments.

Declared Mrs. Taylor:

It seems to me when we have not included the schools that rank first, second, third, and fourth in numbers of youngsters on AFDC, there is something seriously wrong with our indicators. . . . AFDC percent-age of enrollment should be more of a factor than the assessment of real estate surrounding a school, especially in those areas where we determine that the surrounding real estate, thought it be of high assessment, does not contribute students to that school.

In private conversations, board members months later were still citing the proposed ranking procedures as symptomatic of the unre-sponsiveness of the school administration to the needs of Washing-ton's school children.

Instead of approving the proposed criteria, the board sent planners back to the drawing boards. It was two months later before new and more equitable selection standards were approved by the board.

That, however, led to another problem. In re-ranking the District's schools following the new Title I criteria, it was found that eight existing Title I schools no longer qualified for assistance. Rather than drop them from the program, the school board included them anyway to maintain continuity of benefits. It did so in the face of warnings from Superintendent Scott that to include these schools and not others that ranked higher in poverty under the revised criteria might trigger another HEW finding of noncompliance.

"We're already under the gun to pay back over a million dollars," he told the board at its December 15 meeting. "This could get us into the same kind of situation all over again." The board ignored the advice.

The Uses

Title I regulations require schools to make a written assessment of each "identified" student's educational needs, then design programs to meet them. The HEW program review team, reporting in June 1971, gave the school system high marks for identifying needs, but the team complained "the projects frequently fail to address the needs so indicated."

Courses in data processing and "Learning Through Aviation" offered at Cardozo High School were acclaimed by teachers at the school, but federal investigators found they were actually catering to the brightest students, not "those children who have the greatest needs for assistance." A number of other programs that did cater to the children of "greatest need" have been discarded for lack of results.

Project READ, a two-year elementary program to boost language skills, was deemed "ineffective" by school system evaluators. It had been designed by a private California company and undertaken with great local fanfare. Locally designed school programs, such as the secondary-level Reading Incentive Seminar, in which newspapers, comic books, posters, and other "relevant" materials were used to awaken interest in reading, were also deemed of limited utility.

Given this poor experience with special courses for the disadvantaged and general disapproval of ability groupings, school administrators adopted a posture of feeding Title I students the same medicine they feed all their classmates, but in slightly higher doses.

At the Cleveland Elementary School, the city's ninth poorest, the regular needs of the 316 children in grades one through six are served by 12 teachers, a part-time librarian, and two part-time counselors. Itinerant teachers, spending an average of two days a week at the school, provide instruction in art, music, physical education, science, remedial reading, and language arts.

In addition to these regular school personnel, there are 11 Title I staffers: five full-time teacher aides (one for every two and a half rooms); three full-time "pupil personnel workers"; two part-time speech therapists; and a part-time social worker. The pupil personnel workers attend to the health and family needs of Title I pupils.

Two hundred fifty students at Cleveland receive free lunches provided with U.S. Department of Agriculture funds. Title I students also may draw on the services of the "Urban Service Corps," a Title I-funded social service agency within the schools that runs tutorial programs (using college students, older school children, and community volunteers), a clothing center, and a summer camp. Last year the corps provided almost 3,700 articles of free clothing, 110 pairs of eyeglasses, and three hearing aids to Title I children.

About 80 percent of Title I funds goes for salaries. Six hundred fifty employees owe their livelihoods to the program, including reading and math specialists, counselors, psychologists, speech therapists, teachers, administrators, and—the largest single category—paraprofessional classroom aides, who take attendance, give tests, work wtih small groups, and otherwise help the teachers. There is one aide for every third classroom in Title I schools—not a particularly favorable ratio, since teachers are nearly unanimous in singing their praises.

Since Title I expenditures by schools are not available, it is hard to gauge the dollar value of the services within a particular school. Cleveland officials estimated the 1970 Title I payroll at almost $51,000, and it has no doubt risen since. Even so, the figure is

incomplete: it doesn't include nonpersonnel expenses such as Title
I field trips or audiovisual services.

Each classroom at Cleveland is equipped with a record player
and a film strip projector. Eighty film strips are available through
the principal's office. Subjects covered range from graphics to
geography, fractions to folk music. "When you're trying to motivate
children," says one teacher, "you try as many different approaches
as possible."

School officials concede that in the early years of Title I, large
amounts of audio-visual equipment were bought with little thought
as to how the equipment fit into the curriculum.

In 1971, HEW investigators charged that "considerable amounts
of equipment" had been purchased through Title I with "no evidence" that it contributed to meeting the needs of Title I children.
Continued the investigators:

> For example, the Bundy school, which has a total enrollment of 247
> pupils in grades three through six, 12 teachers, and 12 classrooms,
> has 10 television sets, 10 filmstrip projectors, 3 overhead projectors,
> 4 calculators, 10 record players, 1 copy machine and 2 primer type-
> writers. This situation seems to indicate that the District educational
> agency is neglecting to assure itself that equipment already purchased
> with Title I funds is being effectively used for Title I purposes.

One 830-student school visited by this reporter displayed in its
library the following list of equipment:

Computer Machine	1
Calculators, Rotary Type	6
Combination Filmstrips	3
Control Finder	1
Tape Recorders	3
Record Players	33
Duplicating Machines	6
Fans	5
Language Master	1
Microfilm Projectors	2
Overhead Projectors	2
Previewers	3
Opaque Projectors	2
Filmstrip Projectors	37
Radios	24

Showtalk Machines	3
Sewing Machines	3
Televisions	3
Thermofax Machines	2
Typewriters	7
Washer/Dryer Combinations	3

As previously noted, the law requires that Title I services go only to those students in Title I schools deemed to be "educationally deprived." In effect, the law demands that teachers and principals stigmatize the slowest learners, or conversely, discriminate against the fastest. It is, for example, a violation of Title I for a teacher to take the whole class on a field trip if Title I pays for transportation or admission. It is equally a violation to let all students view a film strip purchased with Title I money—unless, of course, they are all certified to be educationally deprived.

Obviously, no teacher in good conscience can exclude "nondeprived" children from such activities. To do so would be to draw cruel and humiliating distinctions between classmates. In practice, teachers tend to put their students—Title I and non-Title I—all in the same boat. Indeed, one principal confessed to this reporter she instructs teacher aides to spend part of each day with the "better" pupils lest they feel neglected.

It seems reasonable to ask that the law or regulations be rewritten to allow teachers to treat all youngsters in Title I classrooms equally.

Cause for Despair; Cause for Hope

There is no question that many of the Title I programs are beneficial. The pupil personnel team at Cleveland helps children obtain needed dental care, clothing, and emergency food supplies. Cultural enrichment is almost a necessity for ghetto children who seldom travel outside neighborhood boundaries. (This reporter questioned a fourth grade student who stumbled over the words "tug" and "dock" in his reader. Later, his teacher explained: "You don't find either in Cardozo.")

Yet the final test for Title I has to be whether or not it is teaching children what they need to know to make it in life. And the unequivocal answer to that question is no. For example, a second grade teacher at Garrison Elementary in the Cardozo area says,

It's so wonderful in the lower grades to see the children come in all bubbly with enthusiasm. You can't give them enough. Then beginning about the third grade they seem to reach a plateau and the appetite for learning begins to wane. By the time you see them in grade six, you can count on both hands the number who retain any real enthusiasm for learning.

This teacher, who declined to be identified by name, has taught in the District schools for 32 years. She estimates that 80 percent of the sixth graders in schools like hers are operating behind grade levels. Twenty percent, she says, are barely able to read at all.

Standardized tests, given twice a year to all students in grades one through nine beginning in 1970, show mixed results. On the average, students in the upper grades appear to be falling further behind from one year to the next. For example, ninth graders in September 1971 were a month behind the reading level recorded by ninth graders in September 1970. The average was a grade equivalent of 6.4 years in September 1971, 6.5 years in September 1970.

But these losses seem to be balanced by gains in the elementary schools. Third graders in September 1971 were generally two months ahead (2.1 years) of third graders in September 1970 (1.9 years) in reading.

The real question is whether these gains will continue or whether they will—as in the past—fall off as youngsters move through the system.

For Title I schools, the 1970-1971 tests gave some cause for encouragement. The average second grade students in D.C. schools in September 1971 was four months ahead of the average second grade student of September 1970 in reading. The average gain in Title I schools, however, was seven months. The average reading score for sixth graders in the system as a whole in September 1971 was identical to that of sixth graders of September 1970. But the average score in Title I schools rose three months. Significantly, the school department as of February 1972 had not yet analyzed these results as they pertain to Title I schools. This analysis is my own.

Title I schools still recorded below other schools. It is possible too that growing familiarty with objective tests exaggerated the extent of Title I gains. Nevertheless, there is reason to believe the gap at the lower levels may be narrowing, if only slightly.

Redirecting Resources

These reults underscore the importance of redirecting Title I resources. The real payoff, it seems clear, is in the elementary schools; that is where the program should be aimed. The Total Learning Center concept, which concentrates all Title I efforts on reading and math achievement, would seem therefore to be soundly based.

True, impoverished students need good food, health care, physical exercise, and many other services. But the central purpose of Title I should be to raise academic achievement. Other programs should rise or fall according to their contribution to that end alone. The schools should not try to be all-purpose social service agencies. It will take all their ingenuity and skill merely to teach children what they need to know to survive and compete in life.

A final word about Title I. A reporter studying the local schools looks in vain for some agency in the administration that is vitally concerned with what works and what doesn't work. There is no such agency in the D.C. schools. The Board of Education's attention focuses on which schools should or should not participate; administrators are chiefly concerned with how much money they will have to work with; employees with whether they can hold their jobs from one year to the next; teachers and principals with whether their books and supplies will arrive on time (they often don't).

Yearly evaluation reports have been notable more for their reliance on subjective opinions than their search for objective benchmarks by which actual progress can be gauged. This policy was made explicit by Dr. Mildred Cooper, assistant school superintendent, Division of Planning, Research, and Evaluation, in hearings before the House Committee on Education and Labor, May 1970. Said Dr. Cooper:

> The primary basis for evaluation of the Title I programs was consideration of the changes in the students in them, as measured by classroom performance and school adjustment, in terms of *observable student characteristics* in the school and classroom as evaluated by classroom teacher. A secondary basis for evaluation were such things as cost per pupil relative to other programs, and the extent to which the objectives of the program *appeared to be* accomplished. Additional factors were whether these programs *appeared to be* reducing

absences, and whether or not the programs were really dealing with that part of the target population most likely to drop out of school. [Emphasis added.]

Evaluation reports of Title I, required by law, are usually completed too late in the year to be of help in policy formulation. For example, in January 1972, while school officials were preparing the 1973 budget for submission to the Board of Education, the latest completed evaluation report was for 1969-70. In fact, a contract had not yet been signed for the 1970-71 study.

The lack of concern with results locally may derive from the attitude of the funding agency itself. The U.S. Office of Education carried out only one audit of program funds. Completed in 1969, it covered only the years 1966 and 1967. Only two years after it was completed did the Office of Education get around to demanding that the school department refund the money misspent during those years.

"Congress, in its wisdom, has said that this is a state run program," observes Thomas J. Burns, Associate U.S. Commissioner of Elementary and Secondary Education. "Our job is not to supplant the states or impose our will on them, but to provide technical assistance, to see to it they can do their job better. The rest is up to them."

Title I can best be viewed as a vast funding machine. Congress grinds out the money. The Office of Education funnels it to the states according to formula. As long as the formula is followed, the people who run the machine are satisfied. More and more money siphons into local districts each year. The trouble with the system is there is no incentive to produce, and no penalty for failure to produce. The only pressure is the pressure to spend the money, in as many schools as the law will allow.

There is, as Jerome Murphy has noted, a disconcerting tendency among lawmakers to abhor waste except when officials in their districts are accused of indulging in it.[7] What Title I needs is a Congress less concerned with dispensing dollars to school districts and more concerned with helping children in low-income schools.

---

[7] Jerome Murphy, *Title I of ESEA*, HARVARD EDUCATION REVIEW, February 1971.

ANACOSTIA PROJECT: AN IDEA WHOSE TIME NEVER CAME

When the U.S. Office of Education announced, in October 1971, that it was phasing out the Anacostia Demonstration Community School Project, angry supporters of the program staged a demonstration in the auditorium of the huge granite and glass building that serves as headquarters for federal school aid.

The significant thing wasn't their demand—that the program be reinstated—but their paltry numbers. Barely 200 protesters made the two-mile trek from Southeast Washington, and most of those who did either held jobs in the project or served on local community school boards.

At its inception, in 1968, the Anacostia experiment was hailed by Johnson Administration educators as "a beacon to school systems in other cities of the nation." Three years later, in recommending its demise, education officer Robert B. Binswanger explained:

> It tested the really hot educational item of 1968: Community control. It was an idea of tremendous political ramifications and popular appeal. But it just didn't work out. When we took a hard look at the program, we found nothing encouraging about it.

What went wrong in Anacostia can be summed up in two words: almost everything. It was an experiment in community control that was never delegated the authority to exercise community control. It was designed to be funded at $10 million a year, but instead received $6.5 million over four years. It was conceived—in the U.S. Office of Education—as a scheme for organizing the poor and was implanted in a section of Washington notable for its lack of organization and its apathy.

The federal government's first major demonstration in urban education, the project was originally envisioned as an ideal test of the concept of community school involvement, which had become a strong demand in black and Chicano ghettos following several summers of racial unrest.

Community control had already been tested in several urban settings, most notably in the Ocean Hill-Brownsville section of Brooklyn where a clash between black radicals and the white school bureaucracy provoked a bitter teachers' union strike and sent shock waves throughout New York's five boroughs and beyond.

The Ocean Hill-Brownsville plan was an outgrowth of a task force report, prepared for Mayor John Lindsay by a panel headed by Ford Foundation President McGeorge Bundy. The report recommended decentralizing that city's vast school system into small, locally controlled units. The architect of that report was a Ford Foundation program officer named Mario Fantini. Fantini also became chief consultant to the D.C. Schools—and a major booster of the Anacostia proposal.

As envisioned by Fantini and the U.S. Office of Education, which served as midwife and financial angel, Anacostia would build on the lessons of Ocean Hill-Brownsville. It would run for five years, and be comprised of 25 programs testing not only community control, but also the interrelationships of a host of other educational ideas of the moment: teacher aides, in-service training, new careers, curriculum innovation, and adult education, among others.

In fact, Anacosita opened its doors in February 1969 with only $1 million. It never involved more than 10 percent of the community. And the achievement gains that had been forecast were never clearly demonstrated.

The Anacostia project area consisted of 11 schools with 13,000 students in Washington's most isolated poverty pocket, a deteriorating urban scar, pockmarked by public housing, across the Anacostia River from the rest of the city. Acting under delegation of authority from the D.C. Board of Education, a locally elected community school board would run the member schools and hire "community reading assistants" to help the regular classroom teachers. Using the schools as magnets to bring the community together, it was hoped that local residents would go on to tackle other community problems, such as crime, drug addiction, dilapidated housing, and the shortage of community services. It employed, at its peak, a staff of 205 of whom three fourths were paraprofessionals.

From the first, the project ran into trouble. Its director, a school administrator imported from another part of the city, was immediately suspected of being a spy for the central administration. The project's choice of a headquarters—in a warehouse on the outskirts of the business district—reinforced the project's remoteness. The

Board of Education, acting on the legal advice of the D.C. Corporation Counsel, declined to delegate authority that would enable the project to choose its own personnel and control its own budget. This lack of autonomy, combined with continual underfunding, strained the project's credibility in the eyes of its constituents and severely hampered its managers' attempts to fill positions and start up programs.

The project was marked, too, by an appalling lack of supervisors. The two administrators for the D.C. schools with the largest interest in the project—Superintendent William R. Manning and Deputy Norman W. Nickens—were gone before it was two years old. At the Office of Education, responsibility was shifted from one bureau to another: from the Division of Compensatory Education to the parent Bureau of Elementary and Secondary Education, to the deputy associate commissioner for planning, research, and evaluation, to the Office for Experimental Schools.

"I'll wager," said Anacostia project director William S. Rice in January 1972, "there isn't a person in the Office of Education today who deals with us who was there when we started." Robert Binswanger, the brilliant, brittle former Harvard professor who runs the office of experimental schools, says he can't dispute that statement.

Binswanger says he investigated the project over a period of eight months at the request of U.S. Education Commissioneer Sidney Marland. Director Rice faults Binswanger for doing most of his investigating on paper. Argues Mr. Rice,

> As near as he is . . . he never took the time to go around and visit these schools, talk to the kids and their principals and see how the spirit in these schools has changed. We made them feel a part of their community for the first time, a part of their school. There were real changes in children, in their hopes, in their outlooks, but you can't get a feel for those kind of changes reading neat sterile documents in the Office of Education.

The best explanation of what went wrong was a summary prepared by the Office of Education itself. "All three major sources of responsibility share in the failure of the project to meet its objectives," the memo states. The responsible parties cited are the Office of Education, whose "general laissez-faire attitude made extremely difficult for the project to function efficiently"; the central administration of the D.C. schools, which "failed to provide the support and assistance it required"; and the project directors themselves, who after three-and-a-half years had still not developed the managerial capacity to administer the program properly and document its performance.

What the memo doesn't mention is that in the four years between the conception and the demise of the Anacostia project, the educational establishment itself had changed its objectives. In the District of Columbia, the search had turned from community involvement—using the schools as an organizing magnet—to academic achievement, the inculcation of basic skills in ways that are clearly measurable on standardized tests.

Nationally the action had shifted too. Nixon Administration educators seemed less swayed by grandiose tests of "hot educational items" than their predecessors. "We're a low profile operation," says Binswanger. "Our idea is to undertake practical tests of the results of educational research. There was no educational data base that Anacostia was testing, only a political idea."

In a sense, this makes it all the tougher for the people of Anacostia. "Marland told us it was not realistic to expect a community could do something with its schools that no school system had been able to do," grumbles William Rice. "It's like saying we were programmed for failure."

Anacostia, nonetheless, will have another chance. In affirming the decision to phase out the project as of August 31, 1972, education chief Marland said his office would make available $2.5 million for another experimental effort in Washington. The new project, which school officials say will also be in Anacostia, had not at this writing been drawn up, but Marland said it would operate under "considerably more supervision" from his office.

FEDERAL SCHOOL AID: A BALANCE SHEET

In certain respects, it must be emphasized, the District of Columbia's perspective on federal school aid is unique. Washington has more federal money than other districts; a virtual city-state, its local school board and school administration perform the functions of both state and local officials elsewhere. There is continual confusion even among administrators over these dual roles.

At the same time, the closeness of city and state functions has the effect of avoiding some mistakes made by local school systems further removed from the technical assistance of state departments of education. The Federal Programs Department of the D.C. schools—the state agency—is housed only a few blocks from the regular school administration building. Educators in both buildings work under Superintendent Hugh J. Scott.

The superintendent is answerable to two bosses: the school board and Congress. His relations with the city administration— Washington's presidentially appointed mayor-commissioner and city council—range from cool to hostile. The mayor's office tends to treat the schools at arms length. City hall does, however, trim the school budget each year, a factor which causes some administrators to say they work for two-and-a-half bosses. Finally, the congressional appropriations procedure is long and cumbersome and typically shakes funds free long after the school year is begun.

Federal aid is, for the most part, narrow and categorical. Superintendent Scott and the Board of Education would prefer the greater flexibility of block grants. There is no inherent reason why there need be 25 separate local school programs supported by the U.S. Office of Education.

On the other hand, the revenue-sharing concept proposed by President Nixon would channel education money through city hall. The popularly elected Board of Education opposes any scheme that would enable the politically appointed mayor and council to assert greater authority over the schools.

Revenue sharing would also make the states the leading agent in school reform. It would be up to the states to apportion the block grants received from Washington out to local communities. There is good reason to believe that without tight guidelines from Washington, such an approach would likely result in, first, shortchanging the cities and, second, denying aid to the politically impotent— principally the poor and the nonwhite.

There's no question that state departments of education need upgrading if they are to play a larger role in educational reform. Whether they should have the central role, however, is debatable. A national advisory council considering state education performance in 1969 concluded that more federal supervision was the surest way to safeguard that the revenues provided are wisely spent. The council recommended establishing basic federal criteria that would assure high quality programs. It also strongly urged improved federal monitoring procedures and a graduated scale of penalties for violations of federal education legislation, including, as a last resort, the withholding of funds.

The history of flexible federal money in the District schools gives an inconclusive picture of the likely effect of revenue sharing. Impact Aid has been spent for everything from rent to retraining, but it has not been used to introduce or back up a systematic educational strategy. The lesson of Impact Aid may be that too few guidelines are as unproductive as too many. A better use of flexible aid money is vocational education. By all accounts, this money is used to supplement and support the main thrust of the school system's program of career education.

The most critical need of District schools—aside from internal administrative reform—is for good, sound compensatory education. School adminstrators contend that they could accomplish wonders with more money. But the history of Title I would seem to indicate local problems stem less from lack of money than from lack of imagination, poor planning, and the absence of a concern with differentiating what works from what doesn't work.

George Weber, an authority on compensatory education at the Council for Basic Education in Washington, D.C., argues that Title I has enabled "a limited number of schools that knew what they were doing to do what they could not otherwise have done. The schools that didn't know what they were doing have wasted it."

That sounds to this observer like a fair summary of the situation in Washington's schools. Weber also suggests that the federal government should get tough with school districts that don't produce results with the money they receive. "If after five years," he suggested in an interview, "a school has not demonstrated improved results with Title I, it ought to lose its status and let other schools get the money. The way the laws are written now, schools get the money from now till doomsday whether they produce or not."

Federal aid to the District schools is sometimes misused, often ineffective, yet always needed. There is little prospct that any of those characterizations will change soon.

Chapter Three

HIGHER EDUCATION:
THE REACH EXCEEDS THE GRASP

by Eric Wentworth

> "The most urgent educational need in the District of Columbia is hope."
> —*President's Committee on Public Higher Education in the District of Columbia, June 1964*

> "The name of the game is not hope, it's money."—*Federal City College President Harland Randolph, September 18, 1970*

If the 1960s brought promise and prosperity to the nation's campuses, the 1970s opened with recession, retrenchment, and resentment.

The Kennedy and Johnson Administrations had presided over a national re-awakening to unmet social needs and had encouraged the belief that ambitious federal programs could solve them.

President Johnson, signing the Higher Education Act of 1965, said it would "swing open a new door for the young people of America. For them, and for this entire land of ours, it is the most important door that will ever open—the door to education."

President Nixon, however, found old needs still unsated and fresh ones fast emerging as the new decade dawned. Inflation, by-product of the Vietnam war, was helping drive costs of running a college or university higher at an alarming pace. Private institutions, and often public ones as well, were forced to raise tuitions almost yearly. These higher student costs in turn created hardships for many—and especially for disadvantaged youths with aspirations the federal programs may have aroused.

The government, besieged by myriad demands on the federal dollar yet compelled to control spending as an inflation remedy, elected to limit outlays for education and other programs despite evidence of mounting needs. By one reckoning, appropriations for all U.S. Office of Education programs slumped from 60.5 percent of authorizations in fiscal 1968 to 36.7 percent in fiscal 1971.

DISTRICT'S PUBLIC HIGHER EDUCATION

Not that federal funds for higher education were drying up altogether. The Nixon Administration's budget estimate for the 1972 fiscal year showed that all federal agencies combined were still spending close to $7 billion for "higher education" purposes. In the District of Columbia, private George Washington University alone calculated its fiscal 1972 federal receipts at $15 million in construction grants and loans, plus $12,750,000 for all other uses. Among the District's public institutions, Federal City College (FCC) received $18,800,000 in general operating funds. Washington Technical Institute (WTI) received $7,900,000 in operating funds, plus $13,760,000 for construction, and D.C. Teachers College (DCTC) received $3,200,000 in operating funds.

While such sums seemed substantial, they fell short of needs— sometimes drastically so. Moreover, a number of the basic higher education programs themselves, however well-intended and perhaps successful earlier, were proving outdated at the start of the 1970s. The Administration and members of Congress, recognizing these shortcomings, responded with new—but conflicting—proposals. As 1972 arrived, legislation still languished on Capitol Hill.

The Barren Back Yard

In the District of Columbia, the government's own back yard, higher education shared dramatically in the promises of the 1960s and the frustrations which followed. At the same time, the District had one problem uniquely its own: the absence of state government, or its equivalent, with adequate fiscal resources to spend as it chose.

For more than a century, the states had spent generous sums to create and expand their own public colleges and universities. These institutions, of course, could then share in the proliferating federal programs for student aid, construction and equipping of buildings, research, special academic programs, and the like.

But the nation's capital, under the firm thumb of Congress, had long been a near wasteland when it came to such public investments. Senator Wayne L. Morse wrote in the September 1968 issue of *American Education,*

> From the time of George Washington a dozen or more Presidents have urged Congress to provide a university for the capital city. . . . Over the years no less than six bills proposing the establishment of public higher education facilities in the District of Columbia were introduced, all of them destined for rejection by Congress. Opposition was sharp, some on the grounds that the Federal Government had no business paying for public education; but mostly the bills died for lack of understanding of the real needs of the District and its people.

In fact, the government had precedents for aiding higher education nationally dating back nearly as far as its own origins.

The Northwest Ordinance of 1787 set aside two townships, in the sale of two million acres to the Ohio Company, "for the support of a literary institution"—in due course, Ohio University at Athens. The Morrill Act of 1862 granted public lands in every state of the union as endowment for colleges of agriculture and mechanical arts. The second Morrill Act, in 1890, provided annual federal subsidies for the "land grant" colleges. Neither the first nor the second Morrill Act, however, did anything at the time for the District of Columbia.

The federal government's only real contribution over the years to higher education in the District, aside from supporting Gallaudet College for the deaf, had been subsidizing predominantly black

Howard University, which was chartered in 1867 right after the Civil War.

Major General Oliver O. Howard, one of its founders and soon its third president, was at the same time commissioner of the post-war Freedman's Bureau and thus had a hand in securing federal money for this private university from the outset. By the time the Freedman's Bureau folded in 1872, it had supplied Howard University with nearly $529,000. Congress began appropriating funds for the university in 1879, at the outset with year-to-year authorizations and since 1928 with permanent authority. In recent years, these funds covered roughly three fifths of the university's operating costs.

The Chase Committee: A First Step

In September 1963, at the urging of Morse among others, President Kennedy appointed a special committee to investigate the District's need in public higher education.

This seven-member committee, chaired by Dean Francis S. Chase of the University of Chicago Graduate School of Education, sponsored wide-ranging studies, surveyed the ambitions of high school seniors, interviewed educators and civic leaders, and reported back nine months later to the slain President's successor.[1]

"The most urgent educational need in the District of Columbia," the Chase Committee told President Johnson, "is hope. The public school system is overwhelmingly college-oriented, yet there is no low-cost general college to which its graduates can go."

Like other American cities, the committee said, more than one sixth of the District's population lived in poverty and cultural deprivation. Unlike a growing number of cities, the District offered nothing in public postsecondary education except a small, under-financed teacher-training college. "In consequence," the committee continued,

> a substantial portion of Washington's school population and young adults is now denied—largely because of the meagerness of their own cultural and financial background—all sense of participation in

---

[1] President's Committee on Public Higher Education in the District of Columbia, A REPORT TO THE PRESIDENT (Washington: U.S. Government Printing Office, 1964).

the society for which they are unprepared, and hence largely unneeded and unwanted. Without hope, these persons are in imminent danger of becoming permanently alienated from the dominant culture and values of their community.

The Chase Committee concluded that the District's large private universities—American, Catholic, George Washington, Georgetown, and Howard—failed to meet local residents' needs. "For valid reasons," the committee found,

> none of the five universities in the District addresses itself primarily to District residents. None of them is in a position to extend any tuition advantages to residents of the District, and each feels itself to have a national, rather than a local, mission.

Of 1,837 students who entered District universities from the city's public high schools from 1960 through 1963, the committee reported, 1,166 or 63 percent had enrolled at Howard. A subsequent school system survey of 1965 high school graduates showed about half continuing their education. Of these, less than 40 percent enrolled at the major District institutions; there were 468 at Howard, 150 at D.C. Teachers College, 63 at George Washington, 36 at American, 10 at Georgetown, and 2 at Catholic. On the other hand, of Howard's total student body only 20 percent had come from the District schools. The Chase Committee said it did not believe

> that Howard can or should be obliged to focus its attention primarily on District needs. Unless it were to move in a direction quite different from that defined both by its long tradition and its current aspirations, it could not expect to absorb a greatly increased number of students from the District.

While the private institutions at least struck the Chase Committee as an "impressive array," it found little to praise in D.C. Teachers College which was then under the city's Board of Education. The Committee viewed the school as characterized by "restricted outlook, scope and resources . . . gross inadequacy of its physical facilities . . . demonstrated inability to command the support by which it might have remedied its cumulative weaknesses." Though education at DCTC was a bargain—a $70-a-year general fee and no other tuition—the Committee found the college inadequate for the District's teacher-training needs, much less for a broader mission.

Hence the Committee recommended:

• Immediate creation of a comprehensive public community college offering both vocational-technical programs and two years of general academic work for students who would then take jobs or transfer to a four-year compus;

• Immediate creation of a public liberal arts college, offering both bachelor's and master's degrees, which would take over DCTC's teacher-training mission and develop other specialized programs as warranted;

• Prompt establishment of a public, noncompetitive scholarship program for graduates of the community college who wished elsewhere to pursue special advanced studies which the liberal arts college was not yet offering.

The Committee stressed that the two proposed institutions should have separate administrations and campuses, with the liberal arts college having "substantially higher academic standards for admission." At the same time, both should be governed by a new Board of Higher Education. President Johnson released the report on July 12, 1964, and urged immediate attention from Congress. "There is no more urgent need today," he said, "than to provide the educational opportunities which will permit every young person to develop to his maximum potential."

Congress: An Agreeable Compromise

It took Congress more than two years to enact legislation. The result, as Professor A. Harry Passow of Columbia University described it in his comprehensive 1967 report on D.C. education, was "a mutually agreeable, if not educationally ideal, compromise."[2] Congress elected to combine in Federal City College both the four-year liberal arts college and two-year community college, assigning control to a new board—with members appointed by the D.C. Government—which would also take over D.C. Teachers College.

Thanks to the high priority that Representative Ancher Nelsen (R-Minn.) among others gave vocational-technical education, Congress authorized Washington Technical Institute as a separate

---

[2] A. Harry Passow, TOWARD BETTER SCHOOLS: A SUMMARY OF THE FINDINGS AND RECOMMENDATIONS OF A STUDY OF THE SCHOOLS OF WASHINGTON, D. C. (New York: Teachers College, Columbia University, 1967).

institution, with its own Board of Vocational Education whose members—for prestige—would be named by the President of the United States.

The legislation ignored the recommendation for scholarships. One source, deeply involved in the congressional deliberations, recalled at least two reasons for the omission: blacks saw such scholarships as a device for deporting them out of the District at least for the duration of their studies, and the lawmakers saw campuses elsewhere as overcrowded already.

"No longer," President Johnson stated November 7, 1966, when he signed the measure into law,

> will District children be denied the opportunity, available to high school graduates in every state, to continue their education after high school in a publicly-supported institution.
>
> When the Federal City College and the Washington Technical Institute open their doors, a long-standing educational inequity will be eliminated. . . . I pledge the full support of the Federal Government in making these institutions not only a success, but a model for the nation.

Backlog and Log Jam

Federal City College and Washington Technical Institute opened their doors in September 1968, both charging only $25 a term for tuition. But by then it was already clear that opportunity was far from universal. The Chase Committee—and then Congress—had grossly underestimated the potential enrollment demand. The Committee itself surveyed high school seniors and the teachers, counselors, and principals who could judge their interests and abilities. It concluded that a low-tuition liberal arts college would draw at the outset at least 600 "college-able" new high school graduates each year; a comprehensive community college of the sort it proposed would, it estimated, start off with about 1,400 new students yearly.

The House District of Columbia Committee, for its part, based cost estimates for the two institutions on these projections: at FCC, total enrollments of 1,500 in the two-year program and 2,500 in the four-year program; at WTI, total enrollment of 2,500.

All these projections failed to take into account the countless District residents who had finished high school years before, when further education was beyond their means, and who now would seek a belated college degree. By the February 15, 1968 deadline for students applying to enroll the following September, FCC had an overwhelming 5,280 applicants.

The college ran a computer analysis and found abundant evidence of this educational backlog:

Only 22 percent of FCC's applicants were 17-18 years old, the normal age for prospective college freshmen. Another 30 percent were 19-20; 17 percent were 21-23; 15 percent were 24-28; 11 percent were 29-38; 4 percent were 39-48; and 1 percent were 49 or even older.

And lest these figures appear to indicate unusually old high school seniors, only 38 percent of the applicants were receiving their diplomas that year.

Moreover, only about 75 percent of the FCC applicants had attended District high schools at all; the other 25 percent had gone to high schools all over the United States and in foreign countries.

Finally, a total of 836 applicants had already attended some other college at least briefly, including 236 at Howard, 138 at DCTC, 40 at American, and 26 at George Washington.

Another factor undoubtedly increasing the number of applicants was the Board of Higher Education's adoption of an open-door admissions policy in lieu of greater academic selectivity. Passow's study had recommended such a liberal approach, contending that "The college should be at the cutting edge in channeling disadvantaged youth into the mainstream of higher education."

Confronted with a tidal wave of applicants, the board sought with limited success to gain a larger first-year budget from Congress. At the same time, it decided to admit students from the first 5,280 applicants by lottery, and thereafter follow a first-come first-served system. Thus from the outset, to the keen disappointment of applicants forced to wait their turn, FCC was an "open-door" college in name only—able to open its door to only a fraction of those who knocked.

On the positive side, the launching of FCC and WTI had an immediate effect on the fortunes of D.C. high school graduates. The school system reported that 65 percent of the 1968 graduates continued their education, a sharp leap from the 50.8 percent of the previous year's graduates. Of the 2,248 graduates who entered college, 492 enrolled at FCC, 386 at WTI, 233 at Howard, 174 at DCTC, 60 at George Washington, 55 at American, and 11 each at Catholic and Georgetown.

A comparable study for 1969 high school graduates revealed only a .1-percent increase in the numbers of those continuing their education. But there was a greater increase, from 46.5 percent to 51.5 percent, in the percentage of all graduates entering four-year colleges.

FCC: A Bitter Baptism

The original plan was for FCC to open in September 1968 with a freshman class, then add another class each fall until in 1971-72 it would have a full four-year undergraduate body. But this smooth development was not in the cards. Internal controversy and confusion, beginning with a bitter hassle the first year over demands for a separate "black studies" program and continuing with faculty-administration set-tos and blundered recordkeeping, sapped public and congressional confidence. Money was scarce in any case.

FCC, according to its own records, opened with 1,962 students in the fall of 1968 and by the following spring had 2,181 on its rolls. September 1969 saw the college adding its second class on schedule with total enrollment rising to 5,046. In the spring term, the figure reached 5,370.

Then trouble came. FCC had received a $4.3 million appropriation from Congress for the 1968-69 year, and $10.8 million (against an $11.7 million request) for 1969-70. For 1970-71, the college originally sought $28 million, but the D.C. Government slashed that request to $16.6 million. This sum would allow addition of FCC's third class in September 1970, however, and the college had sent out acceptance letters to more than 3,000 students —still leaving a waiting list estimated at 13,000.

Until Congress could act on the annual D.C. revenue bill for 1970-71, it held FCC's budget to only $11.6 million. In mid-August, with the revenue bill stalled in the House District Committee, FCC reluctantly announced it would send out letters to some 2,500 of the would-be freshmen saying it would be unable to enroll them in September after all. A public-interest law firm responded with a suit against the college on the rejected students' behalf. The suit was settled September 18, 1970, with the already overcrowded college agreeing to admit any students for whom it could find room.

"The name of the game is not hope," FCC President Harland Randolph said that day, "it's money."

While the college enrolled a total of 5,892 students that fall, the money shortage forced it to drop numerous freshman and sophomore courses and shift faculty into third-year courses for students who had been there since 1968. These maneuvers, however, still left many returnees unable to take the more specialized courses they needed.

FCC sought a $3.4 million supplemental appropriation, hoping to salvage a full three-year program when the winter term started in January 1971. The request included $2.7 million for the regular academic program and $700,000 to match land-grant funds from the Agriculture Department for community services. Again, the college was turned down—the revenue bill had not yet cleared Congress. It finally did so December 21, opening the way for still another appropriation bid, this time for $1.5 million. But it was May 21, near the end of the academic year, when Congress finally approved a supplemental money bill with $1.3 million for FCC. (FCC's enrollment, meanwhile, had slumped in the winter term to 5,204).

By then, the ordeal of the college's fiscal 1972 budget had already begun. President Nixon, as usual, sent the Administration's federal budget proposals to Congress in late January. The District's own budget process, however, consumed far more time.

FCC originally asked the District government to include $27.6 million in its budget proposals for the college's 1971-72 operations. Mayor Walter Washington cut that request sharply. The city council then had 30 days to endorse or modify the mayor's decisions. Next, the mayor had an opportunity to accept or veto the council's actions. The council then had another five days to override any vetoes, after which the surviving proposals went to the President's Office of Management and Budget.

Thus, it was April 19, 1971, when President Nixon finally sent the District's fiscal 1972 budget to Capitol Hill. The budget proposed $20.2 million for FCC, $7.4 million below the college's original request but supposedly still enough to let it become a full four-year operation. It was only on December 15, 1971—at the end of a new fall quarter for which FCC with fingers crossed had enrolled some 7,009 students—that House and Senate finally compromised their differences on a District budget with $18.8 million for the college's operations.

In the meantime, FCC produced in August 1971 a revealing analysis of its enrollment. The study disclosed that of the students who originally had entered back in September 1968, only 690 or 35 percent were still enrolled in the 1971 spring term. In terms of quarter hours completed over the three years, 116 were still counted as freshmen, 264 as sophomores, 234 as juniors, and 76 seniors.

Nationally, according to government estimates, some 52 percent of all students who entered public or private colleges as freshmen in the fall of 1969 were likely to gain degrees in the normal four years. But FCC had to concede that only 10 percent of its fall 1968 entrants were likely to graduate in four years.

President Randolph offered several reasons for this record. Some students only went to FCC for the two-year program or for a limited number of courses helping them qualify for better jobs in a particular occupation. Many were dividing their time between the classroom and continuing jobs, taking less than a full course load or only enrolling intermittently. For them earning a "four-year" degree if they wanted it would take a full decade. On the other hand, he might have added, the overcrowding, poor facilities, stunted curricula, and general confusion inflicted on FCC by its budget problems were undoubtedly also factors in many students' lack of academic progress.

WTI: Taut Ship in Tight Straits

Washington Technical Institute began operations at the same time as Federal City College, and had to endure the same tortuous appropriations process to get its funds. It also suffered during the 1970-71 budget crisis, receiving an initial outlay for that year of only $4.9 million against a $6.4 million request. As a result, it had to slam the door on 600 expectant new students, jam its existing classrooms, and crimp expansion of programs. By and large, however, WTI survived its first years with far less scar tissue than its liberal arts counterpart.

"The name of the game is jobs," WTI President Cleveland Dennard had proclaimed at the outset, and the institute set about tailoring an ever-broader spectrum of programs to match the expected market demand. By 1970-71, it could offer 29 majors in a wide assortment of technological fields: air traffic control, computer science, mechanical engineering, urban planning, nursing, criminology, firefighting, social welfare, and many others.

Enrollment started off at 957 in the fall of 1968 and rose to 1,824 in the fall of 1969, 2,146 in the slim-budget fall of 1970, and 3,019 in the fall of 1971.

In December 1971, a tentative list of pending applications totaled 3,156—including, surprisingly, 1,154 foreign students. The number of pending applications, however, reflected in part WTI's deliberate effort to keep enrollment for particular programs in line with likely employment afterward. Thus, the popular computer science program had a two-year waiting list for admissions.

DCTC: A Dramatic Revival

While the federal government's two new ventures in public higher education for the District were getting off the ground, long-undernourished D. C. Teachers College gained fresh appeal too. The newly created Board of Higher Education, following congressional dictate, took over DCTC from the school board in 1969, but put off merging it into Federal City College.

Despite the presence of two new, low-cost public institutions, DCTC's own fall-term daytime enrollment rose from 1,064 in 1967 to 1,357 in 1968, 1,518 in 1969, 1,485 in 1970, and 1,636 in 1971. Its graduating classes grew even more dramatically, from 121 in 1968 to 259 in 1971.

In sum, then, the combined impact of these three public institutions offering higher education opportunities to District residents was more than justifying the Chase Committee's assessment of needs. In the fall of 1963, as that committee began its work, DCTC's daytime enrollment had been a mere 621. In the fall of 1971, FCC, WTI, and DCTC together boasted a total enrollment approaching 12,000—a nearly 20-fold increase.

Moreover, all three were involved in an immense variety of special courses and community services beyond their basic academic programs. FCC in March 1969 began its well-publicized Lorton Project, offering a college education to inmates and parolees of the District's prison in Lorton, Virginia. Through the D. C. Cooperative Extension Service, funded with federal land-grant money, the college helped sponsor 4-H youth programs, nutrition aides to counsel low-income families on improving their diets, and other efforts to upgrade the lives of the disadvantaged.

Brick and Mortar

The three institutions' rapid growth, however, in itself concerned officials interested in sound planning, sensible coordination, and optimum return on limited public funds. The overriding question, in terms of dollars, was capital outlay for permanent facilities. Congress in 1966 had authorized $50 million to construct and equip campuses for FCC and WTI. By April 1971, the District officials estimated the two institutions' capital outlay needs would total $206 million to $220 million by 1980. DCTC, hoping for continued autonomy, began talking about a new high-rise building for its own needs plus a satellite campus in Southeast Washington.

The space requirements of all three were becoming critical. FCC, which had begun in a temporary building once occupied by the Securities and Exchange Commission, spread rapidly into leased quarters at a dozen scattered sites. WTI was crowded into the complex of buildings on Connecticut Avenue it had "inherited" from the National Bureau of Standards. DCTC continued to operate in two ancient and inadequate structures several blocks apart.

President Nixon, in his April 1971 message to Congress on District affairs, renewed a proposal that the District government be authorized to issue municipal bonds for most of its capital needs. At the same time, he proposed that permanent campuses for FCC and WTI be financed with direct federal grants. Congress declined in 1971 to approve Mr. Nixon's proposals. But it did appropriate $13.6 million, far more in fact than had been sought for fiscal 1972, to start construction of WTI's new campus just north of its existing quarters on the site which the President had approved. Final decisions on FCC's permanent campus, however, were still awaited.

Planning For the Future

Meanwhile, on March 29, 1971, the District government let a $250,000 contract to Arthur D. Little, Inc., the Cambridge, Massachusetts-based consulting and research company, for a comprehensive new study of public higher education in the District. The consultants were to gather and analyze information on everything from community aspirations to manpower needs and produce recommendations covering all aspects of the public institutions' future development.

Thus, less than eight years after President Kennedy had created the Chase Committee to survey an academic landscape nearly barren of public higher education, the District government hired consultants to study how the national capital's bugeoning public institutions should best be pruned, shaped, and cultivated.

The establishment and growth of Federal City College and Washington Technical Institute and the rebirth of D. C. Teacher's College were a direct result of the federal government's belated willingness to move toward overcoming a century of neglect. However limited the funds provided, and however unwieldy the budget procedures that produced those funds, federal appropriations in the District—as nowhere else in the country—were directly and almost totally supporting the operations of public academic institutions.

PROLIFERATION OF GRANT PROGRAMS

Aside from the annual operating funds they have received so tardily from Congress, the District's public higher education institutions—like their private counterparts—could qualify for additional federal money through an almost boundless array of grant and loan programs serving particular purposes.

The federal government began pumping large sums into the nation's colleges and universities during World War II, when it recruited hundreds of scholars and financed their work on military and other technological research in campus laboratories. In 1944, Congress passed the GI bill to pick up the tab for veterans' postwar education and training. Male college enrollments hit 1,836,000 in 1947-48, twice the 1945-46 figure, thus signaling a long period of massive growth in students, structures, and faculty payrolls that was to double and redouble the national investment in higher education. Passage of the Atomic Energy Act and creation of the National Science Foundation provided further federal support for scientific education and research.

In January 1958, after the Soviet Union launched Sputnik, President Eisenhower sent "emergency" proposals to Congress aimed at producing more scientists, engineers, and linguists to keep up with the Russians. He stressed national security and called his proposals "temporary."

The resulting National Defense Education Act (NDEA) of 1958 provided 90-percent federal matching grants to colleges for low-interest student loan funds, graduate fellowships for prospective college teachers, and grants for campus foreign language institutes.

Alice M. Rivlin, in her book *The Role of the Federal Government in Financing Higher Education,* called the 1958 Act "a hodgepodge piece of legislation, representing deliberate compromises, and . . . labeled an emergency defense measure, not a permanent program of federal aid to education as such."[3] Nonetheless, the NDEA set the stage for an outpouring of new federal higher education programs in the 1960s and was itself periodically enlarged and extended.

The 1963 Higher Education Facilities Act provided federal grants and loans for constructing campus classroom buildings and libraries. The 1965 Higher Education Act expanded earlier programs and added important new ones, among them: educational opportunity grants and work-study subsidies (already begun as an antipoverty measure) for the neediest college students; government-guaranteed loans for others; grants to the colleges for improving libraries and instructional equipment, developing community service programs, and training teachers; and grants to needy colleges struggling to survive.

In 1966, and again in 1968, Congress further extended, expanded, and refined programs it had previously authorized. The 1966 legislation covered authorization for construction grants and loans, aid to needy colleges, and federal financing of the NDEA student loans. The 1968 measure added new grant programs: spe-

---

[3] Alice M. Rivlin, THE ROLE OF THE FEDERAL GOVERNMENT IN FINANCING HIGHER EDUCATION (Washington: The Brookings Institution, 1961).

cial services for disadvantaged students needing tutoring, counseling, and remedial work to help them through college; "cooperative education" in which students alternated semesters of work and study; improvement of graduate programs; "networks for knowledge" to encourage intercampus pooling of resources; public-service education for students planning government careers; and law school "clinical experience" projects.

Over this same period, a multitude of other federal spigots were pouring money onto the campuses for research, training, and other relatively specialized purposes. Indeed, by 1968 Ronald A. Wolk could lament in the monograph *Alternate Methods of Federal Funding for Higher Education,* which he wrote for the Carnegie Higher Education Commission:

> There is probably no single person—perhaps not even any single agency—in or out of government who can define with accuracy all of the ways in which the federal government channels funds to American Higher Education or the amount of money actually spent or obligated for all of these programs.
>
> The funds come from more than forty agencies; they ride piggy–back on legislation which, at first glance, seems to have no connection with higher education. . . . Budget requests, estimated obligations, authorizations, and actual expenditures all run together, spilling across fiscal years and academic years, commingling loans and grants, and research funds and training funds. Much important information is simply not available, and that which is becomes obsolete almost as soon as it is recorded.[4]

In a broader context, the very question of what in fact constitutes federal higher education "aid" could be confusing. The President's Office of Management and Budget, in a special analysis accompanying President Nixon's fiscal 1973 budget proposals, disclosed that "federal outlays for higher education" totaled $6.2 billion in the 1971 fiscal year. Nearly half this amount was spent for student aid, and the rest was spent on a variety of institutional support and academic research grants.

Grants to District Universities

District of Columbia institutions, like their counterparts elsewhere, received a share of these total federal outlays. The money

---

[4] Ronald A. Wolk, ALTERNATIVE METHODS OF FEDERAL FUNDING FOR HIGHER EDUCATION (New York: Carnegie Commission on Higher Education, 1968).

came through so many channels, for so many purposes, that it was difficult to keep track of it all. A questionnaire by this writer, seeking figures on recent federal aid by source and purpose, produced a timely response from only one of nine District institutions to which it was sent. An official at one of the other eight compuses said the questionnaire "would take about a man-month to complete."

Information from the one institution which did complete its questionnaire on time, American University, offered a prime example of how many channels could carry federal funds to a single campus. AU reported receiving a grant total of $5.4 million in 1967-68; $4.3 million two years later in 1969-70; and $3.0 million in 1970-71 (Table 5).

An AU spokesman explained some of the money's uses in more detail. The Defense funds went largely for medical research and production of "foreign area studies" (cultural-political profiles of overseas countries and regions). The Agency for International Development paid for "exit interviews" with foreign officials, technicians, and students who had come to this country for training under the U. S. foreign aid program. The Department of Transportation financed work on new teaching methods for driver education.

Until mid-1969, Defense funds at AU had also supported the Center for Research in Social Systems, which gained a controversial repute for conducting studies involving psychological warfare, counterinsurgency, and other politically sensitive subjects.

The Justice Department, through its Law Enforcement Assistance Administration (LEAA) began in 1969 to spend substantial sums at AU for training policemen and other law-enforcement and court-system functionaries through the university's Center for the Administration of Justice. The LEAA funds were classified as student aid since they took the form of tuition subsidies for those enrolled.

In the spring of 1970, student and faculty critics claimed that the university was making a "profit" on the program and using this money to subsidize other educational ventures for inner-city youths. Dean Herbert E. Striner of AU's College of Continuing Education, interviewed in January 1972, said that this claim was nonsense.

Table 5

AMERICAN UNIVERSITY GRANTS BY SOURCE AND
PURPOSE, 1970-71

By Source

Department of Interior	$ 33,729
National Institutes of Health	103,100
National Bureau of Standards	7,513
Agency for International Development	187,723
Department of Health, Education and Welfare (includes Office of Education)	442,025
National Science Foundation	186,528
D. C. Public Schools	34,928
Department of Housing and Urban Development	11,660
National Aeronautics and Space Administration	40,727
Department of Justice	410,000
Atomic Energy Commission	11,540
Department of Defense	1,274,850
D. C. Consortium of Universities	28,537
National Endowment for the Humanities	27,000
Department of Agriculture	2,000
Department of Labor	1,668
Department of Transportation	184,555

By Purpose

Student Aid	751,663
Instructional	27,000
Community	125,697
Building, Construction	—
Books, Equipment	50,415
Research	1,995,692
Area Studies	33,672
Departmental	3,944
TOTAL	$2,988,083

Source: American University, Washington, D. C.

Striner said the Justice Department program produced neither a gain nor a drain on the University's books. As he described it, the LEAA funds were based on enrollment and paid directly into AU's general operating budget. The university at the same time reduced tuition charges to the eligible students—in effect providing them grants or loans of varying sizes according to priorities set by the government agency. Among 300 full-time and 2,100 part-time students in the 1971-72 program, for example, an experienced policeman might expect more generous aid than a freshman planning a future law-enforcement career.

Blending the LEAA funds into the general university budget was logical, Striner explained, since the special LEAA students took some courses in other AU departments while a number of regular AU students took special justice and law-enforcement courses. The university paid the professors' full salaries without regard to the particular mix of their students.

AU's overall federal funding figures proved an essential point: that a large portion of the government money was primarily buying services, however worthy, as opposed to subsidizing directly higher education per se. A full two thirds of AU's 1970-71 grant funds went to research. While research projects might attract or retain important professors, provide expensive equipment, and offer useful paid experience to graduate students, they often contributed little if anything to university operating revenues. On the other hand, as many institutions began to learn in the late 1960s, curtailment of government-funded research could leave them to pick up the extra costs.

Overall Impact

The overall impact of this bewildering smorgasbord of federal aid programs on the institutions themselves, individually and collectively, is difficult to assess. One effect, certainly, was growth. When the NDEA became law in 1958, private and especially public colleges and universities were already growing rapidly. The burgeoning of federal programs in the 1960s not only coincided with, but surely encouraged, the arrival at campus gates of millions of young Americans born in the "baby boom" which followed World War II. Federal student aid gave hundreds of thousands of these young Americans the financial resources for a college education which they would otherwise have lacked. Federal construction grants and loans financed the bricks and mortar for classroom buildings, libraries, laboratories, and dormitories to accommodate the horde. Numerous state university complexes attained populations comparable to those of middle-sized towns as enrollments passed the 20,000 mark. Faculties swelled accordingly—as did the endless list of courses they taught.

Beyond these heavy investments in mass education, federal aid programs were mostly designed to purchase the services of the academic community for national purposes.

One basic type of purchased service was the training of skilled manpower in particular fields. Aside from the federal student aid available to undergraduates generally, according to financial need, the government offered fellowships and other assistance, for example, to those who would become scientists or engineers—or would become teachers of others who would in turn become scientists or engineers. The numbers of students receiving this aid and the related federal programs aimed at broadening and improving instructional programs in such high-priority fields helped spur development of an academic production capacity which by the start of the 1970s was turning out more scientists and engineers than the government, private industry, university faculties, and public school systems combined could possibly absorb.

The availability of fellowships and research grants in the sciences also attracted students to those fields at the expense of others. In medicine, for example, many hard-pressed medical school students were lured during the 1960s into research—where money was plentiful—and away from careers as physicians or surgeons where the rewards would be longer in coming. The inevitable concern with a shortage of doctors came later, and was reflected in the 1971 enactment of health manpower legislation to subsidize medical education and boost production of doctors, nurses, and other health professionals and paraprofessionals.

A second, much vaster field in which the federal government bought academic services was in research and development—for the space program, national defense, health, pollution control, and various other domestic and foreign policy priorities. A number of the larger institutions, in fact, became increasingly identified as "research universities" thanks to the scale of government research funds they received; special centers, institutes, and laboratories proliferated on their campuses. Federal grants and contracts became a sort of sophisticated "pork barrel" in which congressmen, senators, and other public officials brought political pressure to bear to lure federal funds to particular institutions. University presidents found it hard—indeed, they seldom dared try—to turn down such federal largesse when it was offered. Big federal grants enhanced an institution's prestige. They attracted distinguished scientists—men who might even teach an occasional course. The government money also brought expensive laboratory equipment which, once in place, might be used for instructional purposes. Graduate students might help finance their advanced learning through paid jobs as research assistants.

On the other hand, the "research universities" which became heavily involved in government work also grew overly dependent on the government money. And when fat years started yielding to lean ones in the late 1960s, when cutbacks in federal funding coincided with soaring costs in an inflationary economy, these institutions were among those hit hardest.

TIGHTENED PURSE STRINGS

The overall decline of American University's government funds from 1967-68 through 1970-71 reflected, to a significant degree, the coming of tight federal budgets as inflation's threat grew. Several new higher education programs authorized in 1968—graduate program improvement, "networks for knowledge," public-service education, and law school clinical experience—were never funded.

Colleges and universities, at the same time, suffered increasingly from rising costs: professors' salaries and janitors' wages, academic programs with uneconomically low enrollments, building maintenance, utility bills, and a host of other factors. With other resources limited, they were forced to raise their charges to students. In the District, private-university tuition and required-fee rates for undergraduates averaged about $1,400 in 1965-1966 and have increased about 50 percent since. Howard University, helped by its federal operating subsidies, held to a $638 yearly rate as long as it could. But for the 1971-72 year, it increased charges to $843 (Chart 4).

Only the public institutions—FCC, WTI, and DCTC—maintained their original low charges (though for 1971-72 FCC sought an increase which was blocked by President Nixon's wage-price freeze.) The growing disparity between their minimal rates and ever-higher ones at the private campuses threatened, if anything, to widen the socio-economic gap between their respective student bodies.

CHART 4: COSTS AT WASHINGTON'S PRIVATE UNIVERSITIES ARE HIGH AND
INCREASING

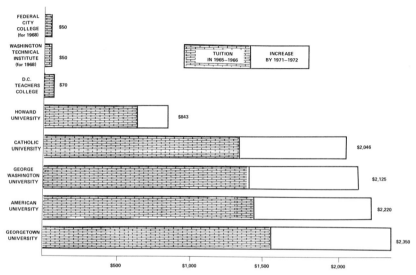

Pittance for Brick and Mortar

Federal cutbacks were particularly drastic in money for matching grants to finance academic construction projects, authorized
by the Higher Education Facilities Act of 1963. Figures supplied
by the D. C. Academic Facilities Commission, created under the
Act to coordinate planning and administer the program locally,
showed the District's private institutions receiving substantial federal money in the early years for science buildings, libraries, and
other such projects. In fiscal years 1965 to 1969, American received $1.9 million; Catholic, $1.0 million; George Washington,
$4.1 million; Georgetown, $1.0 million; and Trinity College, $.02
million (Howard's construction money, like its operating subsidies,
came directly from Congress).

By fiscal 1969, total appropriations had already dwindled dramatically, and the government was trying to shift financing of facilities projects to private loans with federal interest subsidies. District
institutions in fiscal 1967 received $2.4 million out of the total
$453 million appropriations; in fiscal 1968, $1.4 million out of
$267 million; in fiscal 1969, $890,000 out of $416 million.

Total federal grant funds shrank to $71 million in fiscal 1970 and $43 million (for community colleges and technical institutes) in fiscal 1971.

The Reverend T. Byron Collins, S. J., chairman of the D. C. Academic Facilities Commission and federal relations director at Georgetown, disclosed that the $43 million again appropriated for fiscal 1972 provided the District with only $229,000 under the government allocation formula based on high school and college enrollments.

The D. C. commission, he said, allotted $100,000 of that drop-in-the-bucket sum to D.C. Teachers College, which had plans for a $3.4 million physical-education facility. DCTC was theoretically eligible for a federal matching grant of up to $1.7 million.

Georgetown itself was allotted another $79,000 toward a major classroom-laboratory renovation project bearing a total $1.6 million pricetag. The rest of the $229,000 was reserved for WTI under a required allocation for two-year institutions.

Father Collins explained why the government's 3-percent interest-subsidy program for privately financed construction was, by itself, out of the question for Georgetown's first-priority need: a new $7 million building primarily for language instruction. The government program, he explained, would allow Georgetown to borrow commercially up to 90 percent of the project's total cost, or $6.3 million, with subsidized interest. The university would have to put up the other 10 percent of the cost itself.

"We can borrow that from a bank," Father Collins said, "if we can show that we can pay it back out of operating income." However, he calculated, putting up the university's initial $700,000 and repaying the $6.3 million loan would—despite the federal subsidies —force Georgetown to raise its tuition rates by an exorbitant $400.

If federal funds were available, he continued, Georgetown could qualify for a matching grant covering 50 percent of the $7 million, a direct government loan covering another 25 percent, and an interest-subsidy loan bringing total government coverage to 90 percent. That financing package would require a tuition hike of less than $90, he added.

Plight of Two Medical Schools

On another front, the Georgetown official said, government restraints on National Institutes of Health (NIH) research money became a factor in budget crises at the Georgetown and George Washington medical and dental schools.

As Father Collins described it, NIH research grants had been partially subsidizing medical school instructional costs. A given professor, for example, could devote 30 percent of his time to government-financed research and 70 percent to teaching. But federal money for professorial salaries was based on "effort" rather than time, and the professor could claim that he was dividing his effort 50-50. Thus, the government could be paying 50 percent of his salary for only 30 percent of his time. When an NIH grant was curtailed, the university had to pick up the federal share of the professor's salary. Or, when the growing medical school had to hire an additional professor without additional NIH grant money, the university had to pay the new arrival's entire salary itself.

With federal research money restricted, private contributions lagging, institutional reserves drained, tuition rates among the highest in the country, red ink on their ledgers, and costs still mounting, Georgetown and George Washington in the summer of 1970 asked Congress for urgently needed subsidies. A growing number of state governments, they noted, were subsidizing private medical schools. The District of Columbia, of course, was not a state.

The Nixon Administration and the District government told the lawmakers in early September that they opposed such aid "at this time." But by demonstrating need and with astute lobbying, the two universities were successful. The tardy D. C. revenue bill which finally cleared Capitol Hill on December 21, 1970, contained a two-year authorization for grants to the schools of up to $5,000 per medical student and $3,000 per dental student. Georgetown alone received an estimated $3.3 million in fiscal 1971 and $3.5 million in fiscal 1972, the money coming from an HEW emergency fund.

THE OPPORTUNITY PARADOX

In the District and around the country, the start of a new decade focused increasing attention on a glaring paradox. On the one hand, President Nixon, countless lesser public figures, civil rights leaders, student activists, and other keepers of the national conscience were insisting that blacks, Chicanos, and other disadvantaged youths gain greater access to higher education.

"No qualified student who wants to go to college should be barred by lack of money," President Nixon told Congress on March 19, 1970.

> Something is basically unequal about opportunity for higher education when a young person whose family earns more than $15,000 a year is nine times more likely to attend college than a young person whose family earns less than $3,000.

On the other hand, colleges and universities confronted a drastic cost-income squeeze. Besides raising tuition, they were being compelled to freeze hiring, curb salary increases, drop old programs, postpone new programs, and generally tighten sail across the full range of their expenditures. Many ran deficits, including in the District Catholic University and, at one point, Georgetown. Yet experience showed that disadvantaged students typically cost more than others to educate because of their special remedial and counseling needs. Moreover, as tuitions soared, disadantaged students required greater financial aid if they were to enroll at all. And with federal student aid limited, the institutions had to forage for other sources—including their own already tight operating budgets—to find added funds.

The government's student aid programs, however responsive to existing needs when enacted, fell increasingly short of the new demands placed upon them. Total appropriations were inadequate; program limits on what was available to individual students, equally so. Financial aid officers at D. C. institutions, both private and public, reported that federal funds fell substantially short of their requests, that numerous eligible students received less aid than they needed, and that other eligible students received no federal assistance at all.

At issue were four basic U. S. Office of Education student-aid programs:

• Educational Opportunity Grants (EOG), authorized in 1965, offered $200 to $1,000 a year up to four years for college undergraduates of "exceptional financial need." The college had to match each grant with equal aid, for which other federal assistance could qualify.

• College Work-Study (CW-S), first authorized as an anti-poverty measure in 1964, offered 80-percent federal matching grants toward paying the salaries of students employed by the college on campus or by noncommercial agencies off campus.

• National Defense Student Loans (NDSL), dating back to 1958, offered 90 percent of federal matching grants for colleges which set up revolving funds to loan money to needy students at a low 3-percent interest rate. Undergraduates could borrow as much as $1,000 a year up to a $5,000 total—and their debt would be partly erased if they became teachers.

• Guaranteed Student Loans (GSL), authorized in 1965, provided federal, state, or local agency guarantees for commercial or institutional loans to students, with federal interest subsidies for borrowers whose families earned less than $15,000. Students could borrow $1,500 a year.

Additional student-aid programs included Veterans Administration "GI Bill" grants at a basic rate of $175 a month for full-time unmarried students; Social Security grants to children of dead, disabled, or retired beneficiaries; HEW grants and loans to medical, dental, and other health-profession students; and various agencies' scholarships, fellowships, and traineeships for students in other specialized fields. Inadequate funding or limits on individual aid came under fire in some of these programs too.

Needs and Resources

But the U. S. Office of Education programs—primarily aimed at equalizing financial burdens of attending college regardless of the students' past or prospective careers—became the main target of critics and reformers.

The EOG, CW-S, and NDSL programs called for colleges and universities to estimate the federal funds they would need for each program in the ensuing academic year. The institutions forwarded their requests to the Office of Education regional headquarters, where "review panels" comprising student aid officers from that region checked them for "reasonableness" and recommended any adjustments—usually downward.

The total federal appropriation for each program, meanwhile, was allocated among individual states and the District of Columbia.

In turn, individual institutions in each state received a pro rata percentage of their adjusted request. Critics claimed the state allocation formulas were inequitable, with institutions in some states getting a larger percentage of their requests than others elsewhere. For EOG and NDSL, allocations were based on college enrollments in each state as a fraction of total national enrollment. In the CW-S formula, a state's high school graduates and children in low-income families were counted as well.

Annual federal appropriations for these programs came closer to the sums authorized by law than did, say, the outlays for construction grants. Hundreds of thousands of students had benefitted over the years from this money. By the start of the 1970s, though, government funding lagged seriously behind both institutional requests and the "reasonable" sums recommended by regional review panels.

Because the institutions' original requests are pared not only by the regional review panel but also by the Office of Education, actual obligations are far below initial requests. And Washington's colleges and universities have fared less well than have schools nationally (Table 6).

As a result of cutbacks, FCC for one claimed that 245 students accepted for the 1970-71 freshman class were unable to enroll because federal aid was lacking entirely or was insufficient. AU estimated about 50 students were thus barred. Catholic University, on the other hand, reported "none," and George Washington "very few." Georgetown said 479 "needed aid but did not receive it from Georgetown."

To be sure, many students qualifying for federal assistance did enroll, though available aid was less than their circumstances warranted. They received less generous federal support—possibly a smaller grant and larger loan—while the institution contributed other aid from its own limited resources.

Nationally, nearly half the states by the end of 1971 had scholarship programs of their own to supplement the federal support. The District of Columbia did participate in the federal guaranteed-student-loan program, but otherwise offered its residents practically nothing comparable to state student aid. It was common, at District institutions as elsewhere, for financial-aid officers to provide

Table 6

FEDERAL FUNDING FOR STUDENT AID PROGRAMS, 1971

	Initial Institutional Requests	Federal Obligations	Obligations as Proportion of Initial Requests
	(in thousands)		
National	$896,823	$599,749	67%
D. C. Private [a]	3,373	1,926	57
D. C. Public [b]	4,607	2,472	54
Educational Opportunity Grants			
National	244,945	163,586	67
D. C. Private [a]	607	437	72
D. C. Public [b]	1,049	732	70
College Work Study			
National	321,720	199,662	62
D. C. Private [a]	930	367	40
D. C. Public [b]	2,684	1,147	43
National Defense Student Loans			
National	330,158	236,500	80
D. C. Private [a]	1,836	1,122	61
D. C. Public [b]	874	593	68

[a] Includes private institutions: American University, Catholic University, George Washington University, Georgetown University, and Trinity College.

[b] Includes Howard University and public institutions: Federal City College, D. C. Teachers College, and Washington Technical Institute.

Source: U.S. Office of Education.

individual students with an aid "package" which could combine EOG, CW-S, NDSL, GSL, and nonfederal assistance.

Frustrated Aspirations

As educational costs mounted, however, the federal programs' limits on individual aid as well as the total funds federal programs supplied proved especially inadequate at high-cost private institutions. The neediest student, for example, could get a maximum EOG of $1,000, CW-S income from work supposedly limited to 15 hours a week during full-time study, and a maximum NDSL loan of $1,000 (a ceiling unchanged since the program started in 1958).

At the same time, George Washington estimated college-related expenses for its students in 1971-72 at $4,300, which included basic costs for tuition, room and board, books and supplies. At Georgetown, the range for comparable expenses was $3,700 to $4,100. George Washington followed a rule-of-thumb to deny any aid to a student—thus in effect precluding enrollment—unless it could produce an aid package that came within $500 of that student's needs.

Georgetown offered a particularly interesting example of how federal aid's inadequacies affected the enrollment of low-income students. Like many predominantly white, middle-class institutions under pressure to do more for the disadvantaged, it had begun a special program in 1968 to recruit and admit a certain number of students with below-normal academic credentials who came for the most part from poor families.

To provide financial support for students in this "Community Scholars Program," each of Georgetown's various undergraduate colleges and schools was contributing 20 percent of its available scholarship funds, including federal aid. Faculty, staff, church members, and other students also chipped in with money of their own. For the 1971-72 freshman class, the university received about 350 applications from disadvantaged students and admitted a total of 184. But Georgetown officials said only 84 of those students actually enrolled, and they attributed loss of the others largely to insufficient financial assistance.

At the same time, these officials said Georgetown, American, Catholic, and George Washington had jointly sought a $100,000 grant under the federal program of special services for disadvantaged students. This money would have supported counseling, tutoring, and related efforts to help their needy students make the grade in a challenging college environment. But for two straight years their requests had been turned down. A larger grant went instead to Federal City College, which, to be sure, had many more disadvantaged students and thus evidently a higher priority. The Georgetown officials, however, felt frustrated: they were trying to meet what they considered a social responsibility—one evoked by the federal government itself—only to be denied federal funds which they needed.

Under the other student-aid-program, government-guaranteed loans, HEW announced that in 1971 more than one million students borrowed more than $1 billion. Robert A. McCormick, director of the District of Columbia's Guranteed Student Loan agency, reported that in 1970-71, 1,922 D. C. residents borrowed a total of $1,969,310, up from 1,674 borrowing $1,684,000 in 1969-70.

But some loan-program officials around the country were voicing concern whether banks and other commercial lenders could be counted on to continue these less-profitable loans on a large scale indefinitely. McCormick said it was becoming more difficult to sell banks on this "public service" program, though those in the District were fulfilling their pledge to provide $1 million for new borrowers each year (this involved less money than it might appear since, according to McCormick, less than 50 percent of the "old" borrowers sought another loan the following year.) Moreover, the program's critics questioned both the wisdom and public policy of requiring students to rely too heavily on going into debt to finance their education. With federal funds limited, though, the Nixon Administration viewed loans as necessarily carrying a large share of the student-aid burden.

At the same time, the Administration adopted a strategy of "targeting" the available federal funds on the neediest students— those whose families had the lowest incomes and were least able to help pay their children's college expenses. It incorporated this approach in its 1970 and 1971 proposals to Congress. And with Congress failing to act, HEW sought to apply it to the extent possible through administrative rules.

Hard Choices

One particular tactic, effective for fiscal 1972, was to require colleges and universities to file a more sophisticated "institutional need analysis" in requesting federal aid funds for the ensuing year. Frank Williar, the government's student-aid program officer for the region including the District of Columbia, explained that the intent was to make institutional requests more realistic as well as to assist in "targeting" funds on the neediest. To at least one veteran financial-aid director on a District campus, the additional required data simply meant additional guesswork as well as paperwork. Where Williar said the new system should prompt more sophistication in campus financial aid offices, the local director said some institutions had neither the staff nor resources to be that sophisticated. "All you could do," this man said, preferring to be anonymous, "was to crank in figures you thought were fair and accurate."

The "institutional need analysis" forms called not only for detailed information on students' costs for attending the institution but, among other things, for an estimated breakdown of the institution's entire enrollment by family-income categories.

At the U. S. Office of Education, Educational Opportunity Grants program chief Hubert Shaw explained that the government had changed the system for allocating student-aid money among institutions within a state and within the District. Each institution was assured at least 80 percent of the Educational Opportunity Grant and College Work-Study money it received for the fiscal 1970 "base year." But beyond that, the government reserved some of the money to parcel out to those institutions whose students in the 0-$3,000 family-income category still were short of aid.

The most common complaint against the government's "targeting" strategy was that, with total funds limited, the so-called middle-income students were suffering. The student-aid director on one private, high-cost District campus noted that students from families with over $9,000 annual incomes were automatically disqualified from Educational Opportunity Grants. If the required parents' confidential statement showed a student could expect at least $625 a year in support from his family, he too was disqualified. The director reported having to answer to the government after providing a $1,000 grant, plus $2,000 from the institution's own funds, to a student whose parental income was $9,015—though the father was a postal worker with eight children to support.

This aid director said his institution learned from a recent study that students applying for aid came from families with average annual incomes of $13,333 and two children. But at one point, he added, the government said it frowned on having even National Defense Student Loans extended to students with parental incomes above $10,000. He said he simply ignored the dictum for students above that level if they indeed required aid.

By and large, though, most students from middle-income families were expected to depend on the government-guaranteed loans, for which they paid interest up to 7 percent.

It was hardly surprising, then, that in congressional consideration of new legislation the student-aid issue loomed high. There was general agreement that limits on individual student grants and loans should be raised to take account of higher tuitions and other educational costs. There was also accord on the need for substantially larger federal outlays. And there was broad support for creating a "secondary market" in which a government-sponsored agency would buy up guaranteed student-loan paper from banks and thus, it was expected, increase the volume of money commercial lenders were willing to commit.

Targeting vs. Flexibility

A serious dispute developed among Administration officials, lawmakers, and members of the higher education community over "targeting" versus flexibility. The Administration wanted a new law that would incorporate the "targeting" concept: the government, under its proposal, would publish a yearly national schedule indicating the type and amount of federal aid available to students at various levels of expected parental contribution. These contribution levels would take into account family income, family size, the number of children from that family in college, and other related factors. The advantage of this approach, the Administration said, was that students would be entitled to equal federal aid no matter where they enrolled—and would know ahead of time how much aid to expect.

The Senate accepted the "targeting" principle in an omnibus higher education bill it passed in August 1971. However, it proposed greater federal generosity in student grant money as opposed to loans. Students would be eligible for maximum "basic educational opportunity grants" of $1,400 less expected family contributions. In addition, the Senate included supplemental grants for students of both low- and high-cost institutions whose needs were not adequately met by the basic grants.

But the House, where key members paid greater heed to the views of financial-aid directors, included provisions in the bill it passed in November 1971 which gave those officials new flexibility in determining which students received how much federal assistance. The House bill rejected both a national needs standard and greater national program control in favor of letting student-aid directors base their decisions on individual students' particular circumstances.

INSTITUTIONAL AID DISPUTE

A second serious dispute developed over so-called institutional aid. College and university organizations, portraying their institutions' budget problems in often dramatic terms, contended that the government should embark on a costly new program of general operating subsidies. The House bill adopted such a program, including a formula under which two thirds of the money would be distributed to individual institutions according to total enrollment of full-time students (and their equivalent in part-time students) earning academic credits. The other one third would be distributed as a percentage of total federal student aid which the individual institutions received—an approach generally termed the "cost of instruction allowance."

Institutional aid based on total enrollment recognized that many, if not all, colleges and universities were in serious financial difficulty, and that the federal government should help them with general-purpose subsidies without attempting the all-but-impossible task of determining relative needs of individual institutions. The "cost of instruction allowance" approach recognized that institutions enrolling needy students—those qualifying for federal aid—were helping achieve the national objective of equalizing educational opportunity and should be rewarded accordingly. This second approach also recognized that disadvantaged students were often more costly to educate.

The Senate adopted only the "cost of instruction allowance" subsidies, pegging them to the number of federally aided students at each institution rather than the total student-aid money received. The Administration, for its part, first opposed any institutional subsidies on grounds that they would only "perpetuate the status quo" when sweeping academic reforms were needed. It proposed a National Foundation for Higher Education to help finance such reforms. In the spring of 1971, however, the Administration relented and said it could support a limited "cost of instruction allowance" program.

Either form of institutional subsidy, and especially perhaps the total-enrollment approach, carried certain risks for the colleges and universities which, nevertheless, for the most part eagerly sought the new aid. The greater the direct federal contribution to the institutions' operating budgets, the greater the possibility that the government in the future could attach unwanted conditions to is funds which insitutions could reject only at great financial sacrifice. At the same time, the greater the institutions' dependence on such federal subsidies, the greater their vulnerability to the vagaries of annual federal appropriations. A new surge of inflation, for example, could both send the institutions' operating costs soaring and lead the government to reduce its outlays. The institutions' own budgets would thus plunge into deficit as the federal government sought to limit its own budget deficit.

Federal City College, Washington Technical Institute, and D. C. Teachers College were already, of course, almost entirely dependent on federal subsidies Their problems were compounded by the fact that their funding requests were channeled through the District government's lengthy budgeting procedures and then scrutinized by the congressional committees charged with District affairs. Howard University received its federal funds as part of the U. S. Office of Education appropriations bill, which as time went on gained far prompter Capitol Hill approval. To shift the Federal City College, Washington Technical Institute, and D. C. Teachers College funding out of the District budget's obstacle course and onto the more direct route of Howard University's course theoretically held promise of helping both the timing and size of their appropriations. Such a change, however, faced numerous political and administrative objections. Thus, the three public institutions' only apparent hope lay in some drastic overhaul of the entire District budget's handling both downtown and in Congress.

The inherent risks in direct federal operating subsidies for all colleges and universities suggested that massive federal student aid with a limited "cost of instruction allowance" would be preferable. Such aid would have to be sufficient to allow enrollment at high-cost as well as low-cost institutions. Student aid, moreover, would subsidize the institutions indirectly to the extent it allowed more students to enroll and thus yielded more tuition revenues. The student aid program would have to allow increased tuition rates but could control excesses.

Such student aid could be effective, however, only if the federal government were prepared to finance its programs on a far larger scale than it had done in the past. Thus, beyond all questions of policy, the key issue involved priorities—whether higher education in the 1970s could claim a larger share of the federal dollar.

On June 23, 1972, President Nixon signed into law the new higher education legislation which would set the format for federal aid to college students and their institutions over the next three fiscal years. The bill, which survived a months-long controversy over amendments to slow the pace of school desegregation, retained the Senate's "basic educational opportunity grants" and tied institutional subsidies largely to student aid.

The basic grants entitled undergraduates to a yearly $1,400 less family contributions. If the program were fully funded, individual grants would be limited to 50 percent of college attendance costs and could not exceed the student's specified need—that is, the difference between family contribution and attendance costs. If it were less than fully funded, individual grants would be scaled down and in any event could not exceed 50 percent of need (or 60 percent if the program was at least 75 percent funded).

At the time President Nixon signed the bill, estimates of what it would cost the government to fully fund the basic grants program ranged from just under $900 million a year to $1.2 billion or even higher. Such federal outlays seemed unlikely, especially so since the legislation also required annual appropriations totaling $653.5 million for the old student-grant, work-study, and direct-loan programs —which were extended for three more years—before any new basic grants could be awarded.

As for institutional aid, the new law provided a compromise scheme whereby 45 percent of the total funds appropriated would be allocated according to the number of basic grant recipients at each campus, another 45 percent according to the volume of other federal student aid money each campus received, and the final 10 percent according to graduate-student enrollments. The overall ceiling for this aid was $1 billion a year.

However, before any of the 45 percent linked to the number of basic-grant recipients could be distributed, the legislation required that the basic grant program itself be sufficiently funded to assure all eligible students at least 50 percent of the stipends to which they were entitled.

For colleges and universities to receive any subsidies under that provision, in other words, would require a major increase in the government's overall level of student aid funding. For that to occur and for appropriations under all the other new or extended programs to be sufficiently high at the same time, higher education would have to achieve a far more elevated status in the federal-aid galaxy.

CONCLUSION

In fact, the prospects for higher education gaining a loftier rung on the ladder of national priorities seem slim. Federal investments in colleges and their students cannot offer the same sorts of tangible returns as can those in missiles, aircraft carriers, or superhighways. Any contributions of higher education to national security or prosperity tend to be indirect and long-term. Moreover, in the area of human needs, a college education cannot claim to be a necessity on the same plane as health, housing, compensation for the jobless, social security, or, for that matter, elementary and secondary education.

At the same time, the higher education lobby boasts neither the economic leverage nor the political clout to overcome the above-mentioned disadvantages in jockeying for government dollars. The higher education lobby, in fact, comprises mostly college and university administrators and the associations which represent them in Washington. The students—those more than eight million consumers of higher education who should in principle be the most outspoken interest group—have rarely been inclined to lobby for more federal aid. When they have come to the nation's capital in recent years, it has usually been to campaign stridently for ending the Indochina War. The demonstrations they have sometimes mounted to dramatize that cause have hardly enhanced their image as deserving beneficiaries of federal subsidies.

If the total volume of federal aid to higher education seems unlikely to grow dramatically, however, some federal programs even with limited funding will likely continue to influence academic policy. This is particularly true in regard to student aid, where the commitment to bring young men and women from economically, educationally, and culturally disadvantaged backgrounds into the mainstream of American life through equalizing educational opportunities appears firmly rooted.

Meanwhile, the larger universities especially appear destined to continue as service agencies supplying the government with a limitless range of research, advice, and specialized training to meet whatever particular priorities are deemed worthy of funding. One must avoid, however, the notion that federal grants for these purposes can be neatly classified as aid to higher education.

It is ironic, indeed, that amid all the rhetoric of recent years to the effect that colleges and universities should concentrate on their primary mission—teaching, and research related to it—it is the fulfillment of this mission which the federal government seems least willing to support. In fact, of course, as noted in discussing the inherent risks of general institutional subsidies, the government perhaps should not get too heavily into the business of supporting it. That too may be ironic, but it also suggests a basic, inescapable limitation on the federal role in supporting higher education.

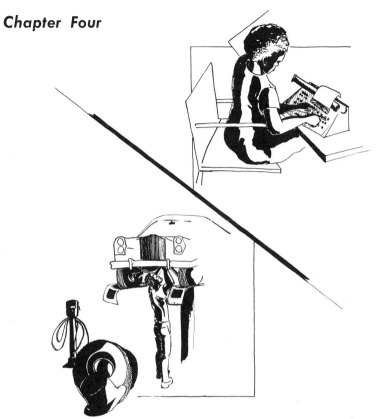

Chapter Four

MANPOWER TRAINING:
TURNING THE UNSKILLED INTO
PRODUCTIVE WORKERS

by Julius Duscha

The difficulties experienced by millions of people in finding work paying adequate wages to support themselves and their dependents has been a growing cause for serious concern. This concern has been translated into expenditures of $4.3 billion nationally in 1972 for "manpower programs"—efforts outside the existing educational structure to prepare people for jobs and provide supportive services, and outside usual hiring channels to create jobs. D.C.'s slice of this pie in 1972 was over $29 million.

THE EVOLUTION OF MANPOWER EFFORTS

After World War II, Congress declared in the Employment Act of 1946 that every American should be able to get a job commensurate with his abilities but appropriated no funds to effect this lofty goal. High unemployment during the 1960 election year and the specter of technological obsolescene, and later the "rediscovery" of poverty and the question for racial equality, spawned a spate of programs to help those who experience difficulties in the market place to find and hold a job. The first commitment of the 1960s was contained in the Area Redevelopment Act, which sought to improve economic conditions in depressed areas with high chronic unemployment. The stereotyped retraining situation envisioned in this legislation was that which would turn an unemployed coal miner ito a highly paid automobile mechanic.

A year later came the Manpower Development and Training Act of 1962, a congressional response to the fear that technological changes in the United States were making long-existing jobs obsolete. Again, as in the ARA legislation, the idea was retreading or upgrading the job skills of persons who had been working for many years but whose skills had been outmoded by machines.

In 1964, with the Economic Opportunity Act designed to fight President Johnson's "war on poverty," manpower-training programs were expanded not only to include workers who found their skills obsolete but also to reach the "hard core" unemployed ranging from unskilled youths to middle-aged and older members of minority groups who had no skills. Reflecting the rise in the number of youths seeking jobs, the programs attempted to emphasize their needs.

New problems have continued to arise and new approaches to be designed. Building on the experience of two smaller attempts, the Work Incentive (WIN) program was begun in 1968 as a major effort to restore relief recipients to economic independence and thereby cut the cost of burgeoning welfare rolls. The shortage of skilled, experienced workers in the tight labor markets of the late 1960s made feasible a hire-now, train-later program, with the government paying private industry for hiring the hard-core unemployed. Although inaugurated by the Johnson Administration in 1968, this JOBS (Job Opportunities in the Business Sector) program was favored for its compatability with Republican ideology by the succeeding Nixon Administration.

The substantial increase in unemployment during the first years of the 1970s brought further changes. Tools which had been useful in tight labor markets proved less sucessful in slack conditions, and the spread of joblessness, coupled with an alleged backlash against antipoverty programs, led to more attention for the victims of the economic recession at the expense of the poor. In addition to these changes in existing programs, a major new Public Employment Program was begun because unemployment was not responding to the Administration game plan.

All the while the cost of this proliferating alphabet soup has been rising: from about $200 million in 1961, to $789 million in 1965, to $2.3 billion in 1969, and to $4.3 billion in 1972.

Administrative Structure

The major new manpower programs are administered nationally through the Manpower Administration of the U.S. Department of Labor, which in turn works with federal-state agencies in the 50 states. When Congress established the U.S. Employment Service in 1933, it decided to make it a federal-state cooperative agency. Only the District of Columbia, which is neither a state nor a self-governing city, was kept solely under federal administration, partly because of its unique status and partly because it was viewed as a close-at-hand opportunity for observation and laboratory testing by the Secretary of Labor and his aides. And it has remained a branch of the federal Manpower Administration.

The federal government picks up most of the tab for manpower programs, its $29 million for 1972 equalling 90 percent of the total cost. The District, like many other states and localities, contributes 10 percent in kind—usually in office space and equipment for the programs.

By being a part of the U.S. Department of Labor, the D.C. Manpower Administration has been free from the federal-state infighting that is so common in programs like the employment services and the federal manpower programs in the states, which in theory are cooperative but in fact seldom are so. In many ways, then, the Washington experience with manpower programs should have been a model. The results of these programs in Washington ought to have been better than in the states because the nation's captal has fewer layers of bureaucracy to deal with than has been the case in the states.

The Economic Setting

The Washington economic setting is also better than that of most states. Washington and its suburbs make up one of the fastest growing areas in the United States. With more than half the jobs in the area accounted for by government, employment is unusually stable. There is little manufacturing, with its seasonal ups and downs, and much of the nongovernment employment is in services, which in the last decade have been growing far more rapidly than manufacturing.

Stable and generally prosperous as the Washington labor market is, it also has its peculiar distortions. The nonprofessional jobs available in the government are generally secretarial and clerical positions which traditionally have been filled by women. Service jobs, whether they be as maids in hotels or as waiters in restaurants, are abundant, but they are often jobs which many youths today view as beneath their dignity. And there are, of course, few well-paid factory jobs requiring little training.

Washington also has a larger percentage of blacks than any other city in the United States. The 1970 census found that 71 percent of Washington's 756,000 residents were black, and the D.C. Manpower Administration estimates that blacks and other members of minority groups (mainly Spanish-speaking residents from Puerto Rico, Cuba, and other Latin American countries) make up a like proportion of the work force.

Though poverty persists to a greater extent in Washington than in most other large cities, the black population is also more affluent than in other major cities. A black middle class has been an important part of Washington for many years. The growth of federal employment and its generally high wage levels have kept pay in private employment fairly high.

Although unemployment for the Washington area averaged under 2.5 percent in the 1960s and in late 1971 was 2.9 percent, this was still only half the national rate. But unemployment in the District of Columbia alone was about 5 percent, and the level is considerably higher among black men and youth in inner-city and other ghetto neighborhoods, where estimates place the unemployment and underemployment rate at from 20 to 30 percent. In a 1968 survey by the D.C. Manpower Administration, 23 percent— 90,000 persons—of the area's labor force was put in the subemployment category. This figure included 17,000 unemployed and seeking work; 12,000 part-time workers looking for full-time employment; 16,000 unemployed who were no longer seeking jobs because of their past inability to find them; and 45,000 persons earning less than $3,000 a year. About 80 percent of the people in all these groups were nonwhite. Around 28 percent were under 21, and 25 percent were over 45.

So despite the stability of the Washington labor market, the growth of the area, and the low area-wide unemployment rate, the District of Columbia still has all the characteristics that have led to the development of massive federal manpower-training efforts— high unemployment in ghetto areas, much underemployment, and large numbers of poorly educated persons with few skills.

THE RANGE OF PROGRAMS

There are four major types of manpower services:

—skill training, adult education, and other remedial measures imparted in an *institutional* setting;

—skill training and remedial measures provided *on-the-job;*

—*job creation and work experience* provided through seasonal or semipermanent work and through new jobs for the unemployed; and

—*job placement and support,* including counseling, recruitment for programs, and related manpower services.

Some programs concentrate on one of these strategies, while others combine various elements. The full range of these services is available in Washington's 11 major manpower programs, through special local efforts in addition to participation in all major national programs (Table 7). Services are provided by the local government, through the manpower agency and other units, and by private for-profit and not-for-profit contractors. Of almost 26,000 enrollees for 1972, over half were put to work with no training, while the others received varying amounts of counseling, basic education, and training in job skills.

The number of programs as well as the number of categories indicates the wide range of manpower training efforts undertaken by the federal government since 1961. All of the major manpower programs have been tried in the District of Columbia not only because its inner-city unemployment problems are severe but also because the District is a handy laboratory for the administrators of the national programs.

Table 7

FEDERAL MANPOWER PROGRAMS IN WASHINGTON, 1972

Program	Federal Expenditures (in thousands)	Number of Enrollees
Institutional Training		
Manpower Development and Training Act (MDTA)	$ 2,400	1,160
Project BUILD	535	410
Opportunities Industrialization Center (OIC)	1,600	1,800
Residential Manpower Center	1,250	185
Concentrated Employment Program (CEP)	5,060	2,500
Work Incentive (WIN) program	2,300	1,540
On-The-Job Training		
PRIDE, Inc.	2,000	1,300
Job Opportunities in the Business Sector (JOBS)	1,000	1,668
Job Creation and Work Experience		
Public Service Careers (PSC)	2,039	503
Neighborhod Youth Corps: Summer	4,500	12,000
In-School	1,500	1,600
Out-of-School	1,800	650
Public Employment Program (PEP)	3,070	500
TOTAL	$29,054	25,816

Source: D. C. Manpower Administration.

Such a large number of programs leads inevitably to less-than-healthy rivalries among administrators for funds and also to duplication of efforts. So many programs also can lead to program-hopping by persons in need of training and to administrators taking the applicants mostly likely to succeed rather than those who need help the most so as to build up statistics of success to use in getting greater appropriations next year.

INSTITUTIONAL TRAINING

Manpower Development and Training Act

The first manpower-training program put into operation in the District of Columbia was a skills-training program under the Manpower Development and Training Act (MDTA) of 1962. Dating back to 1962, it is still the major manpower-training program that emphasizes skills training rather than a balance between remedial and skills training. MDTA investigates the labor market on a systematic basis to determine where job shortages exist before training people and seeks to tailor its training program to job vacancies. The MDTA program is run jointly by the Department of Labor and the Department of Health, Education and Welfare (HEW), with Labor determining areas of job needs and providing payments to persons being trained while HEW supervises the training.

In the District of Columbia a total of $2.4 million was budgeted for MDTA in the 1972 fiscal year. With this money, 1,160 persons were to be trained during the year.

As in the case of most of the other manpower programs in Washington, MDTA's biggest training component is for secretarial-clerical jobs, which are taken almost entirely by women. In addition, MDTA trains men for such jobs as welding and automotive repair. The dropout rate is fairly low—15 to 20 percent—and the placement rate is high—about 85 percent. But MTDA generally is handling a relatively well-educated and highly motivated group of men and women.

The biggest problem facing MDTA in Washington has been the failure to develop an adequate skills-training center. HEW gave this responsibility to the District's Board of Education, which has had difficulty setting up a suitable center. In the meantime, MDTA has contracted out training to private facilities.

As a pioneering and well-structured program, MDTA would be expected to be a mainstay in the manpower effort, but it has not been that in Washington. This is due in part to the fact that many of the unemployment and training problems in Washington stem more from the lack of a good basic education than from merely a lack of job skills, and MDTA is designed largely for skills training.

Opportunities Industrialization Center

Another program that has had a considerable impact on the community—and a large degree of success—is the District of Columbia's Opportunities Industrialization Center (OIC), one of 103 OICs throughout the United States. The OIC motto—"a hand-up, not a hand-out"—is a manpower-training program that grew out of the ideas of the Reverend Leon Sullivan, a black minister in Philadelphia and the first black to become a member of the board of directors of General Motors Corporation.

The Washington OIC received $1.6 million from the Labor Department for the 1972 fiscal year. With that money its goal was to enroll 1,800 persons in its programs. Unlike most other manpower programs, OIC does not pay training stipends, so its per-person cost of $1,200 is lower than in comparable training programs.

Like the other manpower programs that have had some success, OIC has an extensive counseling and remedial-education program. Its skills-training operations cover the usual gamut of jobs favored by manpower programs: clerk-typist, business-machine operator, keypunch operator, auto mechanic, and building tradesman, as well as the expanding field of offset printing.

The OIC attrition rate is low, and its placement record is good. Only a fourth of its trainees drop out, a figure which is unquestionably attributable in large part to the OIC policy of not paying its enrollees. With no stipends available, OIC undoubtedly attracts better motivated persons than some of the other manpower programs, which pay a person while he is learning and often get people who only want the money. There is nothing for a hustler at OIC.

OIC's job-placement record is 87 percent. And OIC does not consider a graduate placed unless he is still on a job six months after taking it. OIC's record reflects the high motivation of a person attracted to a manpower program that does not pay while he earns.

OIC had many things going for it. There is a religious fervor, instilled by the Rev. Mr. Sullivan and by Rev. Edward A. Hailes, the executive director of the Washington OIC. There is the "We

Help Ourselves" motto of OIC, which—although OIC could not do what it has done without government funds—removes some of the handout stigma attached to government-financed and government-run programs. And OIC is dedicated to the Puritan work ethic.

Residential Manpower Center

The District of Columbia also has a Residential Manpower Center. This is a Job Corps Center with a new name and in an urban setting. Located in some of the old buildings at Fort Lincoln once used by the National Training School for Boys, the Residential Manpower Center enrolled early in 1972 a total of 185 youths. Of these, 119 were men, largely from Baltimore and Philadelphia, who were living at the Center. The 66 other trainees were women from the District of Columbia who went to the Center daily for classes but continued to live at home. As of February 1972, the Center was in the process of phasing out the nonresidential program for women and expanding its residential program for men.

The Job Corps was probably the sentimental favorite of the manpower programs spawned by President Johnson's war on poverty. Patterned after the Civilian Conservation Corps of the depression years in the 1930s, the original concept of the Job Corps was to turn ghetto youths into tax-paying citizens by straightening them out in sylvan retreats.

But the Job Corps did not have much success. Not only did its camps lack adequate training facilities; they were also plagued with racial and crime problems. Furthermore, the rural communities near which the camps were located were not very hospitable to the blacks who made up the majority of the Job Corps enrollments.

When the Nixon Administration came into office in January 1969, it closed many rural Job Corps centers and set up facilities in the cities. It was understandable that the Nixon Administration also decided to change the name of the urban Job Corps centers to Residential Manpower Centers. The Job Corps image of unruly youth and failure was not one with which any person wanted to be associated.

But many of the same problems which troubled the old Job Corps centers are facing the Residential Manpower Center in the District of Columbia. Being a residential program, it is expensive and also has a high dropout rate. For the expenditure of $2.5 million over a two-year period from April 1970 to April 1972, the District's Center graduated only 87 enrollees. Many more persons were at the Center for varying lengths of time, but the dropout rate was 40 to 50 percent.

The Center is undeniably dealing with high-risk enrollees. Ninety-eight percent are high school dropouts; many have been involved with the police and the courts; and some are on drugs. The Center emphasizes counseling and basic remedial education as well as training in such skills as clerk-typist, shorthand, office machines, key-punch operator, automotive repair, building trades, and heating and air-conditioning. Training can last from four months to two years, and the Center is obligated to find jobs for all its graduates.

Nevertheless, the high cost of turning out a graduate and the attendant problems of holding the interest of enrollees raise questions about the whole Job Corps concept. The Center in Washington is operated by the Training Corporation of America, a subsidiary of American Standard. The Job Corps and Residential Manpower Centers are business- and profit-oriented. And they have had less success than programs run strictly by the government or programs operated by private nonprofit organizations using government funds.

Project BUILD

A small but fairly effective effort that has had the cooperation of building trades unions as well as contractors is Project BUILD, started in 1968 as part of an effort to get more blacks into Washington construction unions. The program had a budget of $535,000 for the 1972 fiscal year.

Located in an old warehouse near Union Station, Project BUILD had money for a total of 410 men in fiscal 1972. Of these, 160 were to be trained for apprentice jobs; 200 places were for journeymen blacks working below their potential skill level who needed to earn more; and 50 were for veterans or men who needed additional training to qualify as apprentices.

The program is small, but it is geared to what the building trades unions say they can take in any year. The training period is relatively short—three months—and consists of both remedial education and training in construction work ranging from carpentry to the operation of large cranes. Those who are picked for training that will qualify them for apprentice jobs must be high school dropouts, and 60 percent of those entering the program finish it.

Originally, the program provided for six months of training in preparation for an apprentice job, but after some experience with a six-month program it was decided that as much could be accomplished in an intensive three-month program. Everything is geared to making a man ready for a job. He is given just as much remedial education as he will need to function as an apprentice. "We don't give them black history or geography, for example," an administrator of the program said. Every minute in classroom and shop situations is designed to enhance the trainee's abilities once he gets on a construction job.

The program is not without its problems. Up to a third of the enrollees in any one class may be on drugs. There is suspicion among the youths in the program that they will never be able to get jobs because of racism in the building trades. And once the trainees get out on the job they quite often run into race problems. But the directors of the program have a good follow-up system which carefully keeps track of every graduate and seeks to deal with such problems as race as soon as they are detected.

The reasons for the relative success of this program are fairly obvious. There is cooperation among most of the unions and contractors. The size of the program is determined by the demands of the job market. And, perhaps most important of all, every youth knows that the building trades pay well. Skilled building-trades workers are men with a future.

Concentrated Employment Program

The Concentrated Employment Program (CEP) got under way in 1968 to provide the full range of manpower and related services to the disadvantaged in areas with a high concentration of unemployment and poverty. CEP is run by Washington's United Planning Organization (UPO), a 10-year-old antipoverty group.

For the 1972 fiscal year, the CEP budget was $5.06 million. With this money UPO hoped to put 2,500 persons in the CEP program. While CEP can provide a broad variety of services, Washington's project has emphasized classroom education and training.

To be eligible for CEP, a person must be a member of a poor family (less than $4,000 annual income for a family of four) and either unemployed, underemployed, handicapped, a school dropout, or a minority member under 22 or 45 or older. CEP areas must have a high proportion of such persons, but the government tries to keep the target population small enough to be able to demonstrate the results of "concentrated" utilization of resources.

Recruitment is done through community centers run by UPO, and most CEP recruits walk in the doors of the centers looking for help of some sort, often without even being aware of the CEP program. Teams of counselors are used to determine the person's needs, his potential on a job, and the kind of job best suited for him. CEP emphasizes giving trainees options rather than necessarily directing them into jobs that a counselor thinks are best for them.

Under the CEP program, actual training in both remedial education and in skills has moved from specialized or trade schools with which CEP had been contracting to a skills center operated by the District of Columbia Board of Education. Although many persons connected with CEP believe that training often can best be done at a specialized school, the legislation under which CEP operates provides that a centralized skills center should be organized and utilized. The Washington skills center was slow in getting into operation, however, because of an inadequate building which such elementary problems as unsatisfactory heating and air-conditioning systems.

Once a skills center is established, there is a tendency to fill classes, say, for clerk-typists or for automobile mechanics because the teachers are on the job and classroom space is available. But it might have been better for the particular CEP participants who landed in these classes to be placed, for example, in classes for computer skills or carpentry where there were no vacancies at the moment.

The CEP program is a long one, lasting up to a year including follow-up once the person is on the job. Persons quite often move off the CEP rolls into a JOBS program providing jobs in private industry and pay while offering further training. One person who entered the JOBS program is Mrs. Lucille Miller, a middle-aged woman with a tenth-grade education who had spent most of her life working as a domestic in homes and occasionally as a maid in hotels or motels. She has two children and always had trouble finding someone to care for them while she was working. As a result, she was forced to change jobs frequently and had a reputation for being unreliable.

An employee of the Washington CEP talked with Mrs. Miller and suggested that she enroll in an on-the-job training program at a computer company participating in the JOBS program. While Mrs. Miller began a clerical training program, CEP workers arranged for day care for her children, thus removing the primary obstacle to her previous efforts to get steady employment.

After completing courses in typing, mathematics, filing, and other business-office techniques, Mrs. Miller was assigned to the company's accounting department in a position promising advancement with increased pay and greater opportunities.

As the CEP program has evolved, it has enrolled fewer people but has devoted more time to each person. The Labor Department considers the Washington CEP program to be the most successful of the 83 programs throughout the country. The Department's figures show a 70- to 75-percent success factor for Washington's CEP, based on the number of persons who complete training. But UPO officials who operate the program say that a figure of success with one of every three enrollees is more realistic if success is determined by job tenure of three to six months after graduation from the program rather than by mere completion of the program. The fall-off of persons in the early weeks or months of a job is quite high, and CEP has not successfully performed its task if its graduates fail to stay with their jobs.

CEP has money to enroll only a small percentage of the persons who need its help in the District of Columbia. With funds to train only 2,500 persons a year, CEP is not reaching even 10 percent of the 35,000 youths between the ages of 16 and 25 who are estimated to be in need of such a manpower program in the District of Columbia each year.

There is some "hustling" of the CEP program by street-wise youths. UPO officials place the number of youths who hustle CEP at no more than 10 percent of enrollees, a figure they do not consider unreasonable, given the state of the disadvantaged youths CEP is trying to reach.

The problems of "getting people involved" are among the greatest problems faced by CEP in holding enrollees in its program. Not only have the people in CEP seldom if ever tasted success; they also lack motivation. In addition, they have the problems of an unstable home life, inadequate housing, and lack of adequate child care if they are mothers.

So the CEP program has demonstrated that even a highly concentrated and lengthy program to train persons in the reading, writing, and arithmetic that passed them by in schools—or that they passed by—and to teach them marketable skills can have only limited success because of lack of motivation and the feeling that such problems as housing, stability in family life, clothing, enough food, and decent child-care facilities cannot be surmounted.

Work Incentive Program

Also designed to furnish a full range of services is the Work Incentive (WIN) program, begun in 1968 to put welfare recipients to work and cut relief costs. Although fewer than one quarter of all persons leaving WIN nationally have been placed successfully, Washington's program has been nearly twice as successful.

A total of $2.3 million was budgeted for the District of Columbia WIN program in fiscal 1972. This made it possible for the D.C. Manpower Administration to plan to take 1,540 persons into the program in that year. WIN trainees are referred by the Welfare Department to the Manpower Administration, which runs the program. The same procedure is followed elsewhere in the country, but there has been less fighting between Welfare and Manpower in Washington than in other cities, where some welfare departments look on the program as part of an effort to put them out of business.

In the District of Columbia, as elsewhere, each person in the WIN program is given intensive help and training by a group of counselors. In this and the other manpower programs practically all of the trainees and the training personnel are black. The six-man teams of counselors are made up of five WIN specialists plus a social worker who usually has known the trainee as a welfare recipient. The counseling runs all the way from assessing a person's basic needs, which usually include improvement in reading, writing, and arithmetic, to determining what are realistic work goals for him, with considerable emphasis placed on giving the person alternatives.

The training, much of which in conducted in an old colonnaded building high on a hill in far Northeast Washington, generally begins with orientation classes covering everything from personal hygiene and finances to instruction on how to apply for a job. Then there usually is a great deal of remedial training in the elementary subjects of reading, writing, and arithmetic. Finally, the program moves to the skills training designed to put a person into a job.

Little WIN training thus far, either nationally or in Washington, has been conducted on-the-job. Not only do WIN regulations restrict such training to government or private nonprofit organizations, thus excluding profit-making concerns, but loose labor markets have generally stymied attempts to expand on-the-job training. Recent amendments to WIN, however, require far more emphasis on OJT and job creation.

To help keep a person in the training program, which can continue for nine months, welfare payments are augmented by $30 a month. Nevertheless, the dropout rate is high. Some persons simply get discouraged by the slow progress they are making, which may be due to the unavailability of necessary training situations, but most drop out because of health problems, pregnancies, children's illnesses, or unstable housing conditions.

Once a person is placed on a job, his progress is monitored by a job coach, who will do everything from personally transporting the person to his place of work on his first few days on the job to mediating disputes between the person and his supervisor. Such follow-up work generally continues for from three to six months after a person is placed in a job.

An average WIN trainee is in the program for 50 weeks from the day he is accepted to the day his job coach feels he no longer needs to be checked to see whether he is still reporting for his job and getting along reasonably well in it.

Eighty-five percent of the persons in the WIN program are women, a figure which reflects the high incidence of welfare families headed by women as well as the large market in Washington for women with clerical and secretarial skills. The usual job for which a WIN enrollee is trained is clerk-typist, and the average starting salary is $102 a week.

Mrs. Barbara Jones, with three children to support, a tenth-grade education, and only six months' work experience when she enrolled in Washington's WIN, is typical of the program's more successful trainees. Her goal was modest, a job as a clerk-typist.

After three months of intensive work in basic education to improve her reading and clerical skills, Mrs. Jones began typist training. After another three months she was ready to move to a nonprofit professional association for additional on-the-job training. Four months later she was hired by the association as a permanent employee.

The WIN program has concentrated on a small number of people and has devoted much time and effort to each of its participants. The program is better suited to women than to men since it involves classroom work. Its participants have been women, and women seem to adapt much better than men do to classroom situations that are a part of all manpower-training programs. Moreover, as already mentioned the market for women with clerical and secretarial skills is large in Washington. WIN outlays for trainees do not necessarily end with successful placement. Many mothers need expensive child-care services not only during training but also after placement if they are to maintain sustained employment.

Although the original WIN legislation envisioned certain compulsory aspects, the District of Columbia program has never had enough money to train even all those on welfare who have volunteered. But under amendments to WIN which went into effect in mid-1972 the District may be required to increase substantially its referrals and enrollments in WIN or face the loss of federal funds.

In the District of Columbia WIN has demonstrated that welfare recipients, particularly women, can be trained for jobs. But WIN has dealt only with welfare recipients who have volunteered for the program. The results might be quite different if people are forced into the program, as they may be under the new WIN amendments and under President Nixon's proposals for welfare reform.

Whatever WIN's success in enrolling, training, and placing welfare recipients, however, its primary goal of converting welfare rolls into payrolls has made little headway. Not only has the number of AFDC recipients doubled since WIN's initiation, far out-stripping the program's ability to accommodate enrollees, but many of WIN's "successful" completions do not earn enough to leave the welfare rolls.

ON-THE-JOB TRAINING

In contrast to institutional training where an enrollee has no guarantee of finding work even after mastering his course, on-the-job training offers in most cases built-in employment. On-the-job training constitutes only a small proportion of federally sponsored manpower programs, and it plays only a minor role in Washington.

Job Opportunities in the Business Sector

The most prominent OJT program is JOBS (Job Opportunities in the Business Sector). It is operated with government funds by the National Alliance of Businessmen (NAB), set up by business-men at government request to administer the JOBS program.

The JOBS program was established in 1968 as a way for busi-ness to take on the hard-core unemployed. To encourage employers to hire high-risk applicants, the government agreed to reimburse employers for the training and other expenses incurred in taking a person off the streets and putting him to work. But despite a hard selling of the program by the Johnson and Nixon Administrations, it has not been particularly successful. In the District of Columbia, only slightly more than $1 million was set aside by the Labor Department for the JOBS program in the 1972 fiscal year, a one-third reduction from the fiscal 1971 figure of $1.5 million. This cutback reflects a general dissatisfaction with the program. The 1972 funds were to provide money for 1,668 trainees.

The concept of the JOBS program is to hire now and train later. Under the program a company takes on a man and trains him as he works on the job. Because there often is little or no counsel-ing before a man is hired or training and remedial education before the man goes to work, the dropout rate is high—40 to 50 percent, and generally in the first two to four weeks a person is on the job.

As the administrators of other manpower programs have dis-covered, remedial education is often the greatest need of the unem-ployed and unemployable. So is careful and sophisticated counseling to determine the kind of job for which a person is best suited. In addition, the JOBS program is 80 percent male, and, again, as the other manpower programs have shown, training efforts are much more successful with women than with men.

PRIDE: Dealing With the Street Dudes

PRIDE began in 1967 as a neighborhood clean-up and rat extermination program carried out by "street dudes" working in inner-city areas. From those small beginnings it has expanded to a fairly well-structured program that not only puts high-school drop-outs to work but also gives them some basic skills training as well as remedial education so that they can function in today's world of work.

Although some fear PRIDE as radical and dangerous, at least some measure of its success is due to very traditional reasons— emphasis of the Puritan work ethic, a little bit of that old-time religion, and direction from a charismatic figure.

In its formative years PRIDE had received Labor Department funds for both its training and business enterprises, but in the last two years government money has been limited to its training operations. In the 1972 fiscal year PRIDE got $2 million from the Labor Department. With this money it hoped to bring 1,300 youths into its programs. Half of this number, however, were to participate only in a summer work program.

When a youth is accepted by PRIDE, he is immediately put to work, and this is an important reason for the organization's success. Youths walking in off the street to a manpower office think that a job lies behind that door, not more of the boredom of class-rooms that they left behind in high school.

After putting him to work in a laboring, gardening, or painting project, PRIDE starts to deal with the recruit's basic attitudes and problems. He is given tests and a physical examination and put through a work orientation program.

Counseling is generally done by graduates of PRIDE programs who understand street-wise ways. In dealing with the youths, the counselors try to do what is possible rather than ideal. For example, instead of seeking to raise the reading and writing levels of all PRIDE trainees to those of a high school graduate, the program often merely seeks to give the youths the basic education they need to function in jobs.

But perhaps even more important than PRIDE's practical orientation towards uneducated, untrained ghetto youths is the kind of leadership PRIDE has had in Marion Barry, a black who is a veteran of the Student Nonviolent Coordinating Committee (SNCC) activities of the early 1960s and who in addition to running PRIDE has become a significant figure in Washington. In 1971, he was elected to the District of Columbia Board of Education and later became its president. Earlier, he was active in controversies over police relationships with inner-city communities.

A good speaker, Barry has many of the charismatic qualities of a political or religious leader. He is expert at selecting the right issues with which to associate himself and his causes. He knows how to gain access to the media and say things to make page one and the six o'clock news.

PRIDE's success thus is due in large part to the fact that it is not another faceless bureaucracy without a leader on whom its constituency and the community can focus. In the government-run WIN, privately run JOBS, or even in other community-operated programs like UPO's CEP, there is no dominant personality. PRIDE has demonstrated that old-time religion can become an important ingredient in manpower programs.

PRIDE's neighborhood clean-up, landscaping, and painting businesses have had a good deal of success. Its gasoline-station, automotive-repair, and apartment-house-ownership operations have been moderately successful. An effort to start a candy-manufacturing plant failed. Some of PRIDE's problems have stemmed from its efforts to put aid to disadvantaged youth ahead of business acumen. Overstaffing of its gasoline station, for example, has given more youths a chance to learn about a business and to earn some money while making it more difficult for PRIDE to operate the stations at a profit.

Only about one fourth of the youths enrolling in PRIDE programs go on to jobs. But PRIDE is dealing almost exclusively with men, while most of the other programs in the District of Columbia have more women than men enrolled. Also, PRIDE worries less about skimming the cream of the unemployables than do some of the other programs with their emphasis on nice but sometimes rather meaningless statistics.

PRIDE is dealing with the hard-core unemployed "street dudes," 85 percent of whom have had some sort of court action against them before they ever show up at PRIDE's offices. As it has gained more experience in working with the "dudes," PRIDE itself has become more street-wise and has learned much about the best way to proceed in trying to turn the youths into productive workers.

With its emphasis on work and on such enterprises as gasoline stations, automotive repair, painting, landscaping and gardening, and neighborhood sanitation projects, PRIDE is oriented toward the traditional aspects of city life. But PRIDE has run into strident criticism from members of Congress and from the General Accounting Office. PRIDE may not have had the best accounting system, but then neither did the Penn Central in its headlong rush to bankruptcy. Some of PRIDE's ambitious projects have not worked out, and some of Barry's statements may have injured the sensibilities of the white middle class that appears to fear PRIDE. One conclusion would seem inescapable, however: The white middle class who through its federal income taxes is financing programs like PRIDE still prefers black organizers and do-gooders to be a little bit humble. And neither PRIDE nor Barry is that.

JOB CREATION AND WORK SUPPORT

Although public employment still suffers from the image of a WPA worker leaning on his rake and is still unpopular in some circles, the government has undertaken increased efforts in assisting the disadvantaged to succeed in the regular civil service and in creating special jobs to counteract seasonal or cyclical unemployment. Among these efforts are the Public Service Careers (PSC) and Neighborhood Youth Corps programs of the War on Poverty and the Public Employment Program, authorized by the Emergency Employment Act of 1971.

Public Service Careers

The Public Service Careers program is specifically designed to place trainees in the public sector. Because of the government's domination of the job market, PSC is especially important in the District of Columbia.

One aspect of the effort is an on-the-job training program for the public sector. Both District of Columbia and federal government agencies are asked to hire some disadvantaged workers and to train them as they are working. In the 1972 fiscal year $900,000 was budgeted for this part of the program, and 900 persons were to participate in the program. This part of the program has all of the advantages and drawbacks of the JOBS program in the private sector. Counseling and remedial education are inadequate, but a person is put to work immediately, thus quickly fulfilling his need for a job.

The other part of the program in Washington is an effort to move people from WIN or CEP into a government job. This part includes extensive counseling and training. A total of $1,139,000 was budgeted for the operation in the 1972 fiscal year, which was enough money to train and aid 153 people.

Neighborhood Youth Corps

In the District of Columbia the Neighborhood Youth Corps (NYC) programs received more federal money than any of the other manpower programs. Although NYC is considered a manpower-training effort and the funds are administered by the Manpower Administration, it does little more than provide some income for ghetto youths. This is important, but it is a palliative rather than a remedy for the basic education and skills-training problems that so often prevent ghetto youths from getting jobs.

Of the $9.8 million allocated to NYC programs in Washington in the 1972 fiscal year, $4.5 million went for a summer jobs program which was to employ 12,000 youths. The youths were to be hired at $1.60 an hour and put to work in laboring jobs or in positions supervising summer recreational activities at playgrounds and schools.

Another $1.5 million of NYC funds was to be used to pay youths for part-time employment while they were still in high school. A total of 1,600 persons were to participate in this program. The jobs were often in the schools the youths were attending.

The rest of the NYC funds—totaling $3.8 million—were to go for wages to pay 650 youths who were to participate in the post-school work-support program. This program is an effort to aid dropouts and help train them for jobs.

These three programs constitute the bulk of the NYC effort in the District of Columbia, and all three are administered by the United Planning Organization, Washington's principal community action organization.

Public Employment Program

Washington's special relationship with the federal government has been instrumental in making the District's Public Employment Program a "success model." The Public Employment Program is a $2.25 billion job-creation effort, enacted under the July 1971 Emergency Employment Act after more traditional methods of reducing national unemployment had failed. The Washington grant of $3.7 million allowed the District to hire some 600 persons from the 18,000 who were unemployed in August 1971.

The primary goal was to provide the unemployed jobs in the public sector. Several target groups were enumerated, but no priorities were established. Secondary goals include (1) reform of state and local civil service regulations and job structures which had worked against minority groups and the disadvantaged; (2) coordination with manpower programs to prepare these workers for better jobs; (3) the movement onto permanent payrolls of half of those hired, making the program "transitional."

Washington's implementation of these broad and sometimes contradictory goals was sound. This success reflects the sympathetic guidance and supervision provided by federal officials, operating through the Regional Manpower Administrator in the District; the commitment of the mayor to the program's success; and effective and efficient administration at all levels of the District government.

With such support it is not surprising that the city moved unusually quickly, achieving rapid approval, referral, and placement. By the time the District had filled virtually all of its slots, the 20 other largest cities had filled only three fifths. Nor was quality sacrificed for haste. The jobs to be filled, which met previously identified but unfunded needs, were mixed, spanning a range of salary levels, eligibility requirements, and duties. Because of the concentration of need among the unskilled, a significant share were entry-level jobs. Included were 43 percent for health, community education, and social service aides; 12 percent for blue-collar jobs, such as gardeners, plumbers, and mechanics; 11 percent for administrators and school teachers; 10 percent for clerk-typists; and another quarter for a wide assortment of tasks.

The selection of employees similarly coincided with program goals. Adminstrators quickly screened and referred applicants. Agencies were required to justify rejections and were thus under pressure not to "cream" from the referrals. Accordingly, the hires represented a cross section of the city's unemployed and met the program's major targets: 97 percent were nonwhite; 54 percent were veterans; and 62 percent were disadvantaged.

Even more impressive, in contrast to other areas' performance, was the District's success in meeting secondary goals. Most of the paraprofessional aide or trainee jobs (which made up two fifths of the total) provided that experience, rather than diplomas, would justify promotion and permanent employment. For some in expanding areas like corrections, the environment, and narcotics treatment jobs requirements were structured to avoid artificial barriers and to provide upward mobility. However, little reform of the District's already-advanced civil service system has been achieved.

Coordination with manpower programs has been a significant accomplishment, for many of the disadvantaged hires will need education or training to qualify for permanent positions and promotions. All money available for training, though not substantial, was utilized, and District funds paid for extensive counseling and instruction of aides. Moreover, as the program matured, an increasing number of referrals came from other manpower programs.

The District has done well, under the supervision of the Regional Manpower Administrator, in moving "transitional" hires into permanent positions. He insisted that half of all vacancies in the city government be made available to program participants until half of them had been moved into permanent positions. Program administrators have also structured incentives to encourage agencies to hire program participants permanently by threatening to reallocate slots from agencies which have not done a good job.

The District's circumstances have undeniably been conducive to success. It did not face coordination problems with state or other local agencies, and the Public Employment Program encountered little interference from vested interest groups. But these advantages do not diminish the Public Employment Program's solid achievements in Washington.

JOB PLACEMENT AND SUPPORT

Provision for supportive services and efforts at job placement have been recognized as crucial and have been incorporated into most training programs. In addition, the staid "old-timer" among manpower programs, the Employment Service, has been reoriented to enable it to perform its placement services with new tools and for a broader spectrum of the labor force.

As manpower-training programs have proliferated and expanded, the District of Columbia Employment Service has also changed and expanded. The Employment Service has recognized that its clientele has changed and that a higher percentage of job applicants using its facilities are ill educated and badly trained, if not altogether without skills.

To help meet these problems the Employment Service is doing more counseling than it formerly did. In addition, the Service is going out into the community with offices and services looking for people to help.

Moreover, the Employment Service has developed a computerized Job Bank which is updated daily and lists all jobs that have been registered with the Service. It is thus much easier for the Service to match the unemployed with the available jobs. But the Service still cannot match the untrained and unskilled with jobs in a labor market ever increasingly demanding educated and skilled workers.

PROBLEMS AND PROSPECTS

If American society worked better than it does, there would be no need for manpower-training programs. These programs are necessary in large part because of such social ills as racism, family breakdown, bad housing, inadequate public schools, and discriminatory employment practices.

The manpower-training programs evolved over the decade of the 1960s from elementary skills-training efforts to quite sophisticated programs designed not only to train a person for a specific job but also to motivate him and remedy his educational defects.

As experience with the programs has developed and been analyzed, the administrators of the programs have discovered that such problems as motivation and the lack of elementary reading, writing, and arithmetic skills often keep a person from getting a job as much as the lack of a specific skill. Another lesson learned from the manpower efforts is that often a person cannot keep a job because of such factors as a chaotic home life, the lack of public transportation, the lack of health care, or the unavailability of adequate day-care facilities for a worker's children.

These experiences have been put to use in designing new programs. The WIN program, for example, has been carefully tailored in Washington to include extensive counseling to find out whether it is the lack of a specific skill or some social problem that is keeping a person from staying on a job.

But, unfortunately, there has been no orderly progression in the development of manpower-training programs. Except for the EEA, which emphasizes job creation rather than training, the Nixon Administration has not started any important new manpower programs, and EEA has been forced upon the Adminstration by Congress. But the Nixon Administration has also been reluctant to phase out entirely even the more unsuccessful programs of the Johnson Administration such as the Job Corps or revamp drastically some of the less successful programs such as JOBS. In addition, it has stuck with the summer riot-insurance programs of the NYC despite real doubt among manpower administrators as to the value of NYC as anything more than a cynical effort to buy off ghetto youths.

Too Many Separate Programs?

The proliferation of separate manpower programs and the unseemly lack of tidiness in the development and administration of the programs bothers efficiency experts and others who like to organize programs in neat categories and charts. "Eleven significant programs in the District of Columbia! Horrors!" cry the efficiency experts who relish tidy organizational charts.

Well, life itself is an untidy business and it is probably unrealistic to expect government programs to be too orderly. President John F. Kennedy once said that he was more concerned when things were neat and tidy in a government agency than when there were ferment and competition within the agency.

There is unquestionably some duplication in the 11 District of Columbia manpower programs discussed in this chapter. WIN and CEP, for example, are concerned with much the same sort of problems and clientele. So are MDTA and JOBS. And there are many similiarities between PRIDE and OIC.

A large number of projects are in Washington because the District of Columbia has always served as a handy laboratory for the U.S. Department of Labor. But there is also a good deal of cooperation among the programs. WIN and CEP prepare some trainees for JOBS or Public Service Careers slots. Overlap exists, but a little extra help and training will not hurt most WIN and CEP clients. And there seems to be a minimum of program-hopping. Once a person is turned off by one program or considers himself a failure in a program he is not likely to pursue a similar program.

Also, the programs serve many different groups. WIN is for welfare recipients. CEP is a part of the community-wide services of the United Planning Organization. JOBS is an effort to enlist the cooperation of the business community in manpower programs. NYC is aimed specifically at youth. PRIDE and OIC are independent community programs encouraging self-help.

In the name of efficiency, it surely could be argued that if PRIDE and OIC, for example, were combined, less money would be spent on overhead. But such an argument completely overlooks the fact that whatever success the two programs have had is attributable in large part to the *esprit de corps* engendered by the leadership of the two groups, an ingredient that would be dissipated through consolidation of the programs.

Certainly there is duplication, rivalries among program administration, and some program-hopping, but there would still be problems even if the programs were neatly organized. In an area like manpower training where the programs are new and where no one yet knows with any certainty what will succeed and what will not, it may make sense to have rivalries, for the competition may generate better programs.

Under the Nixon Administration revenue-sharing proposals, states and local communities would be given considerable latitude in the use of manpower-training funds and their allocation to specific programs. But whatever their organizational scheme, the programs should help the same target populations being served today.

Creaming the Applicants

Although the manpower-training programs are supposed to deal with people who need help the most, there is a tendency to cream the best applicants. And the worse the job market gets, the greater is the tendency to cream. Success in manpower-training programs means turning the highest possible percentage of trainees into jobholders. The easiest way to do this is to select trainees who are reasonably certain to succeed. The result is that often the people who get the training are the people who need it the least, and Congress funds programs more readily if it is presented with rosy stataistics on the progress being made by them.

None of the programs provides special incentives to trainees or program administrators to encourage the training of those who need it the most and to discourage creaming. Experimentation in designing incentives ought to be developed to induce greater efforts to train persons who genuinely need help.

The question of such incentives raises the problem of motivation, which is one of the most difficult issues facing manpower training programs. On the one hand, many highly motivated persons who voluntarily join training probably do not need much of the elaborate remedial education and training offered to them. On the other hand, program administrators often seem at a loss to try to develop training efforts that will reach the less-motivated persons.

The probability of a steady job with adequate pay at the end of the education and training period does not seem to be enough motivation for some. Monetary incentives during training might help. Coercion to force welfare recipients to take training programs might also be appropriate in special cases.

A Balance Sheet

In the District of Columbia, the manpower-training programs have had some success. They have trained thousands of persons since the first programs went into effect in 1962, and every program has its quota of success stories—of people removed from the welfare rolls, of unskilled workers turned into highly skilled artisans, of dudes taken off the street and turned into productive citizens.

In the District of Columbia, as elsewhere, manpower programs have developed from mere skills-training efforts to sophisticated attempts to provide remedial education as well as training in skills. Administrators of the programs have found that lack of basic education and a basic orientation to the world of work are often as difficult hurdles to a job as the lack of skills.

In addition, the need for housing, day-care centers, and health care as well as the absence of a stable home and personal environment are formidable obstacles to success on the job for a person who is in a manpower-training program. For such programs to succeed, assistance must be povided to enrollees to help them cope with these day-to-day living problems.

Even more difficult is the problem of motivation. Women do much better than men in the training programs, a fact which by now should have led to considerably more reexamination of the structures of the programs. A large part of the motivation problem with men is probably the low-paid, entry-level jobs for which most persons in the programs are trained.

There is a disturbing tendency to mask income-support programs as manpower programs apparently because it is easier to sell such programs to the Congress and the public. The best example is the summer NYC programs, which are basically efforts to prevent summer riots in the ghettos by buying off ghetto youth. There have been no major riots in recent years, but no one knows whether the NYC efforts have in fact helped youths move on to better jobs once they graduate from high school.

There is also a reluctance to give up manpower-training concepts that do not work or that are expensive. The Residential Manpower Center in Washington is a good example. It is an offshoot of the discredited Job Corps program, which had little success in turning ghetto youths into successful workers by taking them out of their ghetto environment and trying to remake their lives in a Center far removed from their homes. In Washington, the Residential Manpower Center is now seeking to do the same sort of thing in, of all places, a former training school for boys. The symbolism cannot be lost on anyone, particularly the participants in the program. The setting on the edge of the city is such that the youths in the program cannot be kept out of the very kind of urban environment that has helped create their problems in the first instance. In addition, the cost of the Residential Manpower Center is inordinately high, in large part because it is a residential program providing board and room as well as remedial education and training. But is the cost worth the results? No one seems to want to face up to this question.

Not surprisingly, programs that can identify with a personality or a mission generally have more success than programs run by a faceless bureaucracy or corporation. Marion Barry's PRIDE and Rev. Leon Sullivan's OIC are good examples in the District of Columbia of what personality and mission can contribute to training efforts. The Residential Manpower Center is operated by a for-profit corporation, but the problems would probably be there regardless of who ran the Center. The JOBS program has not been too successful, not so much because it is run by businessmen as because of the failure of its training efforts to encompass remedial education programs. So, except for the missionary zeal imparted to PRIDE and OIC by the charismatic qualities of their leaders, it is difficult to generalize on the merits of programs run by the government, as opposed to those run by the private sector.

Manpower-training programs are part of a broad-gauged federal effort of the last decade to try to reduce poverty in the United States. The manpower efforts are necessary because of the failure of families and schools and, most importantly, the continuing racial segregation and discrimination in America.

Some Further Questions

How much greater unemployment problems in Washington would be today if there had been no manpower-training programs, no one knows. It is particularly difficult to compare 1972 with 1962 because expectations have changed so much; the percentage of the population in Washington that is black has increased; and businessmen have fled the city for the suburbs, often making it more difficult for blacks in the central city to find jobs to which they can travel easily and cheaply.

Manpower administrators in the District of Columbia believe that, given Washington's generally good economic situation, it has received more than its fair share of funds from the new manpower programs of the past 10 years.

Would Washington be better off in the next 10 years if revenue sharing were in effect and local administrators could decide for themselves how to apportion money for manpower and other programs rather than have rigid programs laid down from the national offices of the U.S. Department of Labor? Perhaps, but not necessarily. In many ways, manpower programs are still in an experimental stage, the most controversial of them being only five to eight years old, and no one yet knows how to deal effectively with the severe problems of the hard-core unemployed. Furthermore, there is no reason to believe that Washington's problems are so unique that they could be handled better on a local basis. In fact, national administrators usually are more alert to new developments somewhere in the United States than are local administrators who often are so concerned with their daily crises that they fail to see the larger picture and the more important developments elsewhere.

The results of the programs in the District of Columbia as elsewhere have often been disappointing, but there have been enough beneficial results to continue most of the manpower-training efforts. The most glaring difficulty probably has been to motivate those who need training most. On balance, it would appear that the programs have paid off. This remains a value judgment since there are no definitive measures to assess manpower programs any more than there are objective means to evaluate education or housing efforts. And it is time for social scientists and government administrators alike to admit this disturbing fact.

Chapter Five

THE AFDC NUMBERS GAME

by Barbara Raskin

There are about 25 million poor people in America—one out of every eight persons. In Washington, D.C., the proportion is higher —about one in six. To meet the income needs of the poor, the federal government assists state and local governments in paying public assistance. In fiscal year 1972, the District distributed about $72 million to 100,000 persons, or about one D.C. resident in seven. Another $7 million was spent to administer these grants, and $26 million more was devoted to providing a variety of social services, including institutional care for adults and children. Because the aged, blind, and disabled constitute less than one fifth of the welfare rolls while more than four fifths receive assistance under the Aid to Families With Dependent Children program (AFDC), AFDC has become synonymous with the generic term "welfare."

D.C. has mirrored national trends in its rapid increase of AFDC caseload and costs. National rolls, which approximately doubled each decade between 1936 and 1966, doubled again between 1966 and 1970, and continue to grow. The District's relief population has grown even faster than national rolls in recent years, with its rolls doubling once more between 1970 and 1972. With 11 percent of its residents on AFDC, Washington now has the ninth highest proportion among major cities. Costs have risen even faster.

A REPRESENTATIVE RECIPIENT

Among the mind-numbing numbers is a 33-year-old heavy-set woman named Catherine Perry. Born and raised in South Carolina, she has lived in Washington for ten years. Like 71 percent of District residents, Catherine Perry is black. She has three children (the average number in an AFDC family), Sondra, 12; Ronnie, 9; and Jimmy, 4 (23 percent of all District of Columbia children under five were on AFDC at the end of 1970). Mrs. Perry has no husband. Charles Perry disappeared three years ago during the winter when his construction team was laid off work, and he has not been located since. (Twenty-nine percent of the black families in D.C. are headed by women. Only 19 percent of AFDC families in America have a father in the home, and only 5 percent of these men are able-bodied.) After her husband's desertion, Mrs. Perry moved in with a relative who remained in Washington for only a year. Then she rented two bedrooms from a neighbor in exchange for taking care of the woman's children all day and most nights. When this arrangement began to disturb her own children, she finally applied for welfare, two years after her husband disappeared.

Catherine Perry lives in a dilapidated, narrow rowhouse in the Shaw-Cardozo area, a ghetto where blacks make up 90 percent of the residents. It forms part of the inner city, far removed from the segregated enclaves west of Rock Creek Park where most of white Washington lives. (It is even farther from D.C.'s 92-percent white suburbs [Chart 5].) Since District rents are high, and because there is an oppressive shortage of low-cost housing (only 25 percent of AFDC children live in public housing in the District), Catherine Perry pays $92 a month to live in a slum. (Thirty-one percent of Washington residents live in severely crowded quarters, a factor which contributes to various forms of social deterioration.) Only 28 percent of District housing units are occu-

CHART 5:   THE POOR REMAIN IN D.C. WHILE THE AFFLUENT MOVE TO THE
SUBURBS (DATA FROM 1970 CENSUS)

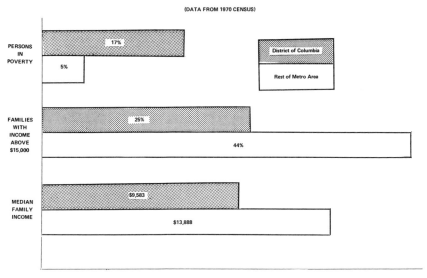

(DATA FROM 1970 CENSUS)

PERSONS IN POVERTY — District of Columbia 17%, Rest of Metro Area 5%

FAMILIES WITH INCOME ABOVE $15,000 — 25%, 44%

MEDIAN FAMILY INCOME — $9,583, $13,888

Source: U.S. Bureau of the Census

pied by owners (a community-stability index) as opposed to the
63-percent national average; so Catherine Perry is one of many
poor people in Washington renting property which is substandard,
too small, and overpriced. Her utility bills average $22 per month,
ranging from $11 in the summer to $33 in the winter because of
heating expenses. Since the District of Columbia makes no routine
furniture grants to welfare recipients, Catherine Perry's two sons
sleep on a mattress on the floor and build little barricades to protect
themselves from rats at night. (Three years after a $939,000
federal grant to fight rodents, there are still more rats than people
in Washington.)

The Perrys are among the two of every three D.C. residents who
live in what the Census Bureau considers a "low income area"
where the proportion of poor persons exceeds 25 percent. In such
areas—which include most of the District—three families in 10
are headed by females. Among four-person families like the Perrys,
that is, those which include children and are headed by a black
female, three of every five live in poverty. The vast majority of

D.C.'s welfare recipients are in female-headed black families, and the odds against women like Catherine Perry, rearing children without a spouse in a society in which an increasing proportion of families have more than one wage earner, are heavy.

D.C. WELFARE BENEFITS

Cash

On the first of each month, Catherine Perry receives a check for $238.50—that is, if no one steals the envelope from her mailbox and if it is not detoured bureaucratically. For a family of four, $2,862 a year does not stretch very far. In fact, it is only three quarters of what D.C. statisticians have estimated as the minimum level of needs for a family like the Perrys, and this standard, in turn, is below the federal government's official poverty level.

In addition to this grant, however, as a relief recipient Mrs. Perry also qualifies for the food-stamp program, which increases her purchasing power for food; for the Medicaid program, whereby the government reimburses doctors for providing certain medical services for her family; and for various social services provided by the D.C. government.

Food

At the beginning of each month, Catherine Perry spends $66 or over one quarter of her check at a neighboring bank to purchase $106 worth of food stamps. (In 1971, about three of every four AFDC recipients participated in the food-stamp program.) Although food stamps expand Catherine Perry's purchasing power by $480 a year, about $25 worth of groceries a week is not sufficient to feed her family. For two and one-half weeks they can have a reasonable diet, but during the remainder of each month the Perrys exist on beans, rice, and black-eyed peas.

Mrs. Perry has grown fat from the starchiness of her diet, plus the fact that she eats laundry starch, a custom common in Washington where there are many southerners who ate clay "down home" to fill their bellies and stop hunger pains. Since clay (she still receives gift boxes of dry clay from a cousin in Mississippi) and starch are low in price, though high in calories, Mrs. Perry can supplement her diet, which frequently descends to a border-line-malnutrition or starvation level, and maintain her energy, if not her health. Since Mrs. Perry's food stamps cannot be used to purchase nonedibles, she must buy necessities, such as soap detergents, napkins, toilet paper, and cleaning supplies, out of her limited amount of cash.

The Perry boys frequently become ill from respiratory infections and other sicknesses afflicting children with dietary deficiencies. On the basis of a physical examination, Jimmy was determined medically eligible for the free Supplemental Food Program. Twice a month Mrs. Perry picks up several bags of evaporated milk, nonfat dry milk, a can of meat or poultry, four cans of vegetables, and two packages of wheat or rice cereal. To carry home these thirty pounds of surplus food she has to take a taxi which costs $1.00 each way; then she must strain to create imaginative recipes that disguise the taste of the canned scrambled eggs with pork so that her youngsters will eat it. However, since children over five are not eligible for this program, Jimmy will be disqualified in a year and a half when his eligibility is reviewed. He weighs 30 pounds.

Health Care

Since the Perry family, like all welfare recipients, are eligible for Medicaid, they receive free hospital, clinic, or private medical treatment, as well as free prescription drugs. The average annual Medicaid benefits for a family of four (mother and three children under 12) in D.C. is $1,162. Although Medicaid cards are supposed to be renewed automatically, there are frequent delays in the issuance of renewals, and medical establishments will not treat welfare clients whose cards have expired. When Catherine Perry did not receive her new card, the Washington Hospital Center would not admit her for a operation until her social service representative guaranteed in writing that her AFDC status automatically entitled her to Medicaid. Nonprescription items such as aspirin, kotex, kleenex, rubbing alcohol, vitamins, and thermometers are not covered by Medicaid. Last September, Mrs. Perry had to purchase a $7.00 vaporizer for Jimmy and was left without a cent of cash for the last eight days of the month. Although Mrs. Perry and her children get free dental care at Howard University, Sondra will not have any orthodontic treatment on her badly formed mouth, since a dentist determined that corrective care would be cosmetically, rather than medically, indicated and thus not covered by Medicaid.

Social Services

The Human Resources Department which processes Catherine Perry's welfare check is also responsible for providing a wide variety of social services. Most of these service programs and institutions are designed for emergency situations when poor people finally fall over the precarious precipice of their wretched condition. But women like Catherine Perry, who use their total life energy "getting it together," have needs for "routine" rather than "crisis" kinds of service programs. Her use of social services (apart from the in-kind food-stamp and Medicaid programs) is minimal and infrequent.

Among the varied social service functions is the administration of locally funded city welfare institutions for delinquent children, the aged, and children in the city's custody. While these city institutions are supposed to be resources to assist their clientele, they often fall short of this ideal. A newspaper series in 1971 exposing the conditions at Junior Village, a shelter for children between the ages of 6 months and 18 years, scandalized Washington. Moreover, mothers have been penalized for using these facilities. In *Getting the Most from the D.C. Welfare Department,* the Mount Pleasant/Cardozo Welfare Rights Organization cautions welfare parents against using Junior Village for emergency child care.

> The Welfare Department should give you Emergency Assistance to keep you from being evicted. It should also provide you with homemaker services when you are in the hospital or unable to care for your children for other reasons. When the Department does NOT do these things as they should, they often advise us to use Junior Village as emergency childcare . . . when we are evicted, or in the hospital, etc.
>
> As we know, Junior Village is not the best, warmest, most comfortable place for our children in an emergency. But there is another point to consider when deciding not to release your children to Junior Village. The Welfare Department *MAY* (even though they shouldn't) consider that your releasing them constitutes *neglect* and may try to hassle you later about it. Although they would probably not be

able to take your children away from you just on those grounds, they may threaten to do so if you release the children to JUNIOR VILLAGE more than once. BE CAREFUL WHAT YOU SIGN, particularly when you are in a stressful situation and your children are involved.

FEDERAL INFLUENCE ON D.C. WELFARE SYSTEM

The District is very much a creature of the federal government, especially Congress. While one set of committees determines the formula by which all states get federal matching money and monitors the various programs, another set pores over the D.C. budget's allocation of "state" funds for welfare and other activities. The city's welfare director has noted in an interview that

> The House Appropriations Subcommittee is acutely aware, especially Congressman Natcher, of what federal funds come to the District, and that has an impact on what the Subcommittee will give in appropriations. The agency that provides the grant monitors it, but the Appropriations Subcommittee considers the impact of those grants in calculating the future D.C. budget.

Thus, as one local official put it, "The D.C. budget has more federal oversight than any other city, since every single budget item is scrutinized by congressional committees." This shadow—cast not by state legislators but by powerful congressmen—hangs heavily over the city government's policy and budgetary decisions. A series of recent developments highlights the extent of D.C.'s obeisance to federal powers and demonstrates how people like the Perrys can get caught in the middle of local-federal power plays.

Tightening Up the System

Fulminations against welfare cheaters have become a perennial event during D.C. appropriations hearings, despite HEW statistics that show only a 5-percent incidence of ineligibility nationwide. But the massive growth of welfare and the admission that support for ineligible families and improper payments to eligible families had cost D.C. somewhere between $5 million and $8 million in 1971 moved Congress to overhaul the District eligibility procedures, initiated with HEW blessings only three years earlier.

In the "traditional" method of determining eligibility, all information submitted by the applicant for welfare was verified by the welfare agency. This process, however, was very costly, and cast the applicant's social workers in the conflicting roles of policeman and counselor. While demeaning recipients by subjecting them to notorious "midnight raids" and other harrassments, long investigations also forced applicants to shift without means until their eligibility was verified. HEW urged states to adopt a "simplified" method of investigating only a 10-percent sample of recipients. This system had been field-tested by the New York City Welfare Department and was also used successfully in checking the eligibility of social security recipients and veterans applying for pensions.

Nevertheless, Congress, annoyed at rising welfare costs, continued to focus upon fraud until welfare administrator Winifred Thompson was unable to resist the "offer" of more welfare investigators by Iowa Republican William Scherle:

> Congressman Scherle: Miss Thompson, is there any request in this budget for additional personnel to assist you?
>
> Miss Thompson: No.
>
> .   .   .   .   .
>
> Congressman Scherle: We should make every effort to make sure the people who receive these funds are entitled to them. Would we be further ahead if we gave you more personnel to do your job better and look into these things a little more thoroughly? Would you object?
>
> Miss Thompson: No sir; I would not. I would feel more comfortable.
> . . .
>
> Congressman Scherle: How many more would you like?[1]

The result of this unrehearsed congressional testimony was that the welfare department gained 45 new unsolicited AFDC investigators.

Congress' scrutiny of the welfare budget made eminently clear its intention to cut back the rolls, ferret out fraud, find deserting fathers, and make the system as tight as possible. Welfare officials were not unintimidated by explicit comments about tightening up procedures when the suggestions were accompanied by implicit

---

[1] U.S. Congress, House Appropriations Subcommittee on District of Columbia Appropriations, DISTRICT OF COLUMBIA APPROPRIATIONS FOR 1972 (Washington: U.S. Government Printing Office, 1971), Part 2, pp. 998-999.

threats of appropriations cutbacks should the local agency not comply. Predictably, in February of 1972, the Department of Human Resources announced a new local effort for welfare reform in the District emphasizing administrative, investigatory, and litigative controls:

> Eligibility will be redetermined quarterly by a check-in procedure; the method of payment will be changed from fluctuating allowances to flat grants; employable recipients will be required to register for job training or employment; a program to obtain meaningful employment for the recipient will be undertaken; allegations of fraud will be investigated and violators will be prosecuted.

> We will institute recertification through regularly scheduled office visits by all recipients able to report. . . . By such review, overpayments, underpayments, and errors by staff or clients will be eliminated. . . .

> The 45 additional investigators provided by Congress will begin an immediate review of improper payments cases. Any cases of fraud will be referred to a new Office of Inspection and Program Analysis. This unit will work closely with the Corporation Counsel to prosecute such cases. The department will also work wtih the Corporation Counsel to recover support payments from fathers who have deserted their families. . . .

> We estimate that this program will save approximately a million dollars during Fiscal Year 1973. Accordingly, we are reducing the departmental request budget which will be presented to the City Council shortly.

Deserting Fathers

Although D.C. welfare mothers are requested to identify their children's fathers, the District uses no coercion to obtain this information. Furthermore, when women complied and cooperated in locating deserting fathers, the local corporation counsel did not have sufficient staff to track the men down and bring them into court for child support orders.

After the recent reorganization of the District court system, however, the function of tracing and prosecuting deserting fathers was turned over to the Department of Human Resources, and additional funds were allocated to triple to 21 the number of staff assigned to finding and prosecuting deserting fathers.

Family Planning

Federal interest in family-planning services, as another means of limiting new welfare recipients, inspired a 1967 Social Security amendment urging that 6 percent of all funds appropriated for maternal and child health services for welfare recipients be allocated to family planning. Although there were neither incentives nor penalties attached to the legislation, D.C. caseworkers were ordered to make regular family-planning referrals to clinics for birth-control information, advice, or devices, and were required to make the initial appointments for their clients. (A member of Planned Parenthood sits in the Intake Office to facilitate this operation.) Each welfare-family folder was to contain the date on which a referral to a family-planning service was made by the caseworker and a detailed follow-up on any action taken by the client. District caseworkers were responsible for follow-up investigations, although forbidden to use coercion.

In the late sixties, however, the social and political climate was not conducive to white and/or middle-class social workers encouraging their clients to pursue birth-control measures. At several staff meetings there were heated debates between administrators who demanded active compliance with the federal emphasis on family planning and caseworkers who were reluctant to offer family-planning counseling. A compromise was apparently reached whereby audits of any folder would reveal a date upon which family-planning counseling was offered plus another date concerning follow-up procedures, while the amount of interest shown by caseworkers was to remain discretionary.

Extending Eligibility

Though the public assistance rolls in D.C. increased annually, local officials did not always utilize available programs to enlarge federal contributions. In 1961, Congress authorized states to qualify families in need of assistance due to the unemployment of a parent (now called the Unemployed Father component of Aid to Families with Dependent Children). But the District did not enact this provision until 1970, and a year later there were only about 3,000 recipients under the program. D.C. still does not participate in the Foster Care Program segment, started in 1969, despite the fact that Junior Village, the institution housing children in the city's custody, was ordered to close by the city council because of inhumane conditions. Failure to implement AFDC components means that federal funds are being lost while needy people are being denied help.

In mid-1969, Congress provided that the wages of low-income working mothers be supplemented so that they would not have to live on less money than AFDC mothers received from welfare. It was not until April 1971, however, and then only at the insistence of the federal Department of Health, Education, and Welfare, that the District complied. Although only about 500 families had received payments supplementing their income from work by the end of 1971, D.C. officials estimated that 10,000 working poor families might be eligible.

Raising the Ceiling

The federal government had long limited its contribution per recipient but not the number of recipients it would aid. This arrangement generally encouraged states to put a ceiling on the level of assistance above which they received no federal contribution. Thin payments were spread across a wider population. Until 1965, the federal monthly contribution per recipient was $15 of the first $18, about $7 of the next $14, and nothing thereafter. Thus, states had to pay only $10 of the first $32, but all additional costs. In 1965, however, states were given the choice of continuing the previous formula or having the federal contribution a flat proportion (from 50 to 83 percent, depending on the state's per-capita income) with no limit. This, in effect, removed the federal ceiling, allowing states to provide higher AFDC benefits at a lower cost; and this, in turn, accounts significantly for the rise in welfare benefits throughout the nation since the mid-1960s.

What happened in the District is a good illustration. With a relatively high per-capita income, the District qualified for the lowest federal matching—only 50-50. Thus, it was cheaper for the District to use the old formula for monthly payments up to $44, but above that level the new formula was more advantageous. Benefits in 1966 averaged $33, and D.C. prudently continued to use the old formula. But when benefits rose in 1970 to $49, it switched. Although the District's outlay is absolutely more for these higher benefit levels, the new system allows a "saving" over the old; savings will increase as benefits grow. At the $56 level in late 1971, the District's portion was $28; but under the old system, its cost to provide the same level of benefits would have been $34. These "savings" of $6 per month, or $72 annually, are substantial when spread across a caseload of 80,000 persons.

Matching Formula

Congress' strong hope that social services will "rehabilitate" welfare recipients is exemplified in the matching system which provides a federal dollar for each state dollar used for cash payments, but $3 in federal money for each state dollar spent on services.

At the national level, the renewed federal bias toward behavior modification of welfare clients as opposed to cash grants is illustrated by the recent allocation to the Social and Rehabilitation Service of the Department of Health, Education, and Welfare of 437 new staff employees who will develop and promote more new social service programs throughout the country and possibly provide a resident advisor in each state. The assumption underlying this allocation is that changing the attitudes, values, morals, customs, and behavior of welfare recipients through social work will diminish recipient dependency and remove people from the rolls.

At the local level, D.C. welfare officials have been aggressive in taking advantage of the matching formula by interpreting any feasibly related administrative, training, consulting, or specialist costs as "services" and charging them to the social services programs component. As a result, the District's administrative costs in 1970 were the highest in the country—26 percent of its budget and more than twice the proportion in any other state. Not only were staff assignments affected by this dual matching formula, but the efficiency of both payment and service programs was curtailed by the effort to take advantage of higher federal payments. There was often staff and client confusion in determining what services actually were being offered or provided.

Separating Cash and Services

The Department of Health, Education, and Welfare strongly urged states to separate the administration of cash payments from social service programs. This request reflected federal concern that local administrators, skimping on time and personnel in processing payments, inadvertently allowed ineligible recipients to slip onto the rolls. In addition, a federal official estimated that in 1971 about one third of federal contributions for services were inappropriately claimed because of local agency confusion as to the nature of its staff work or due to the padding of accounts to get more federal dollars.

Since the most obvious and pressing priority in any local agency is to "get the checks out," there is no way to avoid monumental administrative procedures without seriously damaging the credibility of the department. In 1971 social workers, who handled both the financial and service aspects of their caseloads, spent the majority of their time on income-maintenance work. Consequently, there was inevitable padding and pretense about the provision of services. This schizophrenic practice (of stealing time from payment work to offer a little client counseling which qualified for the higher $3-$1 formula) brought in greater federal subsidies but produced some costly errors in cash payments and caused a loss of services to the clients. Checks were often late or lost and many errors occurred—in the form of both overpayments and underpayments to clients.

Before the separation of payments and services, a D.C. social worker had the responsibility of investigating applications and verifying the eligibility of some 10 percent of applicants, establishing the level of grants, making provisions for payments, and handling any changes in the benefit payments due to changes in the client's situation. The same worker was also responsible for providing information about available daycare centers or services for treating problem or delinquent children. The worker might also make referrals for work-training or employment programs, provide counseling on any and all emotional or family problems, and offer consultation concerning housing difficulties. The worker was to be available to intervene and offer emergency assistance in case of an eviction, to determine emergency grants to meet rent or utilities payments in arrears, and to make all necessary recommendations and arrangements for homemaker services, legal services, etc.

But since the caseworker had an ever-increasing caseload, most of his time was spent taking applications, determining eligibility, getting checks out, and trying to track down missing checks. This situation caused a great loss of morale among D.C. social workers who found themselves dealing almost entirely with clerical and administrative matters rather than with the more human aspects of their cases. Many social workers with advanced degrees became resentful about paper-pushing. Conversely, social service representatives, B.A. degree holders who were hired primarily to handle cash payments procedures, found themselves forced into counseling roles as part of the maneuver to bring in more federal funds. Counseling in cases involving children is a social-work area that historically and traditionally has been handled primarily by professionals wtih advanced training (a justification of the federal formula paying three times as much for these services as for clerical work handled by less-qualified employees). Therefore, the criterion of professionalism was also used to justify the separation of functions so that workers with less training would not engage in psychological counseling.

With the separation of payments and services, 58 percent of the nearly 600 social service employees were assigned to the intake and income-maintenance division, and 42 percent were assigned to the delivery of services. This, however, did not reduce the federal contribution for salaries, even though the majority of workers now fell under the $1-$1 ratio, because new functions were identfiied and charged under the more favorable formula. For example, when emergency assistance is necessitated—due to a late or lost check— the service worker who obtains an emergency grant for a recipient is considered to be engaged in a service rather than a cash-payment activity. Services are considered under the law administrative expenditures, and a local agency need produce only 25 percent of the professional or in-kind salary. It is also easier for the agency to justify such expenditure since it is not involved in granting money to welfare recipients and the funds are used exclusively for salary payment to a professional social worker.

The separation of services and payments programs also was geared toward the eventual takeover by federal administrators of the entire AFDC program. While the adult categories, such as aid to the aged, blind, and disabled, will eventually be administered along with Social Security payments, the intake and cash-payment program for AFDC recipients will be handled separately within the Department of Health, Education, and Welfare. In preparation for possible federalization, D.C. separated these functions several years ago to expedite the eventual takeover.

These administrative changes, however, have not benefited the clients. Although the District government's goal is to develop a unified intake system within a network of decentralized comprehensive centers for services, at present welfare applicants must still fill out lengthy and complicated eligibility forms for each of the separate welfare, food-stamp, and Medicaid programs. Clients complain bitterly about the complexity of these application forms—for eligibility determination as well as recertification—and the fact that each welfare client must now deal with two different caseworkers, one in charge of cash payments and the other in charge of services. This doubling of agency contacts further complicates the client's situation without unifying the intake procedures.

CLIENT RESPONSE TO DELIVERY OF SERVICES

Nor has the delivery of social services been satisfactory. When Catherine Perry first applied for welfare, she was assigned an intake and income maintenance worker who was responsible for determining her eligibility for welfare and a social service representative who was to familiarize her with the various social services available in the District. Both of these workers are with the sprawling Department of Human Resources, which includes not only the Payments Assistance Administration (income-maintenance workers) and the Social Rehabilitation Administration (social-service workers) but also administrations for Community Health and Hospitals, Mental Health, and Narcotics Treatment. These units provide a wide variety of services, including day-care service for welfare mothers enrolled in training, emergency services to families, foster home care, protective services for abused or neglected children, adoption services, and landlord-tenant counseling.

Given the choice, welfare mothers are almost unanimous in desiring higher welfare payments rather than more services or institutions—both of which have failed to provide regular supportive and sustaining types of programs. Perhaps Catherine Perry's greatest need, apart from money, is a free, quality neighborhood child-care center where she could leave Jimmy for a morning, or a communal home where all neighborhood children might stop to play after school. Such a service would be psychologically liberating for Mrs. Perry and infinitely preferable to the gravely limited mental health services now available to welfare clients who suffer nervous breakdowns. Just as a school or church is an ever-present institution in the life of a community, a free neighborhood childcare center would become a routine and psychologically comforting option for the welfare mother who feels oppressed by child-care and money problems.

In addition, Catherine Perry has suggested that programs like the Homemakers Service need shoring up. The Homemakers Service is a private charity which provides trained personnel to enter welfare homes on a round-the-clock basis for nursing or childcare if the mother is hospitalized. There are 130 homemakers for the 40,000 welfare households often in need of such service and care. "Women like me," said Mrs. Perry,

> without any husband or family around who can afford to take off work for a day to come in and help, really need a service like Homemakers. That's more important than Emergency Shelter or Junior Village for my kids. If the welfare people gave us nursing and childcare services, it would prevent lots of worse trouble that costs the city a lot more money. Most of the women I know are so poor that they have terrible nervous problems. Because we don't have any menfolk, we take care of our kids alone all the time and we go half crazy figuring out how to buy a pair of shoes or how to get some food at the end of the month. We can't go see psychiatrists the way rich people do and we have much worse problems. Maybe one afternoon free a month—away from all these worries—would stop some mental breakdowns. I really think that an extra $10 in cash could stop a mother from cracking up and getting shipped off to St. E's so her kids get locked up in Junior Village. Maybe if they cut down some of the other programs or saved some of that administrative money they could give us a little more help. If the Shelter Service would just pay a family's rent one month instead of letting them get evicted so they all have to move into the Pitts Motor Hotel for a few days, they'd end up saving money. But now they've just added 45 new investigators to the welfare department to keep a check on us. That costs hundreds of thousands of dollars and you know none of us have any mink coats stashed away. We were poor yesterday and we'll be poor tomorrow. Why couldn't they just give us the money? Why do they cut off their noses to spite their faces?

Since D.C.'s social services leave much to be desired in terms of appropriateness, availability, and adequacy, their utilization has been steadily declining. Nevertheless, Catherine Perry's social service representative is greatly overburdened. Although his job description called for service work with 65 welfare families, he currently has charge of 500 families. Though his responsibility is to counsel and advise families upon request, he seldom has time to see anyone in person. He explained:

I spend most of each day on the telephone trying to act as a buffer between my clients and the different private or public outfits that harrass them. I don't even have time to think about what I'm doing or what it all means. I just keep answering the phone and then using the other line to call whoever is bugging my clients—you know, taking advantage of them because they're welfare people and black and poor. The most I can offer these 500 families is information about what services are available and urge them to use whatever it is that the city offers. But the services never seem to be the right ones and if they are relevant there's not enough welfare personnel to handle the demand. Anyway, I don't advise many of my clients to get into a training program because they can't find jobs after they're finished with training.

But lots of my clients are getting pretty hip now. They've gotten smart to the system. I think National Welfare Rights helped by pointing out a lot of things to welfare mothers. Why should a woman be a maid—leave her kids in some lousy place for the day—just to earn enough to starve on? What does that get her? Why should she iron Sen. Long's shirts if she ends up getting evicted because she can't make the rent. That's why a lot of women in this city are into Welfare Rights clubs. It's better to be part of something—to organize other poor women and to try out different communal projects or go off with their kids to lobby in congress than to scrub some white lady's kitchen floor for a buck an hour.

For more than five years, Washington welfare recipients have been forming local welfare organizations to protect their rights and interests. Catherine Perry is a faithful member of the Shaw-Cardozo Welfare Rights Organization and has recently begun to assume a role of leadership. "I'm feeling better now," she said,

now that I understand what's happening to me and that it's not my fault that I'm in the welfare bag. My children don't eat too good, but we're not starving to death. I've had a lonely life and it's still hard, but it's gotten a little better now that I know other welfare mothers and now that we've got an organization that stands up for each of us. They'll even get us a lawyer if we have a hearing with the Department. We're not just scared anymore or separated from each other. We've got an organization.

The education Catherine Perry received—about the economic and welfare system in Washington—has liberated her psychologically and politically, if not financially. The D.C. Family Rights Organization has a city-wide membership of 3,000 and is the locally recognized branch of the National Welfare Rights Organization. Another group, D.C. Welfare Rights, has a membership of approximately the same size. Both groups organize, plan strategy and public relations, lobby, demonstrate, and provide supportive help for AFDC mothers.

WELFARE AND WORK

Nationally, one person in 20 receives Aid to Families with Dependent Children; in the District, the proportion is twice as high, reaching up to 50 percent in some neighborhoods. Among the many forces which have contributed to the growth of welfare, both nationally and locally, were legislative extensions of eligibility to new groups such as unemployed fathers and working mothers, court decisions that struck down barriers to relief, and vigorous outreach efforts by welfare rights groups.

Following the 1968 riots in Washington, the political climate changed and the public became more sympathetic toward the financial and other needs of poor D.C. residents. "Mayor" Walter Washington, reappointed by President Nixon, requested in his fiscal year 1970 budget proposal that welfare payments be raised to meet 100 percent of the total basic-needs standards.

Although in 1967 Congress had instructed states to update their "standard of needs," in 1970 Washington was still using such antiquated standards as 1953 rent levels. The dramatic increase when the standard of needs was finally updated produced a great deal of pressure for higher payments (Table 8). Official data finally verified what was already known—that payments were woefully inadequate to meet D.C.'s high cost of living. But despite annual requests to Congress for appropriations to raise benefits, local requests have been denied and city officials have bowed to

Table 8

"NEEDS" VS. PAYMENTS IN WASHINGTON, 1963-1971

	For a Family of Four Receiving Aid to Families with Dependent Children		Percent of Needs Paid
Year	Standard of Needs	Maximum Payment	
1963	$166	$166	100%
1967	182	182	100
1968	184	184	100
1969	208	208	100
1970	280	238	85
1971	318	238	75

Source: U.S. Department of Health, Education, and Welfare.

national political interests and intentions. Nevertheless, welfare benefits in the District have increased rapidly along with the number of recipients and the costs (Chart 6). The level of benefits

CHART 6: THE NUMBER OF AFDC RECIPIENTS HAS QUADRUPLED IN SIX YEARS

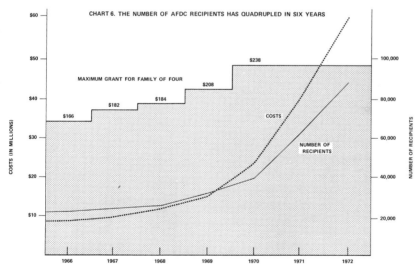

Source: U.S. Department of Health, Education, and Welfare

for a family of four with no other income has risen faster than spendable income for Washington jobholders covered by minimum-wage provisions.

Since D.C.'s welfare payments provide only 75 percent of the officially estimated need, in mid-1971 24 states would have paid the Perrys more than the monthly $238.50 they receive. California would have paid $261; Illinois, $272; Connecticut, $327; and Kansas, $321. The District, even though its cost of living is relatively high, pays less than most northern states but more than those south of the Mason-Dixon Line. This middle-level rank, in terms of the national level of benefit payments, reflects the homogenization of attitudes towards welfare in the U.S. Congress. Washington—the federal city—acts out the positive and negative compromises of national politicians.

With her maximum monthly grant of $238.50, Catherine Perry must pay her rent of $92, purchase her food stamps for $66, and pay her utilities that average $22 a month. Therefore, she is left with $58.50 cash each month, or less than $15 a week, to cover all transportation, furniture, clothing, toiletries, nonedible groceries, nonprescription drugs, and other routine expenditures—such as gym clothes required by the schools—or emergency expenses— such as taxi fare to the emergency room at Children's Hosptial when Jimmy has an asthma attack.

Although Catherine Perry pays no income tax, the less than $15 a week which she attempts to stretch into a survival budget is further trimmed by a 2-percent D.C. sales tax on a loaf of bread or bottle of baby aspirin and a 5-percent tax on sneakers or dungarees. Like other poor people she is also taxed on her public utilities, her telephone bills, and her monthly rental (through property tax passed on by her landlord). Moreover, since large national chains prefer to stay out of ghetto areas, Mrs. Perry must frequently shop in small independent stores where prices are much higher than chain market levels.

Obviously, a woman with three children trying to survive on $238.50 a month, plus $40 worth of food stamps and some other food and medical benefits, would consider finding work to alleviate her difficult financial circumstances. But Catherine Perry, restricted to menial labor by her sex and lack of education or skills, probably could not find a full-time job that would pay more than her current benefits. If she worked as a maid eight hours a day, five days a week, four weeks a month for the going rate of $1.50 per hour, she would earn only $240—$1.50 more than her current welfare check. Her salary would also be subject to taxes, and she would have work-related expenses. Consequently, for Catherine Perry welfare is financially preferable to working at an unskilled job for less than the federal minimum wage.

To encourage welfare recipients to work and thus save tax dollars, Congress has provided work incentives for AFDC mothers. If Mrs. Perry worked full time, she would be allowed to keep the first $30 of her earnings plus work expenses. But a sum equivalent to two thirds of the remainder of her wages would be deducted from her welfare check. This system taxes a welfare recipient earning above $360 a year at the same rate as someone else who earns above $140,000 a year.

Mrs. Perry can earn about $12 per day working as a maid. For the first two and a half days, she is allowed to keep all her earnings, but everything above that after work expenses is "taxed" at 67 percent. Thus, her fourth day's work yields her only $4. There are few people who will claim that 50 cents an hour is a decent wage. Even welfare mothers with more education and training face serious work problems, for blacks in D.C. have unemployment rates more than twice those for whites, and lower earnings scales for all occupations.

In addition to these barriers to adequate earnings is the more immediate concern that when Sondra is in school, Mrs. Perry has no one to take care of 4-year-old Jimmy. Licensed full-time day-care slots in Washington can accommodate only about one sixth of the city's 44,000 children who are between the ages of 2 and 5, and child-care costs are high. Even so, Mrs. Perry would have to make after-school and full-day arrangements during the summer for her other two children. Thus, for lack of training and education, for lack of child-care facilities, and for lack of economic "incentives," Mrs. Catherine Perry is locked into the welfare bag.

WELFARE REFORM

The welfare explosion beginning in the mid-1960s caught the federal government off guard, as related by Senator Mondale:

> In 1967, the Secretary of HEW was in conference with Mr. Califano [White House advisor for President Johnson]. He was asked how many people were on welfare, who they were, and all the rest. Since

we are spending several billions of dollars, one would have thought that information would be available to him as soon as he returned to his office and that he would send it right back. As a matter of fact, it took HEW a year and half to find out who was on welfare.[2]

By August of 1969, President Nixon, more fully informed as to the fiscal crisis caused by increasing welfare rolls and costs, proposed his Family Assistance Plan (FAP). After being buffeted by Congress, the plan was reintroduced in 1971, with Administration support, as H.R. 1. Its provisions were designed to ameliorate the national welfare "crisis" by reducing Catherine Perry's monthly check of $238.50 to $200 and eliminating her $40 food-stamp benefits. The District government would have an option to pay some additional benefits out of local funds if congressional committees approve.

By law, Catherine Perry would be required to register with the Labor Department for either work or training as soon as Jimmy turns six and goes to school all day. She would be forced to accept any job or training program offered to her unless she is sick or immobilized by lack of public transportation or child-care facilities. She would be required to accept work that pays only three fourths of the federal minimum wage of $1.60 an hour. Thus Georgetown housewives may reduce their $1.50 average hourly wage for dayworkers to $1.20 and have maids sent over free of employment-service charge—compliments of the federal government. Under the proposed plan Mrs. Perry could be forced to work eight hours a day at $1.20 an hour, or $9.60 a day. If she refused to work for these wages, she would be penalized by having her guaranteed income cut by $800.

While this penalty for not working is harsh, the incentive for working is not much better than the current one. Mrs. Perry would be allowed to earn up to $60 a month without being "taxed," but she would no longer be permitted to deduct work-related expenses. The "tax" on all income above $60 would still be two thirds. Thus, full-time work at $9.60 per day would increase her gross income by approximately $100 a month, an average hourly rate of 65 cents from which she would have to deduct work-connected expenses.

---

2 Congressional Record, January 25, 1971.

With perhaps 16,000 other welfare mothers in search of work, jobs will be scarce even at $1.20 an hour. Catherine Perry may be lucky to get one of the 200,000 new (but only temporary) jobs to be created by the federal government to handle this flood of women on the national labor market. But probably not, because Catherine Perry is not a very lucky person. Therefore, she may be placed in a training program to increase her employability. She may learn to be a keypunch operator and, after completion of her training, compete with other newly trained keypunch operators for some nonexistent job. D.C. program administrators have experienced difficulty in placing their trainees so far.

Mrs. Perry has no illusions about the flowery rhetoric being used to peddle welfare reform: "off welfare rolls and onto payrolls"; "full opportunity"; "good jobs that provide both additional self-respect and self-support." Given little economic incentive to work and disabused of the dream of "social mobility" which for so long motivated the poor to work at poverty-level wages, Mrs. Perry has discarded the idea that domestic housework leads to high-paying Gal Friday secretarial jobs on Capitol Hill. Politically she has begun to question the economic system which provides only dead-end employment for the oppressed of American society. Catherine Perry now sees that unskilled labor leads nowhere except back to poverty, and she understands that she is locked into poverty whether she works or not.

Under H.R. 1, the District of Columbia, which currently spends nearly 15 percent of its operating budget on welfare, would obviously save a great deal of money since it would no longer be required to give Catherine Perry anything. The District has the privilege of supplementing her $200-a-month guaranteed income to bring it back up to the level of $238.50. If it chooses to do so—and perhaps provide another $40 to make up for the lost food-stamp bonus—it can make Catherine Perry a cash grant of $78 a month—after agreeing to have the federal government administer the supplemental payments. If the District decides to maintain Mrs. Perry's 1972 grant of $2,862 (of which the federal government paid half), it would have to pay Catherine Perry only $462 a year. The District of Columbia could save $15.5 million per year. That's a lot of money saved. Where will it go?

And who else will save a lot of money? Forty-five other states besides the District of Columbia. And who else? Employers who might be able to increase their profits by paying lower wages to more people. And who else? Mrs. George E. Town who will now have an endless supply of cheap maids at her disposal. She will now have to pay only $1.20 an hour for domestic help, and the federal government will subsidize her maids, butlers, chauffeurs, and gardeners with FAP, guaranteed-to-keep-them-alive-and-working annual income.

And who loses? Catherine Perry. And Sondra and Ronnie and Jimmy.

Chapter Six

YOU ARE WHAT YOU EAT: FEEDING D.C.'S HUNGRY

by Mary Lynn and Nick Kotz

"FOOD STAMPS ARE NOT A WELFARE PROGRAM"

Until a cold January day in 1972, Jean Johnson had never asked for food stamps, welfare, or any other kind of public assistance. Tiny, white, and Appalachian-proud, only the lines around her green eyes and her work-hardened hands suggest that she is as old as 41. Hard times, really hard times, are new to her. Her husband, a skilled mechanic, worked regularly until near-blindness suddenly crippled him. The Johnsons have no children.

"All I want is food stamps to help us get by until the VA comes through," Mrs. Johnson explained as she prepared to apply for food stamps in Washington, D. C.

A few minutes later she sat down across from the interviewer in his cubicle in the central food-stamp certification office, located a few blocks from the U. S. Capitol at 122 C Street, Northwest. This,

143

her third cross-town trip to apply for food stamps during two frustrating days, was the first time she had reached an interview. Despite the damp, cold weather, she wore cotton slacks and a thin jacket.

"When was your husband's last paycheck?" the interviewer asked.

"May 28," she answered.

"How have you been living since then?"

Pause. "Relatives and friends have helped us out."

"Please write their names and the amounts they have contributed."

"I don't think my relatives would wish to have their names put on any list."

"But we have to know how you have been living. You say you have no income. Have you been paying rent?" he asked.

"Yes, $75 a month."

"Please give me the receipt for this month's payment."

"I paid by money order. But I brought a receipt for August when I paid with cash."

"We must have the latest rent receipt. You should have brought the stub."

"But I didn't know to bring a money order stub. All they told me was a rent receipt."

"Food stamps are not a welfare program. They are an income supplement program. Now in order to receive food stamps we have to know how you have been managing and how you plan to manage. We could certify you if you apply for public assistance so that we know you will have some income."

"Mr. Johnson and I do not wish to go on welfare," the lady stated.

"But we cannot give you food stamps if you have no way to manage. You should go over to the public assistance office and apply for emergency assistance."

"But I do not *want* to go on welfare. All we need is some food stamps."

"But how do you plan to manage? We cannot give you food stamps if you have no future income."

"Well, we have applied for Veterans, but they say it takes about a month."

"Do you have a copy of your application?"

"No, I didn't know I was supposed to bring it."

"Well, if you will return with your application for VA benefits then we can process your application for food stamps. We cannot process your application until you show proof of future management."

"You mean I can't get food stamps?"

"Not unless you indicate which relative will support you, and the amount of that support, or unless you apply for public assistance. I urge you to apply for public assistance."

"Then I guess I just won't be able to get the stamps then. I'm not going to sign my brother-in-law's name to anything." Tears welled up in her eyes, her voice rose determinedly.

"I'd rather go hungry than go on welfare." Mrs. Johnson said.

Under the 1971 Food Stamp Act, Jean Johnson and her disabled husband were clearly eligible to receive $60 a month worth of food stamps. If the Johnsons were completely without a source of funds, the stamps would be free. If friends and relatives were providing $100 monthly in aid, the Johnsons would have to pay $23 to get the $60 in stamps. The amount of aid, under this federal program, varies with a poor person's income. After being certified for the program, the Johnsons would receive a food-stamp card. Then, semimonthly or monthly, they would take the card to a specified bank or credit union to receive stamps with which they could purchase food from grocery stores certified to accept them.

But Mrs. Johnson gave up.* A newcomer to the social service system, she had little experience in answering official questions from a cool, impersonal interviewer. To "sign up on a list" or "go on welfare" was anathema to her. She did not know how to volunteer information about her husband's sudden blindness, the depletion of family savings, the fact that he had worked steadily as a mechanic for 25 years, or, indeed, how she had managed to scrimp and eat on "no income" for five months while he was in a veterans' hospital. Nor was she asked. ("Mouthwash," she told a writer. "You have to give up things like mouthwash. And the second cup of coffee. And the cigarettes. . . .")

Neither could it possibly have occurred to her to question why

* The Johnsons later did get food stamps after the program director was questioned as to why they had been denied help.

the D. C. Food Stamp Certification office suddenly was making it so difficult for people with no income to get free food stamps. For Mrs. Johnson's experience was not an isolated case. The District of Columbia government in 1971 and 1972 was rigidly rejecting "no-income" families who probably were eligible for food-stamp aid. Only if they applied for emergency public assistance—a few dollars to buy food while the welfare investigators checked them out—could they be certified.

The Federal Cornucopia

Food stamps are the largest federally supported food program. Eligibility and benefits are set by the Department of Agriculture. Families are eligible for benefits if their monthly income is under $300 or under their level of "needs" as determined by the state ·welfare agency. Families with very little or no income receive the stamps free; other eligible families pay more as their income rises but should have to spend no more than 30 percent of their income to purchase a "nutritionally adequate" diet. For example, a family of four with less than $30 monthly income receives free stamps worth $108 monthly. A family of four with $200 monthly income pays $60 to receive $108 worth of stamps.

State and local governments, such as the District, administer the food-stamp program for the federal government. In addition, the District benefits in varying degrees from most other federal food-aid programs, all of which are administered federally by the Department of Agriculture. These include:

• The Special Milk Program, which subsidizes part of the cost of an extra half pint of milk for most American school children. Children are eligible for the low-cost milk regardless of their family income. The program is strongly backed by the dairy industry which believes milk disposed of through this means helps prevent a price-depressing surplus for the dairy industry. The District participates fully in the program, as do most other urban school districts.

• The National School Lunch Program, which supplies both financial and food commodity aid to schools agreeing to operate a federally approved program. In return for the aid, schools are supposed to make lunches available to all children who desire them and supply free lunches to poor children. A similar breakfast program serves only poor children. Until recently, the District did not participate in the school program in any meaningful sense. The District has, in the last few years, made great strides towards feeding poor children, but still reaches fewer children than most urban school systems.

• The nonschool feeding programs for children, which supply financial and food aid to local governments and private agencies for the feeding of children in day-care centers and in school or recreational settings during summer vacation. This program has had a short and erratic history in which Congress has blocked Nixon Administration efforts to cut back on benefits. The District, along with most metropolitan areas, has made use of whatever funds have been allocated.

• The Supplemental Feeding Program for Infants and Nursing Mothers, which supplies special foods to state and local health agencies for distribution to those most vulnerable to permanent damage from malnutrition.

In addition to a quarter of a million dollars for administrative expenses, $325,000 for equipment at five dozen schools, and $476,000 worth of food donated to the breakfast and lunch programs, costs for the above efforts in the District totalled $20.4 million in fiscal 1971 (Chart 7). Nationally, these programs cost over $2 billion in the same year.

D. C. Is a Creature of Congress

The reasons behind Jean Johnson's rebuff at the food-stamp office illustrate one characteristic problem in administering federal grant-in-aid food programs in Washington, D.C. Her case and the "tightening of the program" reflect the D.C. government's and the Secretary of Agriculture's overreaction to congressional criticism of possible fraud in the District program.

A number of congressmen, including Representative Jamie Whitten (D-Miss.), chairman of the House Appropriations Subcommittee controlling Agriculture Department funds, read in local newspapers highly misconstrued figures indicating that the District had been lax in qualifying people for free food stamps. Whitten, a veteran opponent of liberalized food aid, severely reprimanded Agriculture Department officials appearing before his committee. Rep. William Natcher of Kentucky, also a member of the Agri-

CHART 7:   THE DISTRICT'S POOR RECEIVED FEDERALLY AIDED FOOD ASSISTANCE
           IN MANY WAYS, 1971

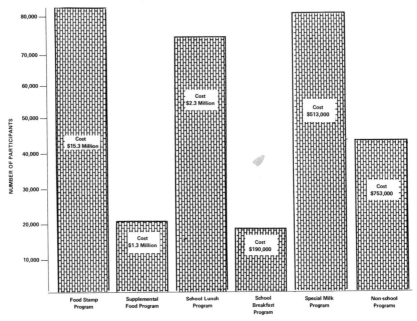

Source: U.S. Department of Agriculture

culture Committee as well as chairman of the District of Columbia
Appropriations Committee, entered into the April 1971 colloquy.
The Department of Agriculture and the D. C. government responded by making it virtually impossible for a penniless family
to get free food stamps.

"We didn't mean for them [the District government] to take our
suggestions so literally," said USDA administrator James Drake,
who helped D. C. "tighten" its Certification Procedures. "D. C.
overreacted" in driving away the eligible poor.

Top-level pressure beginning in Congress, which came five years
after the food-stamp program was in operation, succeeded in
streamlining the D. C. food-stamp program. By 1972, more than
100,000 persons per month were receiving food stamps. However,
the proximity of the District government to the White House, the
Congress, and the executive departments does not guarantee that
the federal government always will react sensitively to the opera-

tion of federal grant-in-aid programs in the District. Aside from crackdowns against the poor, the federal government generally has been insensitive to defects in federal programs run in its most immediate presence. This insensitivity to program defects provides a dramatic illustration of how little attention the federal government pays to program effectiveness once social legislation has passed Congress and has been signed by the President. Liberal advocates and lobbyists have been guilty of the same lack of follow-through to see if the programs they fought for actually were helping the poor. The vast failings of the original 1965 Food Stamp Program and 1946 National School Lunch program should have been obvious to any federal official who read the local newspapers. The failure of these programs did not have to be unveiled until 1967 in Mississippi where hunger suddenly was discovered as a national issue. In that year, and in the two previous years, local Mississippi newspapers had reported lines of people queuing up for food stamps at 4 o'clock in the morning; hungry people not being able to afford food stamps; and children whose one meal of the day was served at school.

The District of Columbia was one of the first communities to apply for the new federal food-stamp program when it became effective in 1965, and the District's early experiences should have informed the federal government—but did not—that the original program would badly need modification if it were to help the hungry poor.

In June 1965, about 9,000 District families were benefiting from another food-aid program—surplus commodity distribution. In this program the eligible poor went monthly to a government storehouse where they received a small and varying number of basic food commodities such as lard, peanut butter, flour, and occasionally cheese or canned meat. The foods available depended on the desire of the Agriculture Department to prop up the price of crops then in surplus. Neither the Agriculture Department nor the governing Agriculture committees of Congress concerned themselves much about whether the commodities program served the nutritional needs of the poor—which it didn't.

Expectations were high that the poor would fare better when the food-stamp program was introduced to the District on July 1, 1965, as a replacement for the commodity program. Instead, the program switch produced a wave of suffering. At the end of 1965, only about 3,500 families actually were buying food stamps, compared with 9,000 families who earlier in the year had been receiving free surplus commodities. The drop in food-program participation should have been readily explainable. The original food-stamp law (since liberalized in 1969 and 1971) simply required the poor to pay too much for food stamps and provided too little food in return.

"No wonder they didn't fall all over themselves to get food stamps at first," explains Thelma Rutherford, a compact, compassionate social worker who is chairman of information and referral at the city's private Health and Welfare Council.

> In Washington, rent is so high and the landlords are so unsympathetic. Transportation costs a lot. Children have to have clothes. When your income is not enough to cover the pressing other items in life, people cut back on food first. That's why all the people who are certified to buy food stamps don't always use them.

The initial food stamp program, in the District as elsewhere around the country, contributed to the frustrations of the poor. It represented one more case of inflated promise and unmet expectation. Ironically, this frustration was heightened in the District because community leaders like Mrs. Rutherford and nutritionist Mildred Brooks had from the outset launched an ambitious and effective campaign to inform and involve the poor. Between them, these two ladies got the District to apply for food stamps and organized one of the nation's first citizens' food-stamp advisory committees to involve the public.

"We started out as a nutrition education committee," stated the elegant, silver-haired Mrs. Brooks. "But our first objective was to get community involvement and to spread the word about food stamps."

Within three months after the program's inception in the District, any conscientious or concerned federal official should have become sensitive to the fact that this federal grant-in-aid program was not working adequately. The community-based Food Stamp Advisory Committee and the poor themselves quickly noted that the stamps cost too much and provided too little food. Scattered stories in the Washington newspapers always stressed the poor's complaint about prohibitive costs and inadequate benefits. For example, a family of four with a $100 monthly income had to pay out $44 in a lump sum to get only $78 worth of food stamps, less than three fourths of the amount needed to buy a minimally adequate diet for a full month.

But in 1965 official Washington did not look at these obvious food-stamp program defects. The energies of liberals advocating aid for the poor were not concentrated on the Agriculture Department, the administrator of the program. And at that stage, USDA officials and the Agriculture committees of Congress frankly were not interested in finding out whether the program helped the poor get a healthier diet. Agriculture's interest in the food-stamp law was concentrated solely on the law's use as a device to help the farmer in the marketplace by means of increasing consumer purchasing power. Farm-bloc congressmen and Agriculture Department officials stressed repeatedly that the program was not a "welfare" program but a "food" program designed to improve purchasing power. Any and all complaints that stamps cost too much were summarily rejected with the comment, "Well, it's not supposed to be a welfare program."

The farm state congressmen were sincere in this statement. They most strongly opposed welfare aid to anyone, except, of course, farmers. Their desire to help the farmer but avoid another welfare program created an insoluble program conflict for the Agriculture Department. Its original attempt to resolve this conflict helped neither the farmer nor the poor: Food stamps were made so expensive that they couldn't possibly be regarded as a handout; so expensive, in fact, that the poor couldn't participate to get more food and thus could not help the farmer sell more food.

Ironically, however, the food stamp program was administered at the state and local level by welfare departments. At the outset, welfare departments, including the District's, regarded the program as an unwanted administrative burden, since the federal government did not pay any costs of administering it. State and local welfare departments resented having to deal with yet another federal department, particularly one as alien to social welfare as the Agriculture Department. Furthermore, most welfare workers philosophically opposed food stamps as an "in kind" aid program, when what people really needed was more money. Food stamps were considered a competitor for scarce funds when welfare itself already was starved for adequate funds.

Food Stamps Come to Washington

In this atmosphere, the food-stamp program came to Washington. A small food-stamp staff was created by the welfare department and located across town from the central welfare administration. The food-stamp operation was isolated in more ways than one. Less than a handful of new personnel were added as the food-stamp program inherited the former commodities-program staff. And "commodities," according to District welfare workers, was known as the Siberia of the welfare department. Under federal civil service, people weren't fired. They were sent to "commodities." The food-stamp office was buried administratively in the welfare department hierarchy.

The new food-stamp program functioned in obscurity for several years. Local welfare department officials seemed unaware of the program's inadequate food aid and inaccessibility. Persons wishing to apply for the program had to make their way to one relatively inaccessible certification office.

But during late 1966 and 1967, the atmosphere began changing in the streets, if not in the office of the D. C. welfare director. Even with the restrictively high payments, the District program began to grow rapidly until 20,000 persons were receiving stamps in early 1967. The program's small staff was nearly engulfed by applicants who began lining up as early as 4 a.m.

During this same period, hunger in America began to catch on as a national political issue. The late Senator Robert Kennedy and the Senate poverty subcommittee left their D. C. offices to uncover hunger and food-program inadequacies in Mississippi and Appalachian Kentucky. Seeing the possibility of new support, the already-active food-program advocates in the District began to beat the bushes in Washington ghettoes to inform people of the program. And John Saunders, who believed his mission was to "sell" the program to the community, became the District's food-stamp certification officer.

> But we didn't need a census to know that people needed food. We spoke to community agencies, church groups, published a food stamp newsletter and tried to find out what people needed. We knew we had to open branch offices in the neighborhoods where poor people lived. They just can't afford to travel across town to wait all day for food stamps. We were able to open only two branch offices in

1967, and we could only staff them one day a week. The problems were growing as fast as the number of customers. I begged the Department for more staff positions, more community offices. Certification officers were quitting because they couldn't stand the pressure, or were not able to cope with the long lines of waiting poor people. And the poor really started complaining not only about the price of stamps—but about service. We were way across town, however, and the welfare department seemed not to be aware of the pressing needs we had.

Then in 1968, the physical transfer of the food-stamp office rapidly produced both new perceptions and new politics for Washington city officials. The office was moved from its remote location to the central welfare office near the Capitol. The problem of inadequate staff now become more than an irritating complaint vaguely transmitted from across town. When ranking city officials came to work in the morning, they were greeted with the sight of hundreds of food-stamp applicants waiting in cold, rain, or heat. The most detached city welfare official could no longer ignore the predawn lines, the confusion, the protest demonstrations, and the breakdown of any semblance of orderly administrative efficiency. Several members of the District's city council, which is appointed by the President, also became concerned. Finally, the insistent and effective "outreach" work of the Food Stamp Advisory Committee began to achieve some results.

The response of the city government and Congress to the publicized lack of an adequate food-stamp staff illustrates one of the problems of administering federal grant-in-aid programs in Washington, D. C. The District is a creature of the federal government, with Congress deciding the most minute details of budget and personnel policy. The handling of the staff-shortage problem in 1968 showed the inability of the city to respond to legitimate citizen complaints when the city is governed by congressmen from Kentucky and South Carolina.

Food stamp director John Saunders requested 24 new staff positions for the fiscal 1969 budget. He sought to cut down the long lines of applicants, to open branch offices located nearer to the poor, and to anticipate further growth in the program. Saunders' staff request was slashed in half before it even left the welfare building. Winifred Thompson, then the city's welfare director, was a canny student of the congressional appropriations subcommittees that controlled her funds. She anticipated their attitudes. She pared the requested 24 staffers to 12 in the process of whittling away at various requests from below in her department. Food Stamp Advisory Chairman Thelma Rutherford pleaded for their reinstatement before the city council. At this point, the city council, led by Councilwoman Polly Shackleton, intervened and restored the appropriations request for 24 staffers.

On Capitol Hill, however, the food-stamp staff request met a sadly predictable fate. The House Appropriations Subcommittee responsible for District spending knocked out the entire request for 24 staff positions. The comparable Senate subcommittee approved four of the positions. The final Senate-House budget agreed to eliminate all the proposed positions from the budget.

Some government observers do not regard the District's problems, such as this one, as unique. It is argued that government relationships in administering federal grant-in-aid programs in the District are really not that different from those in other local governments. The argument goes that Congress serves as the equivalent of a state legislature for Washington, D. C. If so, it is before anything else a state legislature without a single voting member representing the District. At least in Albany the problems of New York City are represented by a sizeable legislative delegation. At any rate, the administrative funds for the food-stamp program are in most jurisdictions provided not by the states but by county or city government. Other cities also have shortchanged the food stamp program by providing inadequate staff, but most responded to publicized needs as citizens generated enough pressure on city hall or the county courthouse.

If two committees of Congress chose to ignore the problems of food in D. C. for 1969, another committee zeroed in on the problem. The Senate Select Committee on Nutrition and Human Needs, which had been holding hunger hearings all over the United States, finally decided, in April 1969, to take a look in its own backyard. Senators George McGovern, Walter F. Mondale, Jacob Javits, and their staff members went on a tour of the Shaw, Cardozo, and Bruce Elementary School areas in Washington and discovered hungry people, especially hungry children. They were accompanied by Dr. Charles Upton Lowe, a pediatrician at the National Institutes of Health.

In one house Senator Mondale held a child in his arms, a child described by Dr. Lowe as malnourished, and listened to the child's mother say, "The food stamps cost too much money for us to buy."

Another mother, whose husband was a city employee earning $115 in take-home pay every two weeks, dropped out of the program because the family was behind in its bills and could not afford to pay $42 twice a month for $62 worth of stamps. Why, she was asked?

> I have three children, one of my sisters, and my 14-year-old brother living with us. We have to pay $74 a month on the mortgage, $42 in heat for February, $45 for the electricity. We are behind in our bills. The water bill for six months, $48.91, came due. I was sick last month and had to have a telephone put in, that was $21.40.

The mother went to the Neighborhood Improvement Center for help because "we didn't have anything to eat." She had borrowed $30 from a friend. The evening before the Senators' visit, the children had been fed potatoes and bread for dinner. "If my husband brings home a pay check, I'll cook neckbones and beans," she said.

In home after home, the Senators found dire misery and case after case illustrating two major flaws in the food-stamp program itself: that even though the stamps provided a saving, their initial cost was unrealistically high for families too poor to save a large cash outlay; and that the amount of food the stamps could buy was considerably less than what the Agriculture Department considered a "two-week emergency" diet.

At hearings before the D. C. Department of Welfare, Mrs. Louise Earl, chief of nutrition for the Public Health Department of the District, testified:

> For a family composed of a mother and four children—a boy 8, and three girls, 10, 7, and 4 years of age, the Agriculture Department figures for a low-cost budget indicate that the low-cost food plan would cost $121.95 per month. If the same family paid $68 for $100 worth of food stamps it would still be short $21.95, and would probably have great difficulty providing an adequate diet for the family without exceptional knowledge and exceptional cooking facilities.

The 1969 and 1971 laws partially alleviated this problem, but a large family with teenagers still does not get enough food.

On April 16, 1969, the Select Committee held hearings with Senator Edward Kennedy presiding. The Food Stamp Advisory Committee was represented by Mrs. Marjorie Harris, who testified:

> We are not doctors or nutritionists. . . . But we do know our city, its streets and its people. We know hunger is gnawing away here in the Nation's Capital. We know babies are dying here because they and their mothers are malnourished. The shocking evidence of this is the fact that the District of Columbia, seat of the most powerful and richest nation on earth, has been shown in a study several years ago to have the highest rate of infant mortality in the country, except for the state of Mississippi.
>
> . . . These facts, by themselves, are shocking and tragic. Unfortunately, they are made even more shocking and more tragic by the fact that a government-sponsored food assistance program, the food stamp program, which pretends to help these poor people feed themselves is a failure to most of them.
>
> According to the Welfare Department's own estimate, only about 39 per cent of all its public assistance cases are participating in the food stamp program—30 per cent of those on old age assistance, 23 per cent of those on aid to the blind, 48 per cent of those receiving aid and 25 per cent of those on general public assistance.
>
> We can only guess at how many not on public assistance, not receiving any financial help, are eligible for food stamp benefits.

"To Put an End to Hunger"

A month later, in May 1969, President Nixon himself embraced the problem with an historic message to Congress pledging "to put an end to hunger in America for all time." The President called for reform of both the food-stamp and school-lunch programs and for a White House conference to study the problem of malnutrition and recommend further action.

The December 1969 White House conference included a special panel on problems of the District of Columbia. The panel declared: "A state of hunger emergency exists in the city, an emergency because close to one-third of the District's population subsist on income below the currently defined poverty level, and are hungry and malnourished." The District panel's recommendations dealt both with national problems of the food-stamp program (the stamps cost too much and provided too little food) and with local problems. Specifically, the panel called for better coordination and cooperation between federal and district officials and for a vastly simplified procedure to snap bureaucratic red tape and break the bottleneck at the door of the D. C. food-stamp offices. In his speech to the conference, President Nixon stressed action to help the hungry in D. C.

The federal government reacted in a variety of contradictory ways to the new spotlights on hunger in the District. Responding to liberal criticism, benefits were liberalized and new ones were added. On the other hand, responding to the criticisms of Washington's conservative congressional overseers, the government promptly erased other food-aid benefits. And the Nixon Administration soon revealed confusion and conflict in its own priorities. On the one hand, the Administration vowed to attack the problem of nationwide hunger and to help the District achieve a model food-stamp program. Within a matter of months, however, the Administration switched its attention to a welfare-reform plan that would eliminate food stamps (without replacing lost food-stamp benefits). In the process, the Administration quietly dropped its special commitment to the District's food-stamp program.

The April 1969 congressional hearings on hunger in Washington produced one immediate result—the implementation of a supplementary feeding program for infants and pregnant and nursing mothers, the groups most vulnerable to lasting injury from malnutrition. The District's Health Department had resisted this program, unwilling to take on another administrative responsibility uncompensated by the federal government. However, Senator Jacob Javits of New York, the ranking Republican on the Senate Nutrition Committee, demanded action by the Agriculture Department. The Republican administration, reacting to political pressure from Javits and embarrassed by the Democratic-sponsored hearings, immediately announced that the District would have the largest supplementary feeding program in the country.

The President's May declaration of war on hunger, reaffirmed at the December White House conference, did produce a liberalization of national food-stamp regulations. Purchase requirements were relaxed slightly, and some families no longer were given less food stamps than others simply because they were poorer.

In D. C. the government responded by establishing a Mayor's Commission on Food, Nutrition, and Health. Confident that they at last had the support of the President, D. C. food-stamp officials felt that their pleas for staff and direction would be heard both by their own welfare director and by the Department of Agriculture. And they were partially correct. A top-level meeting was scheduled between Winifred Thompson, the District's director of Social Services (Welfare), and Isabelle Kelley, director of the Agriculture Department's food-stamp program, to ask for help in improving the delivery of services to the District's food-stamp customers.

This request for help, and the response from USDA, raised hopes initially that service would be improved, staff would be enlarged, and more efficient administration would be developed. In a classic example of intergovernmental relations between the District and the federal government, however, the federal "assistance" backfired so greatly at the expense of the District that one USDA official said it was unlikely that another local government would ever ask for help again.

Stamp Out the Cheaters

The federal aid backfired for the District because the first result of the meeting was a federally conducted audit, which led to unfair charges of fraud in the District program and to harrassment of USDA officials in Congress. And once the program was attacked, District officials reacting defensively tightened eligibility requirements so that many eligible poor were excluded. At any rate, other local government officials were not likely to run the risk of inviting the federal government in to criticize them.

The District's administrative problem from the outset was its inability to cope wtih a growing program expanded through community "outreach," which became far more attractive after the Administration liberalized benefits in late 1969. In an attempt to speed services to customers, the welfare department had opened 10 neighborhood certification centers, but the problem was the same: intolerable waiting in line at each center and harrassed certification officers. Six of the offices were open five days a week and the other four were open one day a week. But there were only 13 certification officers to spread around the centers. The addition of 13 temporary staff workers, borrowed from other departments, later eased the problem somewhat. But as late as August 1970, the *Washington Star* reported that "city officials concede that, in most of the District's 12 Certification points, prospective food stamp recipients who don't get there by 6:30 a.m. need not come at all."

Further complicating the food-stamp division's problems were the maze-like chains of command to which it reported in the city and the federal governments. In theory, the District food-stamp program was under the federal direction of USDA's New York regional office. In practice, Washington officials sometimes intervened in the program's direction, yet all changes had to come through New York. In the city government, the food-stamp division was buried several layers deep in the Department of Social Services (Welfare). Add to this administrative chain the occasional sharp intervention of congressional committees and one comes up with a cumbersome, erratic administrative apparatus not well suited to problem solving. As John Saunders recalled,

> The food stamp certification system was a nightmare. For two years we had been pleading with the Welfare Department for more staff; for two years we had been pleading with the New York office of USDA to give us some guidelines on handling our clerical system.
>
> With the decentralization to branch offices in the community, our problems only increased. At one point there were 50 percent vacancies on the certification staff. Certification officers don't need all the education of equivalent welfare workers (GS 5-8), so I asked USDA to relax the regulation concerning certification officers. They refused. Every time we asked New York to help us solve an immediate problem, they answered with a strict quotation of regulations. If the problem was not covered by existing regulations, we got no help with our problem.

The delayed and often-denied justice received by the poor at food-stamp certification offices was almost matched by the cumbersome system for issuing food stamps. Once a person finally qualified to receive food stamps, he had to apply for them monthly or semimonthly at a specific District bank or credit agency. The banks, despite making a profit on the transactions, subjected the poor to various inconveniences and humiliations such as receiving stamps at limited hours of the day and standing in special lines, including lines only at outside bank windows. Every time a bank complained it was handling too many food stamp recipients, the welfare office reshuffled hundreds of people and required them to go to another bank, often at a far greater distance from their home. It's little wonder that virtually every group that has reviewed the food-stamp program in the District or elsewhere recommends that stamps be delivered by mail or at post offices.

Understaffed and pressured by the long lines of applicants waiting to apply for food stamps, the District was issuing food-stamp certifications over the counter to applicants on the basis of their own statements, rather than first subjecting them to the long wait required for verifying the information about the applicant's income and family size. "There were too many people crowding into the offices, too few officers to certify them," said Saunders. "People were hungry. They couldn't wait for us to investigate every case. With all the chaos we started to attract some addicts and some falsifiers."

The problem of maintaining proper computerized records on food-stamp recipients was further complicated by the lack of an efficient central filing system and by lack of communication in the District government between the food-stamp office and computer office. Nor could the Food Stamp Department get the Justice Department to prosecute the few known "cheaters."

It was against this background of problems that District food-stamp officials, through Director of Social Services Thompson, went to the Agriculture Department, requesting an audit as a basis for organizing a more efficient delivery system. But instead of a more efficient delivery system, the Food Stamp Department rather unfairly got a black eye, and the poorest of the poor found it harder to get benefits.

A series of 1970 audits conducted by the Welfare Department and by USDA's Inspector General variously claimed "irregularities" in 23 to 44 percent of the cases studied. The methodology and basis for the sample were never announced. The audits, however, were taken badly out of context in publicity criticizing the District program. The Inspector General estimated that the federal government might lose $600,000 in fiscal 1971 unless the District took immediate action to prevent persons from fraudulently obtaining duplicate food-stamp cards.

Then, Agriculture Secretary Hardin announced in a Midwest political speech that he was "cleaning up" the food-stamp program in the District and several other cities. The House Agriculture Appropriations Subcommittee thereafter slashed into USDA officials for permitting widespread abuses in the District program.

Even though the percentage of fraud was far less than implied originally, in 1972 the initial charges still reverberated to the detriment of the poor.

There were scattered cases of fraud in the D. C. program, but its proportion was far less than anything indicated by unfair interpretations of the audit reports. First of all, the audits concentrated almost solely on a small, unrepresentative fraction of the food-stamp population, those persons who claimed they had no income. Second, a detailed reading of the audits showed that a majority of even those cases of improper benefits did not result from deliberate fraud but from haphazard administration, particularly in the computer programming. The number of "irregularities" in relation to the entire food-stamp population was actually closer to 3.3 percent—far less than the 23 percent reported in the newspapers. The amount of actual fraud discovered in both the District's food-stamp and welfare programs was less than 5 percent. In both programs, investigators have discovered a higher percentage of improper payments resulting from administrative errors than from fraud, but these errors have resulted in underpayments as well as overpayments to the poor.

Nonetheless, the damage was done. Saunders, who had responded to the President's call to feed the hungry, was demoted and replaced by Norman Bush, a former policeman whose admitted principal interest is to keep the unworthy poor from getting food stamps. In an interview early in 1972, Bush professed ignorance about recommendations to improve the food-stamp program in the District from the White House conference, from the Mayor's Commission, and from the federal Task Force. Shown the list of recmendations, Bush's only comment was a repeated: "We can't do that. It's not in the regulations."

As a result of the audit reports—as interpreted by officials who had never read them—the District stopped the practice of giving immediate food-stamp aid to "emergency cases," people without any source of income. This regulation caused immediate hardship for hundreds of those who found themselves jobless in early 1971, particularly since the District still had not perfected a computerized system to process applications quickly.

The Mayor's Commission on Food, Nutrition, and Health, led by the persistent Mrs. Brooks and Mrs. Rutherford, challenged the results of the audit and protested the hardships caused by the new regulation. Assistant Agriculture Secretary Richard Lyng admitted to the Commission that flagrant abuses in the D. C. food-stamp program probably were more faults of administration than of consumer fraud. And Mrs. Rutherford, who had begged the Department of Welfare, the city council, and the D. C. committees of Congress for three years to notice the program's need for staff, was especially furious.

Partially to appease the outraged Mayor's Commission, and partly to utilize a White House Fellow who had been assigned to his Department, Assistant Secretary Lyng announced that a Departmental-level task force would study indices of hunger in the District and would reshape the food-stamp program in the District of Columbia to make it a model for the nation.

Dr. Melvin Copen, assistant dean of business administration at the University of Houston and the guiding light of the task force study, was the White House Fellow. Copen was urged to utilize all modern business techniques, including computerization, to improve the operation of the food-stamp program. According to Copen,

> It was not that D.C. was being singled out, although the New York office and the Office of Inspector General felt political concern about the D. C. program. Actually, most cities do not have effectively administered programs. We hoped to set up a model for D. C. that we could pass along to other states, as an operational "package."

> We asked around, nationally, about such a program. We found that everybody was positive about the idea of the Feds coming in to help. One of the biggest problems between the local operations and regional USDA offices is that they don't get information back in a timely fashion. The local administrators are always looking to the federal government for help in solving problems, and there is a great similarity in their requests.

The task force was announced with great fanfare, to the delight of the Food Stamp Advisory Committee and the Mayor's Commission on Food, Nutrition, and Health. Months later, the two citizen's groups were bitter that no citizen participation was allowed and that the District government's representative was a welfare department investigator.

In early 1972, a year after the task force was announced, Dr. Copen explained that the model plan had still not been prepared. He stated,

> This Department takes its cues politically. When we first undertook the study, there was great national interest in feeding programs. The President had made a statement, and it was a rapidly expanding program with great national similarities in the problem areas.
>
> Our initial report was designed to streamline things. It would have involved changing Agriculture Department structure and urging the welfare department to change its structure. The report went initially to the New York regional office, and evoked a typical bureaucratic response to innovation. Their answer was "that to change structure would involve changing USDA regulations and the legislation itself." Neither could be done, they insisted.

To protect their own jobs, the USDA bureaucrats in the Food and Nutrition Service were wisely wary of the task force. Most task force members felt that the food-stamp program more properly belonged in the Department of Health, Education, and Welfare so that cash and in-kind food-stamp payments could be coordinated with welfare aid. At least some progress has been made, however, since the District and other local governments were given permission to have food-stamp payments deducted from welfare checks, and—in some cases—to mail the stamps along with the welfare check. But according to Dr. Copen,

> The Food and Nutrition Service of USDA, which could change regulations, took a long, long, time to respond to our recommendations. The time frame dragged out. The President seemed to be interested in other programs. And in the middle of all this, it looked as if Congress and the Administration were going to abolish the food stamp program entirely, which would make the whole study futile. Everybody slowed down.

James Drake, the USDA management consultant who worked on the task force study, commented: "Unfortunately, we picked a bad program to run a systems analysis on. When we picked food stamps to study, the issue was hot. But our interest span on anything in this country is short."

The short attention span of the Nixon Administration and of the nation could produce bitter hardship for millions of poor Americans who finally have been able to achieve a more nutritious diet, thanks to the improved food-stamp program.

The Proof's in the Pudding

The task force helped D. C. in a number of ways by eliminating the "bugs" in computerization and by streamlining procedures somewhat. Despite the administrative problems which still plague the program in the District and elsewhere around the country, the program's value to the poor has been proven by its phenomenal growth. During the five years between 1967 and early 1972, the number of program participants grew nationally from less than 2 million to more than 10 million. In the District, participation increased from 20,000 to 116,000. And the recipients now put more than $2 million a month into D. C. grocery stores.

Beyond any question, the District has made great progress in reaching a larger percentage of its poor population with food-stamp benefits. In early 1972, there were, as mentioned, some 116,000 participants in the program, a fourfold increase in about two years. As in most parts of the country, the District program was hampered in its early stage by resistance from the welfare department and by a conservative stamp-allotment formula that did not serve the poor. The USDA task force reported that the District had the most initial "outreach" in the country. As elsewhere, the District was deluged with applicants—and unable to process them speedily—when the program was liberalized and began to grow. As of early 1972, the District was reaching somewhat less than 50 percent of its eligible poor population with food stamps, and this record closely parallels the national pattern. The District is "different" to the extent that its program is occasionally scrutinized by high federal officials. Unfortunately, this special federal scrutiny has more often produced a "reign of fear" on local officials, rather than an improvement of the program.

All District food-aid programs, along with others around the country, have suffered from fluctuations in Nixon Administration policy. On at least 10 occasions between 1969 and 1972, the Administration sought to cut back aid under either the food-stamp, school-lunch, supplementary-feeding, or nonschool aid food programs. In virtually every instance the Administration backed off under the fire of congressional criticism or action, but the confusion deterred orderly program development. The greatest threat to food stamps still lay ahead in early 1972.

Food stamp benefits could be wiped out by the Nixon Administration's Family Assistance Plan, which eliminates food stamps completely and guarantees a family of four only $2,400 annually in welfare aid. About 90 percent of all welfare recipients now receive more money from the combination of welfare and food-stamp aid. For instance, a family of four in the District received more than $3,000 in combined aid. All welfare recipients except those in the few states with the lowest payments will lose under the Nixon plan unless their state legislatures agree to maintain spending on welfare and replace lost federal food-stamp benefits. Each of the states and the District could save a considerable amount of money simply by letting the federal government take over the entire cost of welfare. The states are guaranteed only that they will not have to spend more than they did in 1971 if they elect to maintain present total benefits. Considering the pressure on state treasuries and the political unpopularity of the welfare issue, it is reasonable to assume that many states will simply save money at the expense of the welfare poor.

The Administration has sought to convince (or confuse) critics of the proposed food-stamp elimination by contending that it would replace the lost food-stamp benefits by raising its initial proposal for a guaranteed annual income from $1,600 to $2,400. But this claim ignores the fact that the vast majority of the participating poor already get more total income than $2,400 either through a combination of welfare and food stamps or a combination of their below-poverty-level salaries and food stamps.

The Nixon welfare plan for the first time also provides benefits for the "working poor"—making the plan appear to include the foundation of a guaranteed annual income. But those working poor who would be eligible for the new welfare plan are now eligible to receive food stamps. Many would actually lose benefits in the switch from food stamps to the proposed Family Assistance Plan.

HUNGER IN THE CLASSROOM

If the history of the food-stamp program in the District reveals an insensitivity on the part of federal officials to problems of hunger and the operation of federal grant-in-aid programs, then the history of the National School Lunch Program indicates an utter disregard for the hungry in the District.

In 1957, Washington newspapers and a congressional subcommittee documented that thousands of District elementary school children went to school hungry and stayed that way all day long. In the District only the new secondary schools, as they were being built, participated in the then 11-year-old National School Lunch Program, under which the federal government supplies both food commodities and cash aid to school systems that wish to operate a hot lunch program. The schools were required by law to supply lunches free to poor children. But in the District no lunches at all were available for elementary school children, and only 2,000 lunches were served in the secondary schools.

Discovering Hunger

Senator Wayne Morse (D-Ore.) scheduled the 1957 hearings of a Senate subcommittee on District affairs after a moving series of articles by the late Eve Edstrom appeared in the *Washington Post*. "Hunger haunts the young in Southwest Washington," her series began.

> It is no ghost. It can be seen in every step. It is in the listless body of the four-year-old whose head and hands droop forward after he delivers his mother's note, which says "could you lend me two car tokens to go to the welfare." It is in the pinched pale face of the 7-year-old who clutches a pound of butter under his coat—and runs.

The subcommittee heard medical testimony that more than 1,000 elementary school children had been diagnosed as malnourished in routine physical examinations given during only one month in 1957. Yet Congress and the District government refused to heed the plea of Senator Morse or to establish a lunch program for District elementary school children, including free lunches for the needy.

The District's inaction in 1957 was probably a product of the times. Poverty had not yet been discovered in affluent America, and many supposedly responsible officials refused to take the issue seriously. For example, School Superintendent Hobart Corning scoffed at the 1957 hearings:

> What do we mean by hungry children? I am a parent and a grandparent and all our folks are hungry all the time. You cannot keep them filled up. If anybody was unwise enough in this investigation

to ask children if they were hungry, I would say the response would be tremendously large because everybody would say they were hungry. I am getting a little bit that way myself.

Corning rejected the testimony of his school principals, of doctors, and of the poor themselves. Like many other school administrators around the country, he saw neither the poverty problem nor the need for schools to provide food services to children.

Prior to the unsuccessful Morse hearings in 1957, food for hungry children in the elementary schools had been donated sporadically and sparingly by charitable organizations in the District. During the Depression and early New Deal days, Mrs. Franklin Roosevelt had personally set up a program at the Greenleaf Elementary School. Ironically, this effort died down after World War II just at the time that the federal lunch program was enacted and the District had increasing need for a lunch program. The "out-migration" of the white middle class in the 1950s and the influx of poor, black refugees from the South greatly increased the number of poor children in District schools.

The 1957 congressional hearings, newspaper stories, and impetus for private efforts to feed children during the next few years stemmed primarily from the efforts of two affluent Washington women, Mrs. John F. Davis and Mrs. Lawrence Lesser, volunteer workers at Barney Neighborhood House.

In 1957, the volunteers were preparing daily soup and sandwiches for about 30 elementary school children. As Mrs. Lesser recalled,

> Our program was started because Mrs. Davis read about a hungry child and invited her to her home for two weeks. When the little girl came back for a weekend in the fall, Mrs. Davis became alarmed at her obviously undernourished condition. Because of TB in the family, the child had been ordered on a diet rich in eggs and milk. But when Mrs. Davis asked what the child was getting for lunch, she was told, "a cup of tea and toast." The family had been on relief, but the father had taken a job. The job didn't last, and then it took a long time to get back on relief. We were shocked to find that there was no place where a poor child in Southwest Washington could get a free lunch.

When Congress and the District government ignored the 1957 hearings, the Barney volunteers, spearheaded by Mrs. Lesser, increased their push at Greenleaf School. The volunteers brought in the "Jayne Cees" to start a similar program at Syphax School. Mrs. Lesser said that everywhere the volunteers went

> the bureaucrats tried something to stop us. At Syphax school, the Health Department said we couldn't serve lunch—we'd have to get screens on the windows, doors to block off the tables from the rest-rooms, sinks, and heating facilities. Well, we did.

> The next year, we raised money, and took the children over to Jefferson Junior High School, where we bought them a 25¢ lunch. The teachers selected their neediest children, and we were able to feed about 200 kids.

Aided by Mrs. Wallace Luchs, whose advocacy for lunches for school children has spanned 12 years, the group began a Christmas Drive for the 1959-60 school year. "Instead of a Christmas basket, sponsor a child," began the letter soliciting funds from the business community. With more hungry-children stories appearing in the press, the group collected enough money to feed 1,000 children for a year and urged every contributor to "go to Congress and complain that you, as a private citizen, should have a right to your children and the children of your community receiving the school lunch program."

Again, the school administration and Agriculture Department provided stumbling blocks instead of food. USDA ruled that the proposed bag lunches violated regulations of the school-lunch program, which required that each Type A lunch include "one cup" made up of two or more fruits or vegetables. "They wouldn't change that 'one cup' to include an apple, an orange or a carrot," said Mrs. Luchs. "Therefore the lunch had to have a plate and cutlery, involving dishwashing personnel and expense. We were able to feed fewer children with our funds."

The Agriculture Department's insistence on "one cup" really symbolized its attitude about the program, which the Agriculture committees of Congress had proposed to help dispose of surplus commodities. USDA rigidly enforced the specifications of its required "Type A" lunch not so much out of concern for the feeding of children as out of its congressional mandate to help utilize specific surplus food commodities. The Agriculture Department's and the farm committees' basic attitudes were revealed by their mutual agreement to ignore two parts of the 1946 National School Lunch

Act. The law required that individual states must spend $3 for every $1 of federal aid and that poor children be given free lunches. Neither provision of the law was enforced. And a majority of Congress was not concerned that the one city which it ruled directly did not participate at all in the program.

After a bitter battle in 1960, which included opposition in Congress and in the District government, a pilot program finally was established to feed 2,000 children. The program was expanded to feed 4,800 children the following year.

The introduction at last of the much-needed lunch program for needy children was accompanied by another problem, which still has not been resolved in the District. That problem is the setting apart, singling out, and stigmatizing of poor children. Because the Agriculture Department rigidly insisted on its regulations governing the content of meals, needy elementary children had to be marched to eat in cafeterias at nearby high schools. The children were called "hunger marchers" and were taunted by other children.

The attention span on public issues is usually a short one, and the school-lunch issue practically disappeared in the District once the embryonic 1960 program was started to feed a few thousand children. Perhaps politicians got tired of the issue, and reformers, except for a few dedicated ladies, decided they had solved the problem.

Unfulfilled Promises

The failure of Congress and the District government to follow through on its 1960 pledges did not become apparent until hunger blossomed into a national political issue eight years later. Only after food-aid reformers focused on national failings of the school-lunch program did Congress, the District government, and the news media again look closely at the District lunch program. What they found was shocking. Only a fraction of District pupils had the opportunity to buy a school lunch. Less than 20 percent of poor children were being given free lunches. School officials blatantly discriminated against the poor children by giving them different colored lunch tickets, requiring them to stand in separate lines, or requiring them to eat in rooms apart from other children.

Discriminatory singling out of the poor continued in 1972 in the 88 District elementary schools without school cafeterias. Seventy-three of these schools, with 43,000 pupils, bring in meals only for the poor children, thus automatically distinguishing these children from fellow students, who either must go home or bring their own school lunches. Because of limited dining space, the poor often eat their meals in separate rooms. Barbara Bode of the Children's Foundation told District school officials that they were discriminating against both the poor and the nonpoor with this feeding arrangement. "The overt identification of free lunch recipients is particularly offensive in schools in which only a small percentage of the children receive free lunches," she said. "The exclusion of the borderline poor and the nonpoor from the federally-supported lunch program compounds the fault."

In 1971, however, a new system was installed to bring in "airline" type lunches to 17 of the elementary schools. Students are fed meals which are brought chilled to the school in individual trays, refrigerated, then heated in convection ovens. School officials hope eventually to serve all the elementary schools by this "Chill-pack" method.

"It is simply impossible at this time to provide lunches for every District school child, no matter what they pay for it," replies Joseph Stewart, director of food services in the District public schools. "It is simply the lesser evil to feed the poor child and not let him go hungry, than it is to worry about whether he will be stigmatized by being among the only children in the school who receive lunches."

The District made considerable progress after the hunger issue focused on schools in the late 1960s. In 1971, the District was feeding about 61,000 of its 147,000 school children. Between 1969 and 1971, the number of free lunches provided to poor children rose from 19,000 to 44,000. Yet community leaders such as school board member Evie Washington and Mrs. Lillian Huff, chairman of the Mayor's Commission on Food, Nutrition, and Health, contend that thousands more children should be receiving free lunches. "The system will be discriminatory until every child in the District can be offered a free lunch," stated Mrs. Huff.

The school-lunch service system was operating far beyond its capacity in 1972, said program director Stewart.

All the meals we send out to elementary schools without cafeterias are prepared in high school cafeteria kitchens which are already serving their own schools—and that's 18,000 more meals than those kitchens were designed to produce!

Stewart continued, "I believe that every child is as entitled to a free lunch as he is to free textbooks. How can a hungry child hope to learn?"

The District's school-lunch program has been plagued by the same contorted administrative arrangements that beset the food-stamp program. The same congressional subcommittees that have refused to provide enough administrative funds for food stamps are also constantly cutting D. C. school budget requests for food and other items. The school-lunch program traditionally has received low priority from top school administrators and has been buried deep in the school system's organizational charts. "It's one thing to get money for the District program, and another thing to get the money down through the layers of the school administration," said Victor Canevello, a USDA official who organized the District's new mass school feeding program. "The way the District is set up, the main problem in getting anything done is to get through the paperwork."

Attempts at federal cooperation with the District have proven even less successful than in the case of food stamps. The federal Office of Economic Opportunity gave the District $70,000 to study means of improving school-lunch delivery to the poor. According to both federal and District school officials, the project ended up as a fiasco with no results. "People in the District have such close and immediate access to the bureaucracy of the federal government yet they utilize it poorly," said an OEO official about the abortive school-lunch study.

> And the federal bureaucracy should have a special responsibility to the District, but it doesn't. Government functions poorly in the District and the political pressures to force the government to be responsive just don't exist.

The OEO-financed study of the District's school-lunch programs flopped for a number of reasons. The staff hired by the school system generally was unfamiliar with the District, inexperienced with the lunch program, and—according to some critics—incompetent to conduct the study. In addition, District school system officials did not cooperate but, rather, placed obstacles in the way of the fact-finding process. Finally, there was a dispute within the District government about whether the study was to be directed by school officials or by the more aggressive Mayor's Commission on Food, Nutrition, and Health.

Amazingly, even the critical comments of the President have not galvanized District and federal officials into more effective action. Addressing the White House Conference on Children in December 1970, President Nixon pointedly described the discrimination in feeding witnessed by his daughter Tricia as she worked as a volunteer in an elementary school. The President referred to one of the many schools in which the poor children are lined up for meals, while other children watch and then are forced to go home or eat meals brought from home.

Yet, with the nation finally focused on the issue of hunger in the classroom, most advocates of food aid for the poor acknowledge that tremendous progress has been made in the District, just as it has in other parts of the country. The number of children receiving free lunches tripled in the District in the late 1960s, and a similar tripling occurred in this period for the nation as a whole, the number of free lunch recipients rising from two to six millon.

Progress toward caring for nutritional needs of the District's children has been stimulated in considerable part by a slow reshaping of District government to permit a semblance of home rule for D. C. residents. A noticeable improvement in the attitude of District school officials about free school lunches occurred after District residents were permitted to elect their own school board in 1968. Elected school board members such as Evie Washington, a community worker in the antipoverty program, have been far closer to the school-lunch program and far more sensitive to it than the previous appointed members. School Superintendent Hugh Scott and Food Service Director Stewart also have demonstrated a far greater determination than their predecessors in feeding school children as an integral part of the education process. In the past, the school board seemed oblivious to the fact that almost one half of the school population were poor, black children. Mrs. Washington, Stewart, and Scott all are both black and aware. Even if they weren't, it is likely that community leaders in the inner city would soon sensitize them to problems such as hunger.

A GREATER AWARENESS AND BETTER RESPONSE

The school-lunch program as well as food-stamp and other federal food-aid programs are beginning to have an impact on the people and the institutions of the District of Columbia. It was possible in 1957 for a District school official to laugh off the problem of hunger haunting school children. No official today could dismiss the poor in such a manner, if at all. If the Johnson Administration poverty programs did nothing else, they helped poor people assume leadership roles in their communties. The District's various community-action agencies and welfare-rights groups are in touch with problems of poverty and know how to transmit their concerns about nonfunctioning food-aid programs to the public and to responsible officials.

Responding to its first elected board members, to community pressure, and to a general national awakening about the existence of hunger amidst affluence, the District schools have made huge strides in providing free meals for poor children. Yet, the District still lags behind most metropolitan school systems in its inability to serve meals to all children.

Two general conclusions about federal grant-in-aid programs in the District are warranted from this study. The first is that the needs of District residents have been poorly served by the various forms of government which have not permitted citizens a voice in the operation of their own services. The battle for home rule in the District has been fought for years, and the winning of it won't prove any panacea for solving the many problems which Washington shares with most other large cities. But the evidence is strong that needs of poor children and hungry adults would be better met by a system of self-government. The election of school board members and of a nonvoting delegate to Congress generally has produced officials more knowledgeable about inner-city needs.

The second conclusion is that the federal government logically should develop broad-based, well-financed monitoring of federal grant-in-aid programs in Washington, D. C. It seems only logical that Washington is the most convenient and suitable laboratory to see whether social legislation works or doesn't work. Congress, the executive branch, and the general public should all be involved in the appraisal of the District programs. Hopefully, Washington could become a "model city" in meeting the problems that affect urban life in America today. At the least, it could be hoped that the noble aims stated in social legislation would not be forgotten quite so soon after the Congress has acted and the President has signed the laws.

Chapter Seven

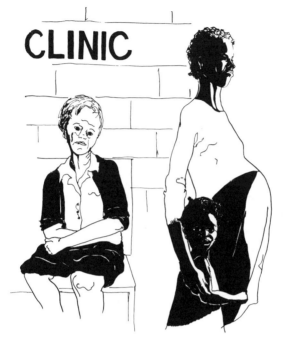

POVERTY AND POOR HEALTH

by David Swanston

The District of Columbia has more than 35 separate health programs receiving federal funds. Most of those funds come from the Department of Health, Education, and Welfare and, as a result, an examination of that Department's health budget gives a pretty clear picture of how the federal government divides its health dollar in the District. In fiscal 1971, HEW split $267 million among six major areas (Chart 8).

In addition to HEW, the Departments of Agriculture, Housing and Urban Development, and Justice and the Office of Economic Opportunity fund District health programs. All told, the federal government spent more than $350 million on health in the District.[1]

---

[1] Department of Health, Education, and Welfare, STATE TABLES OF 1971 BUDGET ESTIMATES (Washington: U.S. Government Printing Office, 1972), pp. 5-12.

CHART 8:   HEW SPENT $267 MILLION FOR HEALTH CARE IN WASHINGTON, 1971

TOTAL = $267 MILLION

Source: U.S. Department of Health, Education, and Welfare

However, less than one sixth of the funds will go to the District government in the form of grants-in-aid. The rest will be spent by agencies outside District government control. About half of the federal funds that the District government gets are for the Medicaid and Medicare programs. The rest is divided among health delivery programs (including experiments); construction; narcotics treatment programs; and support of existing health facilities, training, and environmental health projects.

The need for these federal health funds is great because Washintgon's health record is among the worst in the nation. The general health status of District citizens is "deplorable," the Mayor's

Task Force on Public Health Goals reported in 1970. Specifically, the Task Force reported that:

• Infant mortality in the District was "worse than any state except Mississippi."

• The maternal mortality rate in Washington was "generally more than twice as great" as the average rate for ten cities of comparable size.

• The mortality rate for tuberculosis in the District was greater than any state and was higher than the national average and the average of ten comparably sized cities.

• The District's death rate for cirrhosis of the liver was more than three times the national average.

• The mortality rate for pneumonia in the District was more than one-and-a-half times the national average.

There are many reasons for the District's severe health crisis, but at the root of them all seems to be poverty. A large proportion of Washington's population is unhealthy because a large number of Washington's citizens are poor.[2]

"A basic fact of poverty is that poor health and poverty reinforce each other," the Office of Economic Opportunity reported to Congress in 1967.

> The poor get sick more often and stay sick longer and recover less frequently and less completely than the more affluent. General mortality, infant mortality and various diseases are much higher for the poor than for the non-poor. Adults in poor families have several times as much disabling heart disease, arthritis or mental illness as those in families earning $7,000 or more per annum.

The proportion of poor in the District remains above the national average. Nationally, one person in eight lives in poverty; in the District, the proportion is one in six. And, as the 1970s began, Washington had a population that was increasingly black and young.

To meet the widespread needs of the nation's poor, the Johnson administration launched the War on Poverty in 1964. A year later, Congress passed a wide-ranging program of legislation to meet the poor's medical needs as well.

---

[2] D.C. Department of Human Resources, REPORT OF THE MAYOR'S TASK FORCE ON PUBLIC HEALTH GOALS (Washington: D.C. Department of Human Resources, January 1970), p. 59.

"We can—and must—strive now to assure the availability of and accessibility to the best health care for all Americans regardless of age or geography or economic status," Johnson said in his 1965 health message to Congress. To meet that goal, Congress departed from the traditional pattern of research, training, and construction and passed a series of programs for health care.

In the five years beginning in 1965, Congress passed 26 major pieces of health legislation, designed to serve numerous clienteles, including the elderly and the poor. Legislation started research, established scholarship and loans, and supported medical schools. Under legislation passed during those five years, neighborhood health centers and local mental-health clinics were established and the problems of alcohol and narcotics were confronted.

Many of these programs brought federal health funds into the District, and many of the projects the funds made possible were successful. However, because the funds come from so many different federal sources, and because the projects are administered by so many different agencies, and because there are so many programs, it is difficult to say exactly what the federal dollars are buying and how much good they are doing.

It is possible on the other hand, to examine how the District spends its grants-in-aid and to evaluate specific federally funded programs. In general, the District uses about half of its federal health funds for direct payment of health services. About 30 percent goes for health delivery programs (including experiments); 8 percent for narcotics treatment; 5 percent for construction; and 7 percent for support of existing facilities, training, and environmental projects. These figures include only federal grants-in-aid but do not include District funds (such as operating funds for D. C. General Hospital) or federal funds that go to other agencies (Table 9).

Table 9

FEDERAL GRANT ASSISTANCE TO THE DISTRICT, 1972

(Amounts in thousands)

Grant Program	Funding Agency	Grant Estimated
Medicare and Medicaid		
1. Health Insurance Benefits	HEW	$ 40
2. Medicare Program (Including Assistance to Medically Needy)	HEW	24,000

Grant Program	Funding Agency	Grant Estimated
Preventive Services		
1. Maternal and Child Health	HEW	372
2. Crippled Children	HEW	301
3. Venereal Disease	HEW	39
4. Children and Youth Project	HEW	1,068
5. Comprehensive Health Services	HEW	662
6. Comprehensive Health Planning	HEW	107
7. TB Control	HEW	752
8. Immunization	HEW	136
9. Maternity and Infant Care	HEW	1,664
10. Consumer Health Planning Survey	HEW	158
11. Plan for Health Maintenance Demonstration Project	HEW	30
12. Emergency Medical Service	HEW	71
Mental Health and Treatment of Alcoholics		
1. Mental Health	HEW	82
2. Community Mental Health Centers—Staffing Area C	HEW	229
3. Development and Staffing of Mental Health Center—Area B	HEW	306
4. Community Mental Health Centers—Staffing Area D	HEW	131
5. Community Mental Health Centers Staffing Area B—Growth	HEW	1,360
6. Community Mental Health Centers Staffing Area C—Growth	HEW	456
7. Contract to Screen and Evaluate Patients for Study on Alcoholism	HEW	25
8. Kalorama House	HEW	42
Environmental Health		
1. Air Pollution	HEW	234
2. War on Rats	HEW	885
3. Water Pollution	Interior	88
4. Meat Inspection	Agriculture	443
Treatment of Narcotics		
1. Executive Direction	Justice	870
2. Legal Services to Addicts	Justice	29
3. Addiction Services to Youth	Justice	58
4. Narcotic Addict Treatment Facilities Staffing	HEW	821
5. Anacostia Juvenile Drug Project	OEO	483

Grant Program	Funding Agency	Grant Estimated
Vocational and Rehabilitation Services		
1. Section II	HEW	4,186
2. Disability Determinations	HEW	317
3. Social Security Trust Fund	HEW	84
4. In-Service Training	HEW	6
5. Sheltered Workshop	HEW	25
6. Drug Addiction	HEW	100
7. Specialized Community Aides	HEW	22
8. Selective Placement and V.R. Public Assistance	HEW	13
9. Facilities Improvement	HEW	20
10. Initial Staffing Grant	HEW	14
11. Work Adjustment	HEW	45
12. Employment Evaluation and Service Center	HEW	139
Education and Training		
1. Nursing Student Loans	HEW	15
2. Opportunity Grants for Nursing Education	HEW	13
3. Phasing Out Capital City School of Nursing	HEW	246
4. Medical Dental Apprenticeship Training	HEW	19
5. Higher Education Facilities	HEW	339
TOTAL		$41,545

MEDICAID

Of all the federal-local health programs in the District, Medicaid involves the most money. But few would argue that the program is the most effective. There is general agreement that the program has improved the quality of health care available to the poor, but there is also a good deal of agreement that the program will have to be much more effective to live up to its promise.

Medicaid began in Washington in the fall of 1968—18 months after it was launched nationally—and has grown into a massive program involving 125,000 patients and $49 million a year. Medicaid, enacted as Title XIX of the Social Security Act, had three basic objectives:

—To provide persons receiving public assistance with a broad choice of medical services by allowing the patient to visit the doctor or institution of his choice;

—To increase the number of persons entitled to medical assistance by covering persons who were not on welfare but who would not be able to pay medical costs without going on welfare;

—And to include a wide range of services under the program, so low-income persons would have "complete continuous family-centered medical care of high quality."

Measuring each of these promises against performance in Washington gives a very mixed set of results. For example, when Medicaid went into effect in the District, only 11,000 people were added to the pool of residents entitled to receive assistance even though the D.C. eligibility rules were more liberal than those for about half of the states.

The program was supposed to allow the poor to choose their doctors—just as others do. But it hasn't worked out that way in Washington. There are few doctors practicing where poor people live—and for the poor who must rely on public transportation proximity is a very important factor. Doctors' offices in Washington are concentrated in the downtown areas where there are office buildings and hospitals, or in the wealthy, white areas west of Rock Creek Park. Specifically, the largest concentration of doctors in the city is in the downtown area where the ratio of doctors to population is 1,832 to 100,000. In areas of the city where the poor are concentrated, the ratio is 28 to 33 doctors per 100,000 residents.

The hope that Medicaid would reverse the flight of doctors from the ghetto has not been fulfilled. As *Washington Post* reporter Henry Aubin observed in June 1971:

The three-year-old Medicaid program, which reimburses doctors for treating the poor, has encouraged a few doctors to settle in disadvantaged areas.

But Medicaid payments are low, the disadvantages to these areas are many, and not enough doctors have come into these areas to compensate for the greater number who have left or are leaving.

Problems of robbery, vandalism, and poor pay drove doctors from the inner-city. One physician told Aubin he was making $15,000 a year and worrying about getting mugged when he practiced in the ghetto. He moved to the suburbs, quit worrying, and doubled his earnings. Clearly, Medicaid isn't enough to keep this doctor—and many others—in town. And some who stay in town refuse to see Medicaid patients, as several doctors reported in a confidential D.C. Medical Society poll.

"I instruct my secretary to discourage all Medicaid patients from making appointments to see me because the remuneration is too low," one doctor confided, and "the billing procedure necessitates . . . an office overload for which there's no compensation."

"I had originally joined" another wrote, "out of a sense of social responsibility, but the bureaucratic approach to the program has killed it for me."

And a third doctor responded, "I do from time to time see Medicaid patients. I don't send a bill. It's much easier that way."

Because of these and many other factors, only about 750 doctors—one of every three physicians in private practice in Washington—participate actively in Medicaid. Clearly, the poor aren't getting a very broad choice.

Finally, Medicaid was supposed to offer the poor a wide range of services. The lack of participating physicians in Washington also limits this goal and budget problems have limited it even further. For example, three years after the program began, Medicaid patients in Washington were not eligible for dental care, prosthetic devices, hearing aids, or private duty nurses—services available in many other states.

In short, Medicaid has not been an overwhelming success in the District. Philip Rutledge, Washington's top health official until late 1971, concludes: "Medicaid has probably done more to inflate the cost of medical care than it has to improve the quality of medical care in the District."

A GROUP HEALTH EXPERIMENT

To try to solve both problems—to stem the rising costs and provide better care—Washington launched an experimental comprehensive prepaid health-maintenance program for 1,000 of the city's poor. Under the program, a model of the Nixon Administration's Health Maintenance Organization (HMO) proposal, 1,000 Medicaid patients from 330 families were integrated into the regular Group Health Association (GHA) program. GHA, a large, comprehensive, prepaid medical care program, agreed to provide the patients with a complete package of medical services. Under the agreement, the city paid GHA $350 per patient per year—about $25 more than the average level of support for Medicaid patients outside the program.

One reason that the GHA experiment costs more is that GHA patients receive more services—including dental care—than do Medicaid patients outside the experiment.

The program began in July 1971 and is scheduled to run for three years. If it proves successful, the District will attempt to extend it. Early reports indicate that the program is working. "The people who use the system seem to like it," says Samuel Morch, Director of the Office of Medical Care Planning of the D.C. Department of Human Resources. Of the 1,000 who started the program, only 31 dropped out in the first six months.

One of the main values of this approach—and that of the Kaiser and other prepaid plans—is the high degree of reliance on preventive medicine. Finding problems early and treating them early—or preventing them altogether—avoids many costly treatments later. In pure money terms, Dr. Paul B. Cornely, past president of the American Public Health Association, says that one dollar spent on prevention saves as much as ten dollars in treatment.[3]

If these tests are successful, the District would like to have Health Maintenance Organization centers across the city. However, D.C. officials are wary of carrying the plan too far and putting all of the poor into one GHA-type program. "We don't want to create another poor people's agency," says Dr. William Washington, Director of the city's Hospital and Medical Care Administration, Ideally, he adds, the city would like to have 40 percent of its Medicaid patients in HMO's and the rest seeing private physicians. Whatever the formula, he stresses that "the city is committed to going to one level of health care for everyone."

---

[3] Henry Aubin, THE WASHINGTON POST, June 24, 1971.

But, until that day, Washington's poor will have to rely on private physicians, hospitals, or one of the District's neighborhood health centers.

NEIGHBORHOOD HEALTH CENTERS

The District runs eight neighborhood health centers using federal grants of some $3.6 million a year and District funds that have ranged from $5 million to $7 million in recent years.

The neighborhood-health-center concept gained national prominence in 1966 with OEO support. The centers were touted as solutions to nearly all of the poor's health-care problems.

In 1966, OEO claimed:

> Neighborhood Health Centers will offer virtually all non-hospital medical services for all members of a family within one centrally located facility in a designated poverty community. The coordinated medical services to be offered include preventive medicine, diagnosis, treatment, rehabilitation, dental care, drugs and appliances, mental health services, family planning and health education.

The same report added that the neighborhood health centers would give "patients a positive voice in the operation of the health center and the type and manner of health services to be offered."

When Dr. Murray Grant, then District Health Director, announced Washington's version of the Neighborhood Health Center scheme in September 1967, he gave a local version of much of the OEO rhetoric. The centers would reduce the unmanageable patient load at D.C. General Hospital's emergency room, Dr. Grant said.

He added that the centers would give the poor a place where they would want to go for their medical needs. "They've got to be able to go to one place. They have got to feel 'That's my health center. That's where I go,' " Dr. Grant explained.

Somehow, it didn't work out.

In July 1970, *Washington Post* staff writer Aaron Latham explained the Centers:

> The health department started six comprehensive health clinics in 1968 then added two more to ease the crush in D.C. General Hospital's emergency room.
>
> The crush at D.C. General hasn't eased.
>
> The hospital's emergency room still looks like a railroad station during a holiday rush.

Almost a year later, Senator Edward Kennedy conducted an investigation of Washington's clinics and hospitals and found that D.C. General's emergency room still was overtaxed. Kennedy asked doctors at D.C. General whether they thought the eight neighborhood health centers had eased the emergency-room caseload.

"They've helped some," replied Dr. Robert Santangelo, chief of the emergency room, "but, strangely enough, people still come here . . . they're used to coming here because, as bad as it is, they know they can get care if they wait long enough."

Part of the problem may have been, as Dr. Santangelo contended, that people were used to going to D.C. General and didn't want to go anywhere else. But another reason for the small patient loads at the neighborhood centers was that many people didn't know there was anywhere else to go except D.C. General.

Evelyn M. Clark, a volunteer working with the H Street Clinic, found considerable misunderstanding about the clinic's services when she went door-to-door talking to residents. "Some of them didn't seem to know that there was a health center," she said, "or thought it was only for mothers and babies."

The misconception about the nature of the centers also was reflected in an analysis of who visits the facilities. The analysis shows that, instead of providing care for "all members of the family" as OEO had predicted, the Washington centers were providing service that was nearly limited to women and small children. A 1969 survey of the centers revealed that more than half of all persons receiving services were under six years of age. The next year, according to the study, general medicine visits, the only type appropriate for adult males at neighborhood health centers, accounted for about 23 percent of all visits.

Clearly, the Washington neighborhood health centers were not meeting the national goal of caring for the entire family, or the local goal of easing the burden at D.C. General.

Then, in 1970, the Mayor's Task Force on Public Health Goals reported that the neighborhood health centers were failing in another important area as well. The Task Force noted that the centers were generally not widely used, observed that the lack of laboratory facilities made the comprehensive-health concept unworkable, and then added: "In addition to the above problems, there has been almost total failure to establish a mechanism for effective citizen participation in promoting utilization and improvement of center services and for registering satisfaction or dissatisfaction."

In short, in their first years of existence, the Washington neighborhood health centers didn't measure up. However, the picture seems to have become a little brighter. D.C. officials reported that the neighborhood health centers have gained more acceptance, as was reflected in the dramatic rise in the number of patient visits. In 1971 visits to established centers rose by 8 percent, and the opening of two new centers in Anacostia resulted in a 49 percent increase in total visits to all centers.

The increased visits offer a little encouragement, but even more encouraging is a project by a nonprofit foundation in Washington that is funded by a $2.2 million grant from OEO. The nonprofit group, the Community Group Health Foundation, Inc., is providing health services for some 8,500 residents of the upper Cardozo area.

The board of directors of the foundation is composed of representatives from CHANGE, a community action agency; Howard University; and the Group Health Association.

The foundation, which is building a new clinic, provides the community with these services: medical treatment; preventive medical care; general physical examination; nursing care; home-care services; psychiatric care; ophthalmological, orthopedic, and other special care; counseling; a supplemental food program; x-ray, laboratory, and pharmacy services; and a full range of dental services.

Among the center's 174 employees are 13 physicians who work the equivalent of about 7 full-time doctors, and four full-time dentists. In the operation of the center, CHANGE provides the links with the community; Howard provides medical support; and Group Health provides administrative support.

With the backing of the community, guidance from a major medical school, and support from a successful health plan, the Community Group Health Foundation stands a good chance of succeeding. It has survived on annual grants from OEO, but once the new clinic is built, Foundation officials believe the operation can be self-sustaining.

The future is not quite as bright for the eight neighborhood health centers. However, their funding is holding steady, and, with more community involvement and greater understanding of their function by the poor, they could become important factors in Washington's health care system.

MATERNAL AND CHILD HEALTH CENTERS

Another key element in Washington's neighborhood health efforts are the maternal and child health centers. The centers are part of a major drive to reduce Washington's severely high infant mortality rate, and they get a large share of the $2.6 million a year spent in the District to care for mothers, babies, and pregnant women. The network of centers provides pre- and postnatal care, infant care, birth-control assistance, and care for handicapped children.

The prenatal care is essentially a preventive program that assists mothers-to-be in overcoming problems that are likely to lead to stillbirth, infant death, or physically or mentally defective children. The program concentrates its efforts on high-risk women—the very young, those over 35, those who have had prior birth difficulties, and those with nutritional problems. Pregnant women account for about 20 percent of the patients served by the maternal and child health centers.

Just under half of all the patients served by the centers are children. All infants and preschool children in the District are eligible for free care at the centers, which includes a wide range of preventive services as well as parental counseling, and which is designed, according to the District, to provide continuous health supervision for "those children of a community whose health would not be otherwise supervised."

The rest of the patient load at the centers is divided about equally between handicapped children and women seeking birth control information and services. Centers in the city's poverty areas see the greatest share of the patients. However, according to the District Department of Human Resources, "the relation between economic need and use of services is not as strong as one would expect." [4]

All in all, the Department reported, "about half of all women needing maternity care and more than half of all children under

---

[4] Henry Aubin, THE WASHINGTON POST, June 23, 1971.

one used public [health] facilities." However, officials added that pregnant women were not coming to the clinics early enough. And, without a good deal of prenatal care, the infant mortality rate will remain high.

Specifically, the Department reported in 1970 that 5,000 to 6,000 women did not get care early enough in their pregnancies. And, since there is a strong link between prenatal care and infant mortality (the infant death rate is more than three times as great for mothers who have had no prenatal care), the Department is trying to persuade pregnant women to come to the centers earlier.

But there well may be more to the problem than insufficient clinic use by pregnant women. Some believe the maternal and child health centers aren't doing the job even for the patients they now have. "The overall view of these programs presents a series of serious problems in all areas—poor planning, lack of communication and at times coordination, duplication of some other program services, equipment, and facilities," the Mayor's Task Force on Public Health Goals observed. "Whenever present, the inadequacies and hence the unfavorable conditions seem to present three categories among those giving and receiving services: dedication and cooperation; demoralization and futility; indifference and hostility."

D.C. GENERAL HOSPITAL

It is vital to the District that the neighborhood clinics and the maternity and child health centers survive. If they don't, D.C. General Hospital will become even more overcrowded, and the level of care there is not adequate now.

Early in 1972, D.C. General got less than half a million dollars a year in federal grants, although it is the main source of medical care for Washington's poor. The hospital treats the majority of the city's Medicaid patients each year, and its facilities are used by other federally funded programs. Although individual doctors on the hospital staff receive research grants for some of their projects, the grants are usually small and the programs reach only a few patients; the hospital administrators have no control over these grants and the District government has no record of where the money is or how it is used. While congressional interest in D.C. General has been high—congressmen frequently tour the facility—

there is little federal money. In fact, the hospital has been the victim of years of federal neglect. Its annual appropriation has remained about $26 million for several years in spite of a growing body of evidence that massive expenditures are needed to bring the facility up to par.

The sprawling 983-bed hospital had 22,600 admissions and 232,061 inpatient days of care in fiscal 1971. It gave 98,293 emergency-room treatments, and had 193,360 outpatient visits. Washington's less affluent citizens made up the greatest share of all of the patients, and there are many reasons to believe that the quality of care they received was often less than adequate.

Dr. William J. Washington, the hospital's former director, admits that services at the hospital are "somewhat below" those at other area hospitals. And many believe that Dr. Washington understates the problem rather seriously.

The Mayor's Task Force on Public Health Goals said that "D.C. General is in a state of emergency," and added: "It is clear that the patient load at D.C. General is greater than can be adequately cared for by the personnel and resources available. . . . The staff has worked to the limits of human capabilities; it needs immediate relief."

In 1970, D.C. General was denied the usual full two-year accreditation, receiving instead a one-year accreditation and a set of 24 recommendations. Although the hospital received full accreditation a year later, Dr. Carlton Alexis of the hospital's governing board explained that accreditation did not imply excellence and should be considered only a base from which the hospital should build. Dr. Washington agreed, and said that the hospital needed a $30 million annual budget—$4 million more than it gets now—to do the job.

And until that $4 million is found, D.C. General will continue to struggle along understaffed and providing the city's poor with health care that would be considered totally unacceptable for the more affluent. For example, doctors at D.C. General say patients frequently have to wait eight hours or more for treatment in the hospital's emergency room.

It is not uncommon for a ward to run out of important medication or for nurses to have to leave a ward unattended to move a critically ill patient.

Citizens have complained that they had to stay at the hospital and feed elderly patients because nurses were too busy to do it. Seriously ill men and women have collapsed and died while waiting for treatment. The shocking reports—especially from the hospital's medical staff—go on and on.

"These young doctors can feed you horror stories for as long as you have the stomach to listen," *Washington Post* columnist William Raspberry wrote in September 1969.

> Stories about the hospital pharmacy being out of quite ordinary drugs; of clerical foul-ups that result in lost time, lost pay, and lost lives; stories of a hospital that has never come to understand just how critical the situation is.

The poor understand just how critical the situation is. But there isn't much they can do about it. They continue to come. Some walk into the emergency room with minor complaints that have no business in the hospital at all. Others are brought by ambulance because the District's private hospitals turn them away.

Each year, about 20 patients die because they are transferred to D.C. General from private hospitals for financial—not medical— reasons. In all, about 2,000 poor people a year are transferred out of the city's 14 private hospitals to D.C. General. The practice is called "dumping" and it has grave consequences—both immediate and long term.

The immediate consequences are easy to spot—dumping is bad medically. People die as a result of it. Babies are born in ambulances who could have been born in a private hospital. Ambulance drivers pass private hospitals to take even seriously injured poor people to D.C. General.

The long-range consequences are not as easily discernible but are just as important—dumping perpetuates a separate and unequal system of health care. As the Mayor's Task Force observed: "The present system perpetuates a double standard of medical care— one in which the poor receive poor health care at an inadequately supported public hospital, and the rest of the population receive a uniformly higher standard of health care at a variety of other hospitals."

Additional federal funds—either through increased D.C. appropriations or through direct grants-in-aid—would go a long way toward solving this problem. But the federal government could be a part of the solution on another level as well. According to the Mayor's Task Force, the District could use local regulatory provisions of several federal health programs to put an end to dumping. The Task Force explained:

> Local regulatory power, virtually unused, could be used to require the private hospitals to accept an appropriate share of indigent patients. In the immediate future, pressure must be brought to bear to eliminate the appallingly unequal utilization of emergency facilities.

MENTAL HEALTH

D.C. General, the District's primary public physical-health facility, and St. Elizabeth's Hospital, the District's primary mental-health facility, are at opposite poles of the federal involvement spectrum. D.C. General struggles along under District control with practically no federal support. St. Elizabeth's is controlled completely by the federal government, and close to half of its budget comes from federal sources. And, although the federal government plays a major role in one institution and practically no role in the other, the net result is the same—D.C. residents get a good deal less than adequate care.

The Mayor's Task Force, for example, called St. Elizabeth's "a visible symbol of the stigma attached to psychiatric help." The 117-year-old, 36-acre hospital was criticized for its dilapidated buildings and for its so-called warehousing of the mentally ill.

A special advisory committee formed in 1969 to study St. Elizabeth's reported that the staff had made several advances in the areas of treatment. But the report added,

> unfortunately, despite these earnest efforts, most of these achievements had little impact upon the day-in and day-out care of thousands of its psychiatric patients. The 19th century buildings in which they were housed were deteriorating and, despite the increasing decrepitude, were not replaced. Further, the new rehabilitative programs designed to enhance the discharge of patients were not supported by those community agencies and fiscal resources upon which the hospital necessarily depends. As a consequence, the hospital continued to operate as an isolated unit and thus it became burdened with chronic patients who received only a minimum of custodial care by the overtaxed staff.

The committee report, which recommended St. Elizabeth's transfer from federal to District control, culminated three years of administrative rearranging of the hospital. In 1967, HEW Secretary John Gardner recommended that St. Elizabeth's be transferred to the National Institute of Mental Health. Fifteen months later, his successor, Wilbur J. Cohen, made the change.

"Large custodial hospitals no longer adequately meet the needs of patients, families and communities," Cohen said. "We can no longer merely fit new methods to old patterns of treatment."

But, as Mike Gorman, Director of the National Committee Against Mental Illness, observed, "coming out and saying a new day has been proclaimed—calling St. E's a model mental health center when the salaries are lousy and the toilets worse—isn't going to change a thing."

In any case, the Nixon Administration decided to give St. Elizabeth's back to the District. While the transfer is negotiated, the District continues to pay most of the costs—$45.3 million in fiscal 1971, or about 52 percent of the budget—and have none of the say in the operation of the hospital.

Recently St. Elizabeth's has started a series of rather significant improvements. The major measure was to reduce the number of patients in the hospital—important since experts believed that more than two thirds of St. Elizabeth's patients could leave if appropriate halfway houses, foster homes, or nursing homes could be found, or if arrangements for care could be arranged at the patient's home. By the end of fiscal 1970, St. Elizabeth's had reduced the patient population by about 15 percent.

In addition, the hospital had moved all patients out of buildings constructed prior to 1900 and had improved its image by removing the fence which had kept the public separated—symbolically and actually—from the building housing the Community Mental Health Center.

Also, in an effort to broaden its program of mental health, the District began, in the midsixties, setting up neighborhood mental health centers. Now there are three area centers, plus four other units for detoxification and treatment of alcoholics. However, only one center comes anywhere near offering comprehensive psychiatric care. And that center, limited by a lack of funds and beset with staff problems, each year treats only about 5,000 of the 250,000 residents in the area.

In the late 1960s, the District enlarged its commitment to treating mental health problems and alcohol abuse. But the major new commitment—growing out of rising law and order sentiments in Congress—was aimed at drug users.

NARCOTICS TREATMENT ADMINISTRATION

By the end of the 1960s, heroin addiction in Washington had grown to epidemic proportions. It was estimated that there were in 1970 about 17,000 heroin addicts in the District—including about 20 percent of all young men aged 20 to 24.[5] And the heroin epidemic, unlike widespread abuse of other drugs, had direct dramatic effects on all of Washington.

According to Dr. Robert L. DuPont, Director of Washington's Narcotics Treatment Administration (NTA),

> the average addict spends at least $25 to $50 each day to support his habit. Very few people can afford this expense without turning to crime. Since the heroin addict begins to suffer symptoms of withdrawal 6 to 10 hours after his last use of the drug, he must take heroin several times a day, everyday, to avoid these symptoms. To produce a high, he needs increasingly larger doses. He has a continuing, urgent need for ready cash, unlike abusers of other drugs such as LSD, speed, cocaine or marihuana.[6]

Addicts in Washington spend more than $200 million a year for heroin, Dr. DuPont believes. An overwhelming share of that $200 million comes from crime, and as addiction rates rise, crime rates go up too.

Specifically, serious crimes in the District nearly tripled between January 1966 and December 1969. And, at least half of the crimes were committed by addicts supporting their habits, officials believe. The police treated the new crimes and the addiction that caused them purely as enforcement problems and had very little success.

Then, two medical developments—coupled with a growing public concern that something be done about the problem—opened the door for a new medical approach to the heroin crisis. One development made possible an accurate urine test for the presence of heroin and other drugs. The other established methadone main-

---

[5] THE WASHINGTON POST, February 26, 1972.
[6] Robert L. Dupont, FEDERAL PROBATION, June 1971.

tenance as a treatment for addicts. Methadone is a heroin substitute that reduces the addict's craving for heroin, allows him to maintain a normal life, and seems to cause no physical or mental damage. Together, the two developments made to possible to take an addict off heroin, let him get a job or enter a training program while he is taking methadone, and test him regularly to make sure he has not returned to heroin.

On February 18, 1970, the District of Columbia launched the country's first major city-wide program of heroin addiction treatment making extensive use of methadone maintenance. The program, developed by Dr. DuPont's Narcotics Treatment Administration, had $185,000 in grants from the Justice Department's Law Enforcement Assistance Administration for its first year of operation. It began with 150 patients in a program that had four goals for each participant:

—to get full-time work or training;
—to stop illegal drug use;
—to refrain from committing crime;
—to stay in the program.

The NTA program makes extensive use of methadone, but Dr. DuPont explains that

> it is not exclusively a methadone program. About 60 percent of the patients are on methadone maintenance, 20 percent on methadone detoxification (gradually decreasing methadone leading to abstinence within 1 to 3 months) and about 20 percent are abstinent.

The individual addict patient, whether he comes voluntarily or is referred from the criminal justice system, can choose not only the facility he prefers, but also the type of treatment which seems most helpful.

The addict patients—about 80 percent of them self-referrals—begin their treatment with a medical examination, program orientation, and discussion with doctors. Once a category of treatment is selected, the patient is referred for regular treatment to one of 17 centers scattered across Washington's urban core.

The treatment center located behind D.C. General is typical. There, in a relaxed and friendly atmosphere, a steady stream of former heroin addicts come in to drink down their cup of methadone-spiked orange juice and give a urine sample. The majority of the patients are young, male, and black. But a fair number of women, whites, and older men can also be found. Many are unemployed and come in old clothes. Others show up in the uniforms they wear as truck drivers, gas station attendants, milk men, mechanics, or clerks. The youngest seem to be in their early teens. The oldest around 50. The old hands joke with each other and with the casually dressed staff members. New patients are quieter and some seem embarrassed. A few patients bring their families for counseling sessions. The whole process—except for counseling—takes about ten minutes.

In two years of operation, NTA's patient load has increased from 150 to 3,300. Federal grants increased from $150,000 to $4.6 million. And, most important, the program seems to be successful.

In May 1971, NTA began a 12-month study of 600 patients who were selected at random from the patients in the program a year earlier. The study revealed that after 12 months in the program:

—55 percent of the patients did not exhibit evidence of drugs;
—52 percent had remained in the program;
—70 percent had remained in methadone maintenance programs;
—76 percent had not been arrested; and
—65 percent were employed.[7]

The number of crimes committed in the District began to drop in 1970. While no one factor is completely responsible, it is generally agreed that the NTA program helped significantly. As Dr. DuPont points out,

> many in the city—including the Mayor, the Chief of Police, the staff of the Senate District of Columbia Committee, and the major newspapers—have credited the work of the Narcotics Treatment Administration with at least part of the recent crime drop.

There is still much to be done. NTA is reaching only about 20 percent of the city's heroin users. But Washington—with the help of the federal government—has made a good start toward solving one of its most difficult human problems.

---

[7] D.C. Narcotics Treatment Administration, NTA's MOST IMPORTANT FACTS (Washington: D.C. Narcotics Treatment Administration, November 1971).

FREEDMEN'S HOSPITAL

One of the oldest federally funded health programs in the District of Columbia is Freedmen's Hospital, the teaching hospital of Howard University. The hospital was founded by Congress in 1865 as part of the Freedmen's Bureau to care for emancipated slaves from the South. In its first century of existence, Freedmen's became Washington's third largest private hospital and trained nearly half of all the black physicians in the United States.

Today, the hospital has nearly 500 beds and a professional staff that includes 527 nurses, 383 physicians and surgeons, and 117 medical and dental interns. In fiscal 1970, the hospital provided care for 11,500 inpatients and 115,000 clinic and emergency patients. The hospital, located on the Howard campus at the edge of Washington's inner-city poverty area, is the primary source of medical care for many of the city's poor and is generally credited with having the best emergency room in the District.

As the demands on the hospital grew, as more clinics and laboratory services were added, the 70-year-old hospital building became more and more inadequate. As a result, in fiscal 1971, the federal government gave Freedmen's a $15.6 million grant to begin construction of a new hospital.

The new hospital will be a seven-story, 500-bed brick building located on the Howard campus. To be completed in 1974, the new $33 million hospital will have clinics, teaching facilities, and research areas, as well as facilities for inpatient care.

SMALL RETURNS

All of the programs described above, all of the federal money that they receive has one goal—to give the residents of the District of Columbia better health care. There's good reason to believe that the goal has not been very well met. Morbidity and mortality rates in the District continue to run far ahead of national averages. The poor still crowd into the emergency room at D.C. General and still wait hours for unsatisfactory treatment. The shortage of doctors in the inner city continues. Neighborhood health clinics and maternity- and infant-care programs have not been totally successful in accomplishing their goals. The bulk of the total amount of federal health funds comes into the District without the D.C. government's knowledge or coordination—a practice that clearly works against overall health planning. St. Elizabeth's remains under federal control and the District appears to be far from ready to assume control. And D.C. budget problems and personnel reductions—the Department of Human Resources cut 800 jobs last year—exacerbate the health difficulties.

But there are signs that give rise to hope. The narcotics treatment project is working very well. A new Freedmen's hospital will be completed soon and will effectively serve Washington's inner city. The two neighborhood projects providing comprehensive health care—the privately run Group Health experiment and the Community Group Health Foundation—seem to be working.

The following general conclusions seem warranted:

• A true, prepaid comprehensive health plan purchased from a private contractor may meet the health needs of the poor because it places heavy emphasis on preventive medicine.

• A well-administered methadone maintenance program can reduce the number of heroin addicts and, as a result, reduce the crime rate.

• Federal provisions tied to grants can, and should be used to force private hospitals to accept part of the burden for caring for the poor.

• Medicaid and Medicare have accomplished a good deal by allowing the poor and the old to get better medical attention, but the programs should not be counted on to deliver secondary benefits such as keeping doctors in the inner city.

• The poor must be involved in program planning if projects are to work.

• Federal projects have forced the District to move health facilities out into the neighborhoods where poor people live and, because of that, the poor have access to many more health services.

• Finally, the link between poverty and bad health has been clearly established. And to be ultimately successful, health projects must be only one aspect of an overall campaign to attack the financial, educational, social, and employment problems of the people who live in Washington.

Chapter Eight

COMMUNITY ORGANIZATIONS:
THE VOICE OF THE POOR

by Walterene Swanston

A POWERLESS CITY

Like many northern urban areas, the District of Columbia attracted thousands of poor blacks from the South in search of jobs and a better way of life during and after World War II. For many, the jobs turned to be nonexistent or dead-end, and the promise of a better life hollow. Still they continued to come, adding to the problems of the city and indirectly at least causing affluent whites to flee to the suburbs. Those who fled, fearing that blacks would take over, took their much-needed tax dollars with them and left the city financially unable or unwilling to care for its citizens with problems.

The newcomers found that neither they nor the rest of the District's residents could have much impact on local government because ultimate power—to choose the city's top administrators, to make its laws, and to allocate its budget—rested with the White House and with the Congress.

At the beginning of the 1960s, the decade in which the civil rights movement forced massive social changes elsewhere, the President still appointed the three-member Board of Commissioners who presided over the local government, and Congress approved the District's laws and budget. The upper-class black and white citizens who had any influence at all in shaping local government policy served in "advisory" capacities, but for the most part citizens did not participate in the decision making.

What services were provided for the poor came from the upper classes through charities, settlement houses, and churches. In the early 1960s, the District had more than 700 neighborhood or community organizations (civic associations), but they were small volunteer groups, and whatever persuasive influence they exercised on local government was of little avail to the poor since the associations for the most part did not include or represent the poor.

THE BEGINNING OF CHANGE

The Economic Opportunity Act of 1964 pioneered in inviting poor citizens in the District and elsewhere to participate in the decisions that affected their lives. That legislation, coupled with President Lyndon Johnson's decision in 1967 to reorganize the District government—permitting the city to have an appointed mayor and a 9-member city council—made many District residents more willing and more able to make demands on the local government.

Though 750 of the neighborhood groups still exist, they have little money and less clout and have been overshadowed by four community organizations created and funded by the federal government.

The 1964 Economic Opportunity Act is responsible for the most comprehensive of these four programs—the United Planning Organization (UPO), the District's antipovery agency. Since then three other federally funded programs have extended citizen participation and community organization in the District of Columbia:

—the Model Cities program, which designated a portion of the city to receive special funds to attack its problems;

—the Peoples Involvement Corporation (PIC), a nonprofit corporation which is concentrating on developing the Shaw neighborhood; and

—the Model Inner City Community Organization (MICCO), the advisory arm of the urban renewal agency.

The federal commitment to these four programs carried a price tag of $47.5 million during fiscal 1971. While the District government contributes some resources to these programs, the Departments of Labor; Commerce; Health, Education, and Welfare (HEW); and Housing and Urban Development (HUD) foot most of the bills. The four programs grew out of an awareness in the early 1960s that the poor, crowded into the cities, would no longer sit idly by and permit local government to ignore them and their special needs.

In Washington, the newly recognized urban poor were predominantly black. They had come North with few skills that would land them jobs in the urban work force. They were poor when they came and their poverty was perpetuated by a racist system that kept them out of good jobs, out of unions, and out of first-rate schools.

The black population of the District has been growing at a rapid rate since 1940, and its proportion in the District population doubled in the two decades between 1950 and 1970, rising from 35 percent of the total population to 71 percent (Chart 9). But despite their growing numbers, during the 1950s and the early 1960s, blacks were in the lowest paying jobs in the federal and local governments; many jobs in private business were closed to blacks altogether; and the absolute disparity in income between blacks and whites was increasing. Adequate housing became an increasing problem because low-cost housing in the Southwest and Foggy Bottom was being torn down; restoration of Georgetown and Capitol Hill was forcing blacks to move; and those blacks who were able to buy their own homes were restricted to certain parts of the city. (By 1960, nearly 85 percent of all blacks in the Washington metropolitan area lived in the central city; within the District, the vast majority lived east of Rock Creek Park.) The health and welfare departments could not take proper care of the poor because they were always strapped for money. The schools

CHART 9:   WASHINGTON IS INCREASINGLY A BLACK CITY

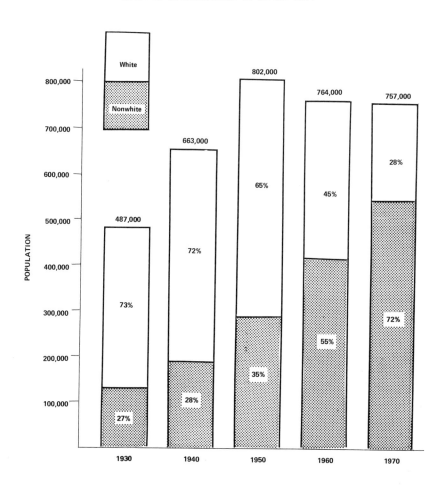

Source: U.S. Bureau of the Census

faced troubles. "The public services that might have palliated some of the evils of slum living were understaffed and ill-equipped," District historian Constance McLaughlin Green said of this period.[1]

---

[1] Constance McLaughlin Green, THE SECRET CITY (Princeton, N.J.: Princeton University Press, 1967), p. 325.

At the beginning of the 1960s, blacks did not have a real voice in the administration of the city.

> The appointment in 1961 and reappointment in 1964 of a Negro as one of the three District commissioners was, it is true, an epoch-making departure from the past, but John Duncan and his two white associates proved unable to do more than pick at the edges of the massive problems confronting them. Whether pleased or disappointed at what they succeeded in accomplishing, the bulk of citizens, white and colored alike, believed that as long as committees of Congress acted as the City Council, the District would suffer from neglect and from biased or uninformed ideas of the community's needs.[2]

There was little incentive for either the Congress or the local government to provide for the poor. For the most part the key members of the Senate and House congressional committees on the District were white Southerners, many of them with rural constituencies, and since local officials were not elected, they could not be thrown out of office for ignoring the community's needs.

Congressional limitations aside, the District government could not deal with the problems of the poor in the early 1960s. District officials had no established mechanism for getting inside the poor black community to find out what the problems were or how to handle them, and the poor distrusted the white local government. Not one major District government department was headed by a black person, and those blacks who were in the local government were in the lower grades and had no policy-making power. For the most part, blacks did not even try to change the local government because they believed it incapable of change. By 1960, the gap between the city's poor and the local government had become a chasm. The needs of the poor were not being met in Washington and many other cities. And, by 1964, it had become clear that local governments either could not or would not respond to those needs.

PARTICIPATION BY THE POOR

It was this awareness that led to the passage of the most far-reaching social legislation of the decade—the Economic Opportunity Act of 1964. It brought the District and other cities federal funds earmarked for the poor, and it gave the poor a voice in designing the programs that could change their lives.

---

[2] *Ibid.,* p. 22.

The Johnson Administration intended that the Community Action Program (CAP) be the very heart of the antipoverty effort. The intent of the legislation was that practically any program aimed at serving the poor could be funded through the Community Action Agency (CAA). Accordingly, President Johnson envisioned that the Community Action Program would

> ask men and women throughout the country to prepare long range plans for the attack on poverty in their own local communities. These plans will be local plans striking at the many unfilled needs which underlie poverty in each community, not just one or two. Their components and emphasis will differ as needs differ. These plans will be local plans calling upon all the resources available to the community—Federal and state, local and private, human and material.

The act's designers evidently appreciated the wide horizons possible for the Community Action Program. Indeed, as Sar A. Levitan has noted, "it is clear that CAP is not a 'program,' but a strategy of combating poverty." [3]

The legislation defined a community action program as an effort which

> mobilizes and utilizes resources, public or private, in any geographical area, in an attack on poverty; which provides services, assistance, and other activities . . . to give promise of progress toward elimination of poverty or a cause or causes of poverty . . .

> —which is developed, conducted, and administered with the maximum feasible participation of residents of the area and members of the group served; and

> —which is conducted, administered, or coordinated by a public or private non-profit agency other than a political party, or a combination thereof.

THE UNITED PLANNING ORGANIZATION

During its early years, the District's Community Action Agency, the United Planning Organization, had problems typical of urban groups around the country. They included:

—extended debate over the meaning of "maximum feasible participation";

---

[3] Sar A. Levitan, The Great Society's Poor Law: A New Approach to Poverty (Baltimore: The Johns Hopkins Press, 1969), p. 109.

—attempts by black militants to "control" the boards of directors and to exclude whites from decision-making roles;

—hastily conceived and badly administered programs;

—charges that too many of the programs were prepackaged and forced on the poor; and finally

—a growing belief by some that there was never enough money allocated to make a dent in eradicating poverty.

At the beginning of 1960, there were 161,000 poor persons in the District, amounting to 21 percent of the District's population.[4] Efforts to find the poor and to plan programs to deal wth poverty in the Washington metropolitan area were either nonexistent or poorly administered.

In 1962, the United Planning Organization was chartered to serve as the center of regional planning for the elimination of poverty and to design community services. Funds came from foundations and private businesses, and its board of directors was drawn from the city's power structure. There were no poor people on the board.

Two years later, under the Economic Opportunity Act, the United Planning Organization was designated as the Community Action Agency for the District and the surrounding counties in Maryland and Virginia. Maryland has since established its own, but the UPO still represents the District and Northern Virginia.

In its eight years as a community action agency, UPO has initiated programs in the areas of health, housing, education, employment, and economic development. These range from day-care centers to emergency food and clothing programs, from mental health clinics to special programs aimed at the Spanish-speaking, and from credit unions to alcoholic rehabilitation programs. Included are not only several prepackaged national emphasis programs—neighborhood legal services, Head Start, day care, early childhood education, and community credit unions—but also locally initiated efforts. Among these programs are two which are aimed at providing more and better housing, two youth programs, a police-community relations project, a drug treatment program, and a preschool program.

---

[4] OFFICE OF ECONOMIC OPPORTUNITY INFORMATION CENTER REPORT, Washington, D.C., 1970.

The Housing Development Corporation, a nonprofit corporation, was set up to buy, sell, rent, build, rehabilitate, manage, and lease housing for low-income families, and to provide jobs in the construction trades and business opportunities for inner-city contractors. The Corporation, which gets part of its funds from UPO, HUD, and the Office of Economic Opportunity (OEO), currently has 1,000 housing units under way in the District.

The other housing program is the Washington Planning and Housing Association which is funded jointly by UPO and the local Health and Welfare Council, the community chest agency. This association is a housing planning agency, which has attempted to determine how much housing is needed in the District and which has also tried to bring about legislative changes that would benefit low-income families seeking adequate housing.

The District government's Office of Youth Opportunity Services began in 1967 as a summer enrichment program. Now operating year round, the program provides community-planned and operated educational and recreational programs for youth. The District operated the program with both UPO and city funds. Formulated by neighborhood planning councils, the programs offered to youth services ranging from preschool educational programs to work-training programs for teen-agers.

The Pilot Police District is funded by OEO and is designed to improve police-community relations in a section of Northwest Washington. Although the program is operated by the District government, UPO serves as its liaison between the city and OEO. The program is planned and monitored by a citizen board. The project has resulted in the employment of community residents in police stations, special training in police-community relations for policemen in the district in which it operates, and a special recruitment program to attract minority group members to the police force.

The Drug Addiction Treatment and Rehabilitation Center began in 1968 with a $600,000 grant from OEO. The program, which includes treatment for both volunteer addicts and those referred by the courts and hospitals, is operated by the city's health department.

The Model School Preschool program started in the District in 1964 before the development of Head Start. The program is part of the District's public schools model-schools project. All five of the preschool programs are for children living in the Cardozo area of Northwest Washington.

For some of these locally initiated programs, the District government provides staff while UPO provides the funds. Many of the programs were planned jointly. While the District government does not maintain a day-to-day working relationship with UPO, the city does have a liaison officer in the Department of Human Resources who represents the mayor in dealings between UPO and OEO. The liaison officer, James Butts, said that the city does have to give final approval to UPO plans before they are submitted to OEO. "We have the authority to veto UPO programs, but it seldom happens. We work out hassles before they get to the veto stage," Butts said.

Between fiscal years 1965 and 1971, District agencies—including UPO—received $109 million in CAP funds. The District received a fair share of the total CAP funds. In fiscal 1970 and 1971, for example, the District got 4.3 percent of all Community Action Program funds. During the 1965-1971 period, the UPO budget grew from $15.8 million to $26 million. And while most of the money for UPO came from CAP, additional money came from the Department of Health, Education, and Welfare, and the Department of Labor in the form of direct grants, and from the Model Cities Program, in the form of subcontracts.

In October 1965, after UPO's first year as a community action agency, *Washington Evening Star* reporter Betty James wrote:

> Several things are clear about the kind of war that is being waged:
>
> It is not a form of the dole.
>
> It is not welfare reform.
>
> Its goal is jobs for the poor and the education and the training to get them. Its goal is justice for the poor and a voice in the decisions that affect their lives.
>
> The most important thing about the first frantic year of the United Planning Organization . . . is that UPO is trying to fight the kind of war that may achieve these goals.

UPO was not without its critics—from both without and within —during its first year. As Mrs. James noted,

> Civil rights leaders and liberal churchmen are among the strongest critics of the program, contending that UPO is too timid to really

take on the power structure represented on its own board, that the poor are not involved in any way that counts, and that UPO, in one short year, has become another bureaucracy.

It was true that there were no poor on the board until civil-rights activist Julius Hobson asked the District Court to take away the board's authority to spend any more public funds until representatives of the poor were included on the board. (In 1966 Congress amended the Economic Opportunity Act to require that a third of the CAA board represent the poor.)

UPO's staff complained that its first executive director, James Banks, "railroaded" programs through the staff and sent them to OEO for approval. A close observor of UPO's progress said that Banks did indeed run a "railroad," but he ran it the way OEO wanted it run.

> He knew what kind of programs OEO would approve and it was those kinds of programs that he submitted. The success of UPO is due to Banks. Some people didn't like him, but he could work with the poor and he could talk to people in a way that was never condescending.

Perhaps more than anyone else, Banks shaped the early poverty program in the District. His successors, Wiley Branton and Jeanus Parks, have not drastically changed the direction of the programs.

Neighborhood Development Centers

The neighborhood development centers have constituted one of the most vital parts of the District poverty program from the start. Scattered throughout the city, the 10 centers provide the poor with much-needed social services within their neighborhoods. Before the centers were established many of the poor either had to travel "downtown" to get services or do without. And many did without rather than stand in long lines or sit in crowded waiting rooms at welfare offices once they got downtown.

There are two types of neighborhood centers—those which existed as settlement houses before the poverty program and then received additional funds from UPO to act as development centers and those which were specifically created and funded by UPO to provide services.

A good example of the former is Friendship House, located on Capitol Hill in the shadow of the Congress. It serves a neighborhood that has changed rapidly in the last 10 years. Many affluent whites are buying and restoring houses in the area, while at the same time much of the Hill's black population lives in public housing or old and dilapidated row houses. Friendship House is a rambling, three-story Victorian settlement house that has been part of the community since the turn of the century. It serves 50,000 residents in the area bounded by East and South Capitol Streets and the Anacostia River.

The building itself houses a day-care center for 80 children; a child-guidance center, which is used twice a week; a food-stamp certification center; a visiting-nurses program for teen-age girls; and administrative offices for the entire development center. The building is open and bustling from 7:30 a.m.—when parents on their way to work drop off children for the day-care center—until 10 or 10:30 p.m. when the last of the community groups meets in the building.

As is typical of the District's Neighborhood Development Centers, Friendship House also runs programs dealing with community organization, consumer action, education mobilization, employment services, credit unions, and legal services. The staff estimates that between 6,000 and 7,000 people a year use Friendship House for some purpose, but their regular clients number about 1,500 a year.

Typical of the centers created by UPO is the one operated by the Near Northeast Community Improvement Corporation (CIC). Founded in October 1965 as a nonprofit organization to promote, administer, and manage programs designed to reduce poverty, CIC gets most of its funds from UPO. It serves a neighborhood of 100,000 persons living in the area that includes the H Street Northeast corridor, one of the areas most heavily damaged during Washington's 1968 riots. Twenty-five percent of the people in the neighborhood have incomes below the poverty level, according to CIC statistics.

CIC operates six major programs—employment, education, consumer protection, housing, alcoholic rehabilitation, and youth. It operates out of two buildings—the administrative offices are on the H Street riot corridor; the service center is two blocks away in a well-worn one-story building on Florida Avenue Northeast.

The Martin Luther King Memorial Center (as the neighborhood center is called) houses CIC's major programs. Of CIC's 23 employees, 10 are neighborhood workers. According to program records, during the year that ended in September 1971, the CIC staff:

—found jobs for 1,692 of the 3,418 persons who applied through their center;

—placed another 282 in job-training programs;

—handled 363 eviction cases, prevented 48, and found emergency shelter for 130 families;

—conducted courses in consumer protection education for 5,446;

—certified 5,713 persons for food stamps and provided emergency food for 255 persons;

— tutored, on a regular basis, 158 students; and

—enrolled 587 persons in adult education classes.

CIC estimates that about 5,000 neighborhood persons a year use its facilities or services and adds that, like most of the neighborhood development centers, it does not have enough neighborhood workers.

"We just don't have enough money to hire as many people as we need." Lawrence Rickard, a young staff member explained:

If we do find somebody that is good at neighborhood work, he wants to get promoted to a better job, so there are always vacancies at the neighborhood worker level. And that's where we need people most.

Because we only have 10 neighborhood workers, they have to stay in the office to handle complaints for the people who come in looking for help rather than going out in the community trying to find the people who need us.

Right now, our neighborhood workers only get out of the office one day a week, and that's only if we're not terribly busy in the office that day.

We could get more neighborhood workers if we could afford to pay them more, but our budget is being either held at the same level or is being cut, so we can't do any better. To meet our last budget cut, we had to eliminate a staff position, and every time we have to do something like that, it creates a morale problem among the other members of the staff, to say nothing of what it does to what services we are supposed to provide in the neighborhood.

Funding Innovative Projects

In addition to causing these specific difficulties at neighborhood centers, the lack of funds at OEO has had an adverse effect on the overall thrust of the fight against poverty. According to Frank Hollis, UPO deputy executive director, budget constraints have forced OEO to push national programs in the District at the expense of locally initiated efforts. He claimed that while UPO officials have tried to get money for some locally initiated projects, "what we get are the prepackaged ones. You can't blame OEO because it is caught up in a time when there is a declining commitment to the poverty program by the Congress and the Administration."

Hollis said that in an effort to capitalize on OEO priorities, UPO is planning to concentrate on economic development in its next phase. "We can tell now that OEO is interested in funding economic development projects, so we will probably try to get money for those kinds of projects here," he said.

Another of UPO's problems, some of its officials hold, is that whenever UPO does establish a good, locally initiated program, OEO takes it from UPO control, removes the money to run it from the UPO budget, and transfers the program to another government agency. According to Hollis,

> Success has not been rewarded; anything but. For example, we started the Washington Institute for Employment Training, a job training program. Last year, OEO decided it was a good program and they took it from us and gave it to the Labor Department. [It is now the Opportunities Industrialization Center.] They also took the $600,000 budgeted for it.

Hollis said that the original intention of OEO to fund programs through UPO and then spin them off as they became successful was a sound idea, but, he added, UPO should be able to keep the money to plan other programs.

Even though Hollis would like to keep the successful programs under UPO, many of the spun-off programs have been more successful and have gotten more funds after becoming independent. However, UPO officials believe they could offer a more comprehensive program if the money from the spun-off programs were left in the UPO budget.

UPO Administration

Because UPO is physically close to OEO and to Congress, it does receive some special attention in the way of the audits and reviews but no special treatment when it comes to funding, UPO officials claim. An extensive review of one of the neighborhood development centers in December 1967 by the General Accounting Office, Congress' watchdog agency, turned up some of the problems that have plagued UPO since it started. The review, made at the request of the Senate Appropriations Committee, examined objectives of the program at Southeast Neighborhood House and also examined expenditures, staffing, recording of program and financial information, and reporting of program operations.

The review team found that the neighborhood workers' monthly statistics were not supported by their daily reports, that little emphasis was being given to education and employment, and that few of the people contacted were referred to other component programs and community agencies established to help alleviate poverty.

The team also found that an increasing number of persons were delinquent in repaying loans to the credit union, that more than a third of the children enrolled in the day-care program were from families whose income was too high to qualify for free care, and that some expenses had been paid twice.

The review recommended that UPO improve its program management, administrative records, and financial controls. Although OEO's own review teams have found similar problems in other UPO programs, for the most part the problems were worked out quietly.

Administrative problems have caused UPO to lose its first two directors and some of its most promising young staff members. Young militants have occupied UPO offices protesting that the organization was too rigid to allow creative programs.

UPO's third director, Jeanus Parks, who headed the neighborhood legal-services program before he assumed his present job, has been trying to iron out some of the administrative problems. Parks contends that the structure OEO established for CAAs created some of the problems.

> UPO was set up so that division heads, in most instances, white, had their own fiefdoms; only in very limited ways were they answerable to the director.

In the past, an agency like UPO was never designed for the director to direct. Before, you never knew who was supposed to do what. You had a lot of people doing their own thing without regard for central administration.[5]

Parks has reorganized UPO to establish a new system of accountability; many of the program's critics claim that the agency may be easier for Parks to run now, but they charge that the reorganization makes no difference to the poor who simply need services where they can get to them.

"UPO administrators now and always have viewed themselves apart from the poor of this city," said Lola Singletary, a District government employee who has worked in the poverty program.

That first board of directors before UPO became the CAP agency, represented the middle-class blacks and whites who had always run things around here. Even though the board now legally has to have a third "representatives of the poor," it isn't the poor who control the board, who decide what UPO does with the money it gets.

On the other hand, one high District government official who has worked extensively with UPO argues that control shouldn't be the issue at all, that the poor should leave some technical decisions to professional planners. He said,

I've never been so sure that the poor, because they have a problem, are the best ones to know how to solve the problem. That's why I believe the professionals, the experts, should play such an important role in designing UPO programs.

The professionals here have abdicated their responsibility. They have, in many instances, been so intimidated by the push for "community control" that they no longer do their job. That's one reason some of the programs that UPO designs don't work.

Another severe critic—a neighborhood worker from Friendship House—charges that

UPO perpetuates itself rather than trying to establish programs that are going to have any lasting effects on the poor in this town. The administrative costs mushroom at the top, and the community gets less and less of the money.

The administrators have set themselves up as a buffer between government and the poor—that puts the poor right back where they started from.

[5] *Interview With Jeanus Parks,* PIC MAGAZINE, Vol. 1, No. 2, 1971.

UPO has become a bureaucracy, and it has become staid. Nonetheless, it has made some changes in the lives of the poor. Its principle achievement has been to make the local government at least conscious of the problems of the poor, and, at the same time, it has given the poor community organizations through which to make their needs known.

Despite the local criticism of the UPO programs, the federal OEO officials who are responsible for UPO seem satisfied that it is making progress toward easing the problems of the poor.

The man closest to the program in the OEO regional office is Charles Howard. He makes three trips a month from the regional office to look at the District's programs. Howard said that while it's still too early to know just how much the very poor will get from the poverty program, he believes that, because the poor are participating in designing their own programs, some progress is being made. And he believes the District's programs are getting better all the time.

"UPO programs have gained sophistication, both in the kind of programs they are developing and in the way they are being run," according to Howard. Howard explained,

> One of UPO's earliest programs set up neighborhood credit unions in which the poor could have small amounts of money and borrow money for certain items. For the first few years, the credit unions were totally dependent on UPO for funding. Now, all of them have become self-sufficient and have been spun off from UPO. They're independent now.

> They started buyers clubs—kind of cooperatives to help the poor buy in bulk and get better prices—and they too were dependent. They are now beginning to become independent.

OEO intended the CAAs to spin off programs so that the independent programs can survive when the federal commitment to OEO programs changes.

PEOPLES INVOLVEMENT CORPORATION

The Peoples Involvement Corporation (PIC) is another program that has been spun off from UPO, though UPO does have some control over its funds. PIC began as a development corporation to serve the Shaw community. In 1969, it became a separate community organization, receiving part of its funds from OEO but other funds from the Department of Labor and HEW. PIC officials said that they formed a separate organization because UPO's funds were being cut back at a time when PIC wanted to expand its services. By severing most of its ties with UPO, PIC became eligible for funds from other federal agencies in addition to OEO money, its officials claim.

PIC now gets some of its money—$125,000—from OEO; $200,000 comes from HEW; and some more comes from Commerce and from Model Cities. Because UPO has projects similar to those that PIC funds in the same neighborhood, there is some duplication of services.

PIC operates in a 1,600 block area of the Northwest. Its board of directors is made up of 39 people, 36 elected members and three appointed by the mayor. Elections for board members are held every two years. The election is open only to members of the PIC neighborhood. The board selects PIC's priorities in consultation with its "outreach" staff.

The PIC was established to concentrate its efforts on families or individuals facing serious problems concerning employment, physical and mental health, involvement with the courts, child rearing, home management, economic development, coordination of services, multiservice centers, and other environmental or personal difficulties.

PIC's main offices are in a large, abandoned bread factory in the midst of an area that is just now showing signs of renewed growth. The offices are located just at the foot of Howard University and around the corner from Freedmen's Hospital.

PIC's projects include a multiservice center, a consumer protection program, a parent-child health center, a day-care center, a rehabilitation project, and a local development corporation.

Although the development corporation has been getting the most attention lately—the corporation recently announced that it will finance, with government funds, a $7 million hotel—the program that works the best is the community facilities multiservice center at North Capitol and K Streets N.E.

The center is in a facility handed down by a church in the neighborhood. The building is shabby, though the thousands of people who use it every week don't seem to care. The center is only temporarily housed in the building and will transfer its activities to another location nearby, which is being constructed. But for now, the center brims with people trying to get help of one kind or another.

"This neighborhood is changing," said Velvin Dabney, director.

This is an area that is being renewed. Churches, with federal loans, are building apartment houses; non-profit housing corporations are building. We're gaining population, and just about everybody that's here now can use some of our services.

The center's most needed services are the health and food services and drug addiction treatment, according to Dabney. Dabney added,

All PIC actually provides is the administrative staff and the building. The District government runs most of the programs. Our community organizers have found out what people in this area need and we try to provide them with the right services.

The center houses welfare programs, an alcoholic rehabilitation program, a public health clinic, a narcotics treatment facility, a family and child service facility, and a home economics program, and it draws about 15,000 people a week. The members of the service-center staff say that they frequently have more people trying to use the facilities than the staff can easily handle.

Dabney, a community organization specialist, says that he has had to make a lot of changes in the way the center operates.

When I first came here, I used to see the people we were supposed to help leave this building crying. And I said to myself this isn't right. So I set out to find out what was going on. I started walking up and down these halls, listening to the welfare intake people humiliating clients, talking nasty to people.

They weren't working for PIC, but for the city; but I am responsible for the kind of services people get here. I tried talking to the people who were not treating the clients right; some of them straightened out. For some of the others, I had to go to their supervisors downtown and together we got them transferred.

Now, I believe the services people can get in this center are very good, the kind they need in a place that is convenient.

At least one of the center's clients, an 18-year-old unmarried mother, agrees. As she sat on a straightbacked chair outside the welfare department office, waiting to see one of the supervisors, she said:

> My mother was on welfare and I remember how she used to hate to have anything to do with the welfare people. She always said they treated you like dirt when you had to go downtown to ask them for something.
>
> I swore I'd never ask them for anything. But last January I had my baby and I didn't want to get married. And I wanted to finish high school. So I had to go downtown to apply for welfare and they said I could also get food stamps. Downtown, at the welfare office, they figured out how much money I was entitled to and then sent me over here to get my food stamps. That's how I found out about this place and I've been coming here for one thing or another ever since. The people, they treat you nice here.

PIC is now working on a second multiservice center for the Shaw neighborhood.

While some of the PIC programs—like the multiservice center— seem to work quite well, other projects have not. For example, Project Square was designed to renovate 51 row houses in Shaw. The houses were to be remodeled and offered for sale to the people who used to live in them. But so far, only nine of the houses have been finished, and many people believe the others will never be completed.

PIC's most ambitious project now is to build a large hotel to be called Harambee. With a $3.6 million grant and a matching loan from the Department of Commerce, PIC's development corporation is planning to build the hotel in the midst of a neighborhood that is showing signs of recovering from the 1968 riots and years of neglect. The hotel is to be built on Georgia Avenue, in the same neighborhood where PIC has its headquarters. Howard University is planning to expand its campus, and Freedmen's Hospital is planning a new $33 million hospital in the area. PIC officials hope that the other developments will provide clients for the hotel. One of the PIC's critics said of the project, "I can't imagine how they talked the Commerce Department into going for a project as shaky as this one seems." Another of PIC's critics, a Georgia Avenue businessman, said he didn't think the hotel would be a success.

> In the first place, PIC couldn't get itself together enough to finish Project Square, and now they are talking about taking on something

the size of Harambee. Even if they do get the building up, it's going to be in trouble. I know that other businessmen have surveyed this area to see if it is feasible to put up any kind of project like this and none of them thought they could make it work.

Sure Howard University is growing down this way, and Freedmen's is going to build a new hospital nearby. But that is all that's happening right now in this neighborhood, and people are afraid to come around here at night—especially the people they hope to attract to this hotel.

Besides, it appears to me that the project doesn't have that much neighborhood support. It's just another one of those things that someone else is proposing to build here.

PIC will own the land and the building, and lease them to a corporation which will run the hotel. The corporation hopes to employ 200 neighborhood people once the hotel is built.

PIC officials are as aware of the kinds of programs they can get funded as UPO officials are. One PIC official said, "This is the year for economic development. The money is there and that's why we went after it to build Harambee."

Although most of the evaluations of PIC have included only general audits and reviews, the General Accounting Office did make a special audit to check on the money for Harambee, PIC officials said. At the time of the audit, PIC had not received any of the money for the hotel. GAO never issued a formal report.

Unlike UPO, PIC gets to keep its more successful programs. One such program, which is aimed at infants and their parents, has gotten good evaluations for three years, and every year it has received slightly more money, according to a PIC staff member.

But PIC does have problems. One of its major problems is created by its funding sources. Because the money comes in from so many sources, PIC needs additional accounting services to handle the bookkeeping the funding agencies require. And PIC officials complain that both the District government and OEO are so slow paying their bills and approving extensions or reprogramming of programs that it causes unnecessary problems. PIC is asking its funding sources for more money for accountants, and that may solve some of its problems. Its other problems will be solved only by experience.

MODEL CITIES PROGRAM

While UPO has gone after the problems of the poor in the entire city, both PIC and the Model Cities program, which is another source of federal funds in the District, have limited their areas of operation to selected neighborhoods.

Whereas UPO's community action programs try to find the poor throughout the city and provide for their special needs, the Model Cities program concentrates its efforts on a "target" neighborhood with well-defined boundaries in which significant numbers of poor people live. The District's Office of Community Services oversees programs proposed and administered by both groups and sometimes acts as a liaison between the two groups.

The District's "Model" neighborhood is 1,500 acres of poverty in the heart of the city. It encompasses the communities of Shaw, Trinidad, Stanton Park, and Ivy City. Although several other communities were in competition for Model Cities funding, only those mentioned met the HUD criteria. HUD required that the model neighborhood contain no more than 10 percent of the city's total population, that it already be receiving some federal money, and that there be a mixture of residents. Anacostia, located across the Anacostia River in Southeast Washington, was considered, but it was too saturated with public housing to contain the mixture of residents HUD required.

The Model Cities program, in the language of the Department of Housing and Urban Development, is "designed to concentrate public and private resources in a comprehensive five-year attack on the social, economic, and physical problems of slum and blighted neighborhoods." Authorized by Title I of the Demonstration Cities and Metropolitan Development Act of 1966, its purpose is to upgrade the total environment of such neighborhoods and significantly improve the lives of residents.

The District applied for Model Cities money in April 1967, and was accepted as one of 156 cities to share in the funds. The federal government put up 80 percent and the local government 20 percent of the funds to plan a first-year "action plan."

HUD placed the responsibility for getting the community involved with the principal local executive (mayor, city manager) and provided for an elected governing body (city council, commission). In December 1968, Mayor Walter Washington established the D.C. Model Cities Commission to "provide the citizens of the model area direct access to the decision-making process by involving them in the development of a Model Cities plan and its implementation to the end that they may be partners in the effort to improve the quality of our urban life." Eight months later, the 140 elected members of the Commission submitted a $10 million plan for the first action year of the D.C. Model Cities program.

The District received $9.6 million for its first-year action programs. During that year, the Model Cities Commission funded a wide range of programs for economic and physical development, education, training, child care, and health. While HUD guidelines allow Model Cities commissions a year to plan action programs, the District's action year began May 1, 1970, and ended 20 months later. HUD had to give the city an eight-month extension because the program was badly planned. The second action period, which began in 1972, will also be of 20 months duration to allow proper planning, according to HUD officials.

The D.C. Model Cities project has had administrative problems from its beginning. The District was slow in making its initial application for funding. Although some cities got their programs funded as early as May of 1969, the District didn't get its approved until January of the next year. After that, HUD forced the D.C. commission to revise its first-year action plan five times before giving it final approval. HUD officials said they forced the changes because the plan didn't show evidence of enough citizen participation.

"HUD wants to stay out of the programs as much as possible, but I'm afraid we're going to have to force some other changes in the program in the next few months," said a HUD official responsible for the D.C. program. He went on to say,

> The only thing we're concerned about now is the fact that there are dual administrative staffs—one for the commission and one for the city's Model City Administration. Both of them are responsible for planning and running the program. It's unworkable. The administration is fuzzy; that's one reason the planning is so slow. We're just going to have to force them to change their staffing pattern.

Aside from the administrative problem, HUD believes the program is a good one. "They may not have terribly many new kinds of programs, but we are sure that they are providing for at least some of the unmet needs of the people in the Model neighborhood," the official said. And according to a local Model Cities program official,

> During its first year, a lot of Model Cities programs did duplicate services. Some of them duplicated District government programs, others duplicated Model Cities programs, but just about all of the duplication has been eliminated now.

For the most part, there is not much unusual scrutiny of the program from outsiders. But Congress, during the summer of 1971, became very interested in one controversial summer program for youth. It was called Earn and Learn and was funded by the Model Cities Commission. The program, with a budget of $300,000, paid students who lived in the model neighborhood and who could not find jobs $1.60 an hour to go to summer school. There was an investigation by some members of Congress, but the program was allowed to proceed.

The model neighborhood is showing some signs of improving, but the most improvement is in the services that are now available to the poor in the area. Health care was a major problem in the area, so during its first year, the Model Cities Commission began a community health project, a dental project, a lead-poisoning screening project, and a drug addiction treatment project. The second-year action plan calls for the establishment of two additional comprehensive health-care programs.

> In all but the smallest cities, it is almost impossible to determine what permanent improvements the Model Cities program will make before the 5 years are up. We know there are some good, imaginative programs in the District, but we'll just have to wait to see if they make lasting changes in the way people live,

noted the HUD official quoted above.

MODEL INNER CITY COMMUNITY ORGANIZATION

Although the Model Inner City Community Organization probably won't have as great an impact as some of the other community organizations, it too brings federal money into the city.

MICCO, a private, nonprofit community organization operating in the Shaw area, is the community organization arm of the Redevelopment Land Agency (RLA), the urban renewal agency.

MICCO's plan is to guide the rehabilitation and redevelopment of the Shaw-school neighborhood in the central city. MICCO's charge is to see that low-income housing is provided, that there is subway service, that health and social-service facilities are provided, and that obsolete schools and other public facilities are replaced.

Even its advocates admit that MICCO has not accomplished those goals and is perhaps farther than ever from doing so. MICCO was founded in 1966 by Rev. Walter Fauntroy—then pastor of a church in Shaw, now the District's nonvoting delegate to the House of Representatives—to give the residents of Shaw a voice in the shaping of the urban-renewal area. Fauntroy, who was MICCO's first and only president until he resigned in February 1972, also wanted to prevent the RLA from displacing poor blacks in Shaw with affluent whites as it had done in the renewal of Southwest Washington. HUD has tried to prevent this kind of removal of the poor by requiring the creation of citizen-manned project advisory committees for all urban-renewal projects.

All of MICCO's funds come from RLA, which, in turn, is funded by HUD. Since March of 1967, MICCO has been awarded contracts totaling $1.3 million to advise RLA on the development of Shaw. RLA has spent an additional $3.4 million on planning and another $14 million on acquiring property for redevelopment.

As yet, there is very little to show for it. Only one apartment building—the 108-unit Lincoln-Westmoreland Apartments—has been built. It was built for families with incomes ranging from $6,000 and $12,000 a year. Yet the crying need in Shaw is for public housing—enough for 19,800 people. At present, there is none being built, and only 54 units are being planned.

Still MICCO claims that it represents the poor in Shaw. Its board of directors is made up of 51 members from 134 citizens' groups. Each of the 134 organizations—which include community-based organizations ranging from churches and fraternities to parent-teacher associations and youth groups—elects one representative to MICCO. The board is elected by the member organizations.

Whether or not the board represents all elements of the community is being seriously questioned. A recent study by the Washington Planning and Housing Association found:

> In spite of the numerous community meetings, we get the feeling that there has been no systematic participation by the "little guy" in

Shaw. The decisions are made by relatively affluent businessmen and prominent ministers. In plan-making, MICCO has not organized affinity groups in schools or among tenants for example.[6]

Other critics of MICCO have made similar charges. And many blame Fauntroy for MICCO's faults. Channing Phillips, a former MICCO board member and political rival of Fauntroy who now heads the nonprofit Housing Development Corporation which is building in Shaw, has said that "the only people who come to the MICCO board meetings are those who have an immediate interest." MICCO board member André Bouchard called MICCO a closed club. "That's the way it was conceived—to be a very tight-knit group of people with like interests," and he further charged that the board is a rubber stamp for Fauntroy.[7]

Fauntroy has denied the charges, saying that until RLA restricted citizen participation in the renewal of Shaw, MICCO did represent the views of the people of Shaw. He has also denied charges that MICCO benefits his friends and political associates more than Shaw's poor. He did not deny that some of his friends do make money acting as attorneys for and consultants to MICCO, but he said that it had been difficult to find people who would give the effort required to make MICCO work.

Though there are safeguards to assure citizen participation in the renewal process, they are not always effective. The city council must approve the urban-renewal plans every year; public hearings on the plans are required; the Model Cities Commission must be consulted to make sure development plans are consistent with its plans; and various other District government agencies must be consulted to make sure that, for example, zoning ordinances are obeyed.

Also built into the RLA-MICCO relationship are serious problems over the MICCO's role in the selection of potential developers. RLA has held that MICCO's role is purely advisory and that MICCO should not have a decisive say over selection of developers. Fauntroy has contended that the power to select developers responsive to what he defined as community needs "is what citizen participation is all about." RLA seems to have won the dispute. In late February 1972, RLA forced Fauntroy to resign from

---

[6] Eugene Meyer, *MICCO's Critics*, THE WASHINGTON POST, February 22, 1972.
[7] *Ibid.*

MICCO by refusing to award MICCO any new funds unless Fauntroy gave up his position. At the same time, it was spelled out in the contract between MICCO and RLA that MICCO would continue to be an advisory body. The new contract gave MICCO a budget of $475,000—$7,000 less than the previous year, and only three quarters of MICCO's request.

Some of MICCO's board members say that the RLA decision defining their role as advisory isn't new at all. Before the RLA announcement, board member Watha Daniels said, "MICCO is only an advisory group. We don't kid ourselves that we are anything else, because we realize that it is RLA which has the power to make ultimate decisions about what will happen in Shaw." He said that MICCO's presence will be felt somehow and, he added, the board has been able to have some impact on renewal plans. When asked what the impact of MICCO has been, another board member said,

> Without at least some of us on the MICCO board caring about what happens to Shaw, it might simply have been torn down and paved over by now. I know the rebuilding is slow, but I would rather believe that RLA is at least thinking about what Shaw needs and about relocating families before it does anything.
>
> And the very fact that there is a board helps make RLA respond to real needs of the community.

Whatever else is being questioned, it is clear that MICCO has gotten some citizens involved in the planning of Shaw, and some community needs will be met because of their role. But what happens to it as a broad-based community organization is still very uncertain.

LONG-RANGE IMPACT

Although the four programs discussed in this chapter vary widely in their goals, budgets, and achievements, they all have some things in common. Because all of the programs require citizen participation in one degree or another the people who have participated in designing them have developed a new sophistication in uncovering community needs and in designing programs to meet these needs.

The four organizations are also at least partially responsible for a new policy in the District government which may have some widespread effects on social services in the future. Because of so many new federal programs, some of them with overlapping goals and areas of operation, the District government was forced to look at its own social-service delivery system and redesign its planning processes. Instead of planning on a citywide basis, officials have divided the city into nine service areas. Each service area has a citizen board that works with city officials to plan for the development of the programs for its area. As a result, the District now has the benefit of being able to use the information that the Model Cities Commission gathers on community needs to design its own social-service programs. Because the Model Cities program has already found the gaps in services, the city does not have to duplicate the data-collection process and can plan on the basis of information already at hand.

This added sophistication also is responsible for the District's new policy of holding open community hearings on long-range plans to build new facilities. "What this means is that the citizens will be able to say to the city, we need another school here or we don't want an incinerator built in our neighborhood," according to Diana Josephson, a director of the city's Office of Community Services. She concluded,

> When we held the hearings [for the first time last year], not only did community people come, but they came prepared. They have become very sophisticated in planning how to spend money through their community organizations, and they intend to use that sophistication to make local government respond to their needs for services.

The four organizations discussed have also proven to be a training ground for black administrators. Indeed, some of the District's top officials have gained their experience in these programs. (For example, James Banks, former UPO director, now heads the city's housing administration.) And many of the programs also have provided jobs and a job ladder for people who otherwise might have been left out of the job market altogether.

Many observers believe that while the Nixon Administration's revenue-sharing proposal, which would give the District a block grant to provide social services, would change UPO, Model Cities, and PIC, it would not totally destroy them as community organizations. According to one OEO official,

> There is every reason to believe that these organizations have built up constituencies of their own during their existence. And even if

they don't get money, the citizens who participated in the design of programs which addressed themselves to real community needs will never again let the District government ignore them. They may exist in the form of settlement houses again, but they will certainly be more sophisticated and better equipped to *force* government to respond to them.

Despite the optimism of some, city officials realize that because some Congressmen take a special interest in how federal programs work in the District there may be some interference in the programming of block grants. And, they believe, if this happens, citizen input into the programs may dwindle.

All of these programs were designed to close a gap of one kind or another; whatever becomes of them as federally funded community organizations, they have succeeded in closing those gaps. And in the District of Columbia at least, these organizations have assured that the gap between government and the people will never be permitted to open as wide as it was at the beginning of the 1960s.

Chapter Nine

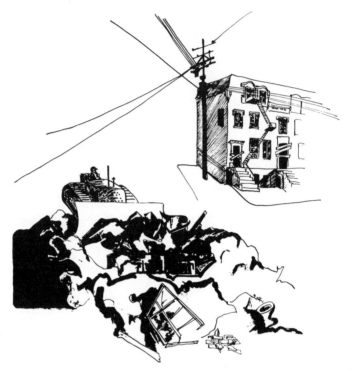

URBAN RENEWAL AND HOUSING: RHETORIC AND REALITY

by Eugene L. Meyer

American legislative history is replete with rhetoric of great promises. American social history, however, has reflected to a large degree the failure to live up to them. Nowhere is this more true, sadly, than in the highly touted programs to rebuild the cities and to provide a decent home in a pleasant environment for all Americans.

From the New Deal to the Great Society, bills have been enacted into law which, their supporters claimed, would eradicate urban poverty or, at least, minimize the physical discomfort of being poor.

In 1934, the Federal Housing Administration (FHA) was created to insure mortgages at below-market rates. The 1937 housing act authorized construction of low-income public housing by new local authorities with substantial federal subsidies. The 1949 housing act promised "the realization as soon as feasible of the goal of a decent home and a suitable living environment for every American family." It sought to do this through urban renewal, meaning slum clearance and grants to lower the cost of land to private redevelopers. The 1950s and 1960s produced other new programs and new rules.

Washington, the nation's capital, has often been the testing ground—if not always the proving ground—for many of the new programs. The District had the country's first large-scale urban-renewal project. It had its own public-housing authority three years before the rest of the country. In the late 1960s and early 1970s it received more riot recovery aid—and sooner—than other American cities (Table 10).

Table 10

FEDERAL URBAN RENEWAL GRANTS TO WASHINGTON, D. C.

(Cumulative Through April 1972)

Southwest	$ 49.6 million
Columbia Plaza [a]	.1
Northwest #1	23.3
Northeast #1 [b]	7.8
Fort Lincoln	12.9
Neighborhood Development Program [c]	96.8
Anacostia-Bolling (proposed)	—
TOTAL	$190.5 million

[a] Begun in 1960, this 18-acre project was overshadowed by the adjacent Watergate complex. Private developers spent $27 million for 800 luxury apartments, 30,000 square feet of retail space, and underground parking for 1,200 cars.

[b] Just east of Northwest #1, this 82-acre area was set aside for commercial and light industrial use. By early 1972, 19 enterprises had been completed, most of them displaced by other urban-renewal projects.

[c] The NDP program, initiated in 1968, funds projects on a year-to-year basis rather than all at once. The NDP areas are Shaw, 14th Street, N. W., and H Street, N. E. (the three 1968 riot coridors), and downtown Washington.

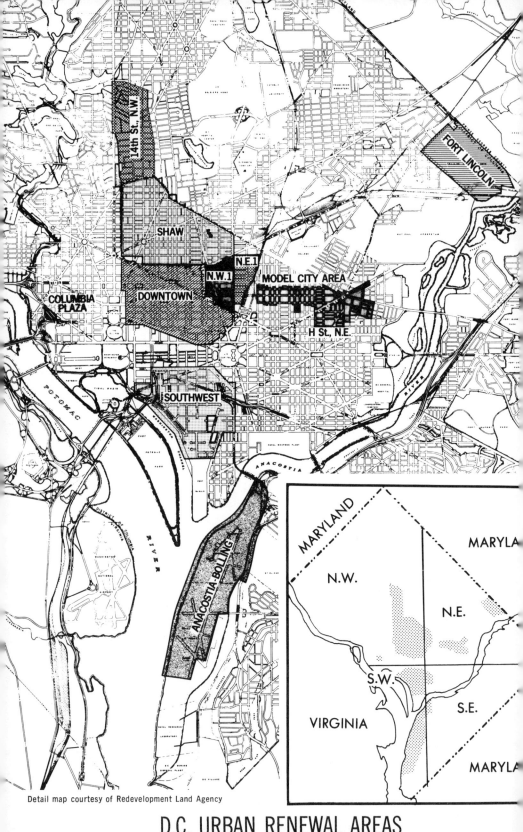

14th St., N.W.

FORT LINCOLN

SHAW

N.E.1

NW.1

MODEL CITY AREA

COLUMBIA PLAZA

DOWNTOWN

H St., N.E.

SOUTHWEST

POTOMAC

ANACOSTIA

ANACOSTIA-BOLLING

RIVER

MARYLAND

MARYLA

N.W.

N.E.

S.W.

VIRGINIA

S.E.

MARYLA

Detail map courtesy of Redevelopment Land Agency

D.C. URBAN RENEWAL AREAS

Yet, for all its head starts, for all the official expressions of concern and federal largesse lavished on it, Washington's performance reflects a mixed scorecard at best. At worst, it is a record of monumental failure.

RENEWAL

Washington's renewal efforts have reflected both the attitudes and the programs that prevailed at different times.

In Southwest Washington, there was large-scale bulldozing and 23,220 people, mostly poor and black, were displaced without being consulted. A new community composed largely of upper-income whites took their place. The outcry created by this upheaval designed in the 1950s led to the zoning out of all luxury housing in the next renewal area in the early 1960s. The plan for this area—building new housing for poor people only without providing necessary social services as well—was then attacked as merely gilding the ghetto.

In the middle and late 1960s, citizen participation became an article of faith in the gospel of the Great Society. In renewal especially, rhetoric seemed to substitute for action—the rhetoric of the streets added to that of the politicians. Community control seemed almost an end in itself. There was only a vague vision that there should be "no more Southwests" nor any more public housing reservations.

For the community groups that played a decisive role in the late 1960s, the pendulum of power is swinging partially back downtown in the early 1970s as the city's renewal authority, the Redevelopment Land Agency (RLA), seeks to reassert its powers. Many of the RLA policymakers are now blacks who feel that citizen involvement got lost in a political thicket. They are determined to find it again.

Meanwhile, nearly $100 million in federal funds has been poured into renewal of Washington's riot corridors. Most has been spent buying up property for redevelopment. Except for interim assistance parks, high-intensity sodium vapor lights installed as an anti-crime measure, and one completed apartment building, there isn't much to show.

Recent housing legislation has created new subsidy programs and tax incentives to speed up production and lure investors into the subsidized housing field. The future of these programs—and of urban renewal generally—is now clouded. New federal policies discourage further concentrations of subsidized housing. Washington's Metropolitan Council of Governments has adopted a voluntary "fair share" plan to distribute such housing throughout the region. New legislation is being considered that would create metropolitan housing authorities.

A maze of disparate alphabet-soup agencies, some technically federal but mainly hybrid and unique to the nation's capital, grapple for solutions. The National Capital Planning Commission does initial planning and, with the city council, approves renewal plans, which the RLA implements.

Funding is almost entirely outside the pale of the District budget process, coming mostly from direct federal grants. The federal government has intervened from administration to administration and project to project. For the most part, however, Washington has been left to sink or swim in its own quagmire.

And behind it all remain the basic questions that are, after two decades of renewal, still unanswered. As expressed by George O. Walker, III, equal-opportunity officer of the D. C. area office of the Department of Housing and Urban Development, here are the issues:

> If you tear down properties, what are you going to put in there? And where will you put the people? Where do you relocate them? Do you build first in the suburbs, then tear down inner city slums? There are blacks with roots planted in the city who want to stay there. What do you do with these people in the meantime, and how many can actually come back?

From Rags to Riches

The same questions were being asked 20 years ago when the planners began looking at urban renewal. They were not asked, however, with the same urgency. The country had different priorities and values then. Washington reflected them. South of the Mason-Dixon line, Washington was a Southern city, roughly one-third black. Its 1950 comprehensive plan called for dual schools, dual parks, dual playgrounds. Segregation was the norm.

In 1946, Congress created the D. C. Redevelopment Land Agency. By 1949, with the passage of urban renewal, the RLA was ready to begin carrying out its mandate to eliminate slum and blighted areas. Southwest was its first, and for a decade, its only project.

Southwest existed as a community before Washington. It was known as Carrollsburg, and, of the neighborhoods within the District, only Georgetown is older. When the capital moved to the Potomac in 1800, Southwest became home for rich and influential people. With the Civil War and Reconstruction, the demography changed. Poor blacks poured into Washington. Many of them crowded into ramshackle "alley dwellings" quickly erected by rapacious realtors. Southwest had more than its share of this unique Washington institution.

Alley dwellings still existed in large numbers as Washington approached mid-20th century. The sight of them silhouetted against the Capitol of the "Free World" made a devastating picture, widely circulated abroad by America's critics.

There was some doubt about whether to tear Southwest down completely or whether to try to preserve the neighborhood and improve it. The National Capital Planning Commission favored preservation. The RLA wanted to raze the slum buildings on the 440-acre site and start all over again. The RLA won. Only seven rowhouses from the Carrollsburg era were restored.

Of Southwest's 5,000 living units, 76 percent were substandard. In 1951, 77 percent of the 23,220 residents were nonwhite; two thirds earned less than $3,600 a year.

The relocation of the first family in 1953 was considered a great cause for rejoicing. The federal urban renewal required that displaced families "be assisted in finding decent, safe and sanitary housing elsewhere." And, indeed, in terms of the housing situation two decades ago, most did improve their housing conditions through relocation. What they lost was their neighborhood.

According to the RLA, 46 percent were relocated to Southeast Washington; only 12 percent stayed in Southwest, east of the urban-renewal area.[1] Today, many apartment houses stand vacant and vandalized in parts of Southeast, the result of crowding large, poor

---

[1] Daniel Thursz, WHERE ARE THEY NOW? (Washington: Health and Welfare Council of the National Capital Area, 1966). Study based on interviews with sample of former Southwest residents.

families into small units, some of them undoubtedly filled with refugees from the renewal bulldozers.

The 2,000 units of public housing in Southwest, of World War II and 1950s vintage, are now among the worst in the city. The public housing is separated from the new Southwest by Delaware Avenue. The low-income tenants call the dividing thoroughfare "The Berlin Wall."

Such "Future Shock" was lost in the euphoria over the pioneer experiment that was Southwest. As urbanologist Jeanne Lowe has written approvingly, "Those who governed the District decided that Southwest should be beautiful." [2]

Southwest would bring back the white families who were fleeing to the suburbs, the boosters argued. The tax base, they said, would be improved. By such standards, Southwest was a big success. Today's resident population of 11,000 is 78 percent white and almost exclusively upper-income. Some 60,000 federal workers commute to the area, mainly from the suburbs. As for the tax base, Southwest yielded $592,000 before renewal. In 1970, the city derived $3.2 million in property taxes from Southwest.

The National Capital Planning Commission's 1951 plan for preserving the old neighborhood was met with a proposal for sweeping change from RLA. In accord with planning principles then in vogue, land use was to be strictly segregated. The grand design called for an affluent residental section, a freeway, a rebuilt waterfront, a shop-lined bridge (known as the Ponte Vecchio, after a similar structure in Florence, Italy) linking the waterfront and an acquarium across the channel in East Potomac Park, and a magnificent raised esplanade from the Mall to the waterfront.

In February 1954, builder William Zeckendorf was engaged to do the final plan. His firm of Webb and Knapp would do much of the building. Zeckendorf promised to give Washington in Southwest "the cosmopolitan atmosphere of a great world capital."

A series of decisions and circumstances combined to change the plans. Highway planners objected to the planned routing of the Southwest freeway along the railroad right-of-way. The road wound up alternately elevated and depressed and slicing Southwest neatly

---

[2] Jeanne Lowe, CITIES IN A RACE WITH TIME (New York: Random House, 1967), p. 200.

in half, dividing federal office buildings and the L'Enfant Plaza office-hotel complex from the residential and waterfront areas.

L'Enfant Plaza and L'Enfant Mall, which grew out of the raised esplanade idea, held much promise. Zeckendorf said the mall would be to Washington "what the Champs Elysees is to Paris or the Piazza San Marco to Venice." It was to be the gateway to Southwest. In the plaza area, there were to be sidewalk cafes, fountains, theaters, skating rinks, a performing-arts center. Below, on a separate level, there were to be large stores and small ones. The Mall was to end in an overlook, with parking underneath.

Several things happened to shatter the vision, or at least alter it substantially. In 1965, Zeckendorf went broke before starting the project. The Rockefellers came in to build the L'Enfant Plaza complex, with the RLA assuming responsibility for the Mall. Downtown merchants opposed any large department stores at L'Enfant Plaza, so none were located there. The performing-arts complex was built in Foggy Bottom instead, as the John F. Kennedy Center. The acquarium and the Ponte Vecchio died in Congress. Without the bridge, there were no bidders for the garage under the overlook. Today, the whole project looks magnificent but empty. The Forrestal Building straddles the entrance to the Mall at Independence Avenue. The Mall leads to nowhere. The offices and 39 arcade-level shops of L'Enfant Plaza are occupied weekdays but deserted nights and weekends. The whole project bears no physical or spiritual relationship to the rest of Southwest.

The waterfront idea changed, too. It was conceived as a promenade of small shops and refreshment stands for all ages and income brackets. Instead, it is winding up with two or three large restaurants and decked parking.

In the residential section, a plan to require that one third of 1,020 rental units be low-income ($17 a room) was dropped in 1959 because there were no subsidy programs then to support such social goals.

Integrated new housing was a revolutionary aspect of renewal in the then-Southern city. Racial integration worked in Southwest, but not economic mixing. The Amidon School, opened in 1960 to serve the new Southwest, is now filled with the children of the poor, while middle-class children—black and white—attend private schools.

Today's Southwest continues to reflect the tensions built into it by the planners. There are no corner groceries and other needed neighborhood services. The shopping is done in one suburban-style center.

The lack of economic mix continues to haunt Southwest. There are only 310 units of moderate-income housing (with a waiting list of 500) in the renewal area and no low-income housing west of Delaware Avenue.

What may be the final chapter in this drama over housing low-income families in Southwest is now being written on a 3.3-acre piece of land across the freeway from HUD. The 50-year-old Southwest Community House, liberal homeowners and tenants, church and civil-rights groups are backing 84 units of low- and moderate-income family housing for the site. Other residents, the L'Enfant Plaza corporations, and waterfront interests favor a 266-unit high rise for the elderly with underground parking for the restaurants.

Before urban renewal, Southwest "was a jungle," says Watson Rulon of Hogate's restaurant. "Any direction was up. The waterfront can be the jewel in the crown of this development or its worst flop." And the setting for the jewel, Rulon says, is parking.

But Clara Brown, a public-housing tenant, summed up the bitterness felt by many over Southwest. At a stormy public hearing over the disputed site, she said:

> The shouting of a few of us is almost over. . . . The scream and pain of living in the servants quarters of this vast Southwest Plantation is unfortunately real. . . . The beauty of Southwest is superficial. . . . Thirty-six congressmen live in this area and hundreds of government officials and you ask yourself . . . where are you going when Public Housing says you are no longer eligible [because of over-income]. . . . Where do you go. Back to the ghetto. . . . Just a few years ago the newspapers were filled and the radio was blasting news about the new Southwest. But today there is silence because the million dollar corporations have taken over Southwest at the expense of human lives.

The Reaction Sets In

The Southwest experience gave America the phrase "Negro removal" and a battle cry, "No more Southwests." By the 1960s, such large-scale razing of neighborhoods and displacement of blacks was out of tune with the civil-rights motifs of the national administrations. It was also bad politics. For every action, there is a reaction. The reaction to Southwest was Northwest One.

The guiding principle in Northwest One—a 117-acre trapezoid a few blocks from the Capitol—was renewal for the residents, who were poor. Further, unlike renewal in Southwest, renewal in Northwest One would be staged so that many original buildings would remain standing until new ones could rise, with the goal of minimizing displacement.

There would be only moderate-income apartments (with 20 percent of the tenants getting an additional subsidy under the federal rent-supplement program) and public housing. There would be no luxury housing. As it turned out, there would also be few services for a population desperately needing them. And while many of the residents who were displaced were temporarily housed elsewhere, the 20 percent that chose to return or remain were the area's poorest. The small middle class, always the people with the most options, never came back.

Of 1,003 dwelling units in Northwest One, 829 were substandard. Forty-five percent of the population of 7,000 was poor enough to qualify for public housing. One small block had over 600 children crowded into some of the city's worst housing. The 1963 urban-renewal plan called for 1,766 units (later increased to 1,780 —710 low-income, 1,070 moderate-income). There were to be 566 units of public housing and 241 rehabilitated homes. The population after renewal would be increased to 8,500.

A public-housing project, Sibley Plaza, was the first building completed in 1968. It contained high-rise apartments, mostly for the elderly, and townhouses for families. A nearby 199-unit project, sponsored by a Catholic church in the neighborhood, closely involved the future tenants in planning. The physical aspects of Northwest One were generally applauded. But social problems soon surfaced.

Three years later, one quarter of the planned units had been built, and the problems remained: lack of schools, lack of medical facilities, lack of shopping. One hundred and eighty businesses, mostly small and family-owned, had been moved out by renewal; many were unable to survive the dislocation.

In October 1970, in a draft report (heavily sanitized in the final version), Roy Priest, the Northwest One project director, described his sense of frustration:

> Northwest One has for all practical purposes zoned out the middle class. For all that this "middle class" American has been disparaged, he is the backbone of the concept of "community". . . . When a family must fight for survival, it does not have time to worry about the quality of education, the lack of commercial development, recreation facilities, drug problems or the lack of job opportunities. . . . Urban renewal has built a concrete jungle rather than a community. . . . Ultimately, the project defeated itself, for NW1 will never provide a suitable environment for its residents.

The final version concluded somewhat less stridently:

> If major economic, social and human resources cannot be amassed immediately for launching an all out attack on the problems of the low- and moderate-income family, then our agency should begin developing new tools for creating diversified social, economic and ethnic communities that have a survival factor greater than zero.[3]

While Priest and others were complaining that renewal had merely gilded the ghetto in Northwest One, others asserted the project did not contain enough low-income housing and that rent in the moderate-income units was inflated. Tyler House, for example, rented one-bedroom units for $130, three bedrooms for $194. Further, the Federal Housing Administration had allowed 20 percent of Tyler House's 298 units to rent to families earning more than the usual $12,200 ceiling.

As Northwest One nears its scheduled 1973 date of completion, its problems persist. The school planners wanted to build a new elementary school at North Capitol and H Streets because, they said, renewal would result in 1,473 more children than originally anticipated. But the city's housing authority wanted to erect 51 townhouses (with 200 more children) on the same site for families displaced by urban renewal elsewhere in the city. If the school were allowed to use some adjacent land for its playground, Northwest One could wind up with both, serving mainly to magnify the dilemma.

---

[3] Redevelopment Land Agency, WHERE ARE WE NOW: AN ANALYSIS OF NW #1 URBAN RENEWAL PROJECT TO DATE, ITS SUCCESSES, ITS FAILURE AND SOME SUGGESTIONS FOR CHANGE (Washington: Redevelopment Land Agency, February 1971), p. 55.

Hurry Up and Wait

> "Mayor Washington . . . has prom-
> ised me a . . . timetable under which
> construction in these areas would
> begin next fall."—*President Nixon,*
> *January 31, 1969*

The Rev. Dr. Martin Luther King, Jr., was assassinated on April 4, 1968. That night and for two successive nights, hundreds of buildings in Washington's black ghettoes went up in flames in a fiery catharsis of black rage and frustration. When the smoke cleared, the damage totalled $12.6 million. Three principle business arteries in black neighborhoods were badly hurt: 14th Street, the heart of Cardozo, suffered $6.6 million worth of damage; 7th Street just north of downtown, the main business section of Shaw, $4.2 million; H Street, N. E., $1.8 million in damages.

These three areas became known as "the riot corridors." After the rioting, they looked like pictures of bombed-out London after the German blitz. The hustle and bustle of these streets were replaced with piles of rubble. Inadvertently, however, the riots served as a catalyst to spur new planning efforts in the areas. Four years after the 1968 riots, nearly $100 million has been spent acquiring properties for redevelopment, but there is little physical evidence of it. The debris has been cleared; 250 damaged buildings have been demolished and replaced with 18 "interim assistance" parks and playgrounds; high-intensity lighting has been installed to deter crime; and a couple of holes in the ground testify to rebuilding just getting underway. But, as of mid 1972, only one new building and 40 renovated rowhouses are completed, and these are in Shaw, which started urban renewal two years before the riots.

"It's easy in a few days to destroy what has been built over generations," says Melvin Mister, executive director of RLA. "But the job of replacement is not done easily or quickly."

But back in the post-riot period of 1968 and 1969, an air of euphoria pervaded renewal circles over the rebuilding of the riot corridors. Citizen involvement was at its height. It was fashionable. It was, to many people, a panacea and an end in itself. There was no hint that the great experiment would be in shambles by 1972.

There was also a great show of activity. Meetings involving citizens and officials were held with much fanfare.

Mayor Walter E. Washington created, in August 1968, the Reconstruction Development Corporation (with a $600,000 Ford Foundation grant) to plan 14th and H Streets using a dozen paid "community fellows" to talk to residents. Shaw already had the Model Inner City Community Organization (MICCO) doing this.

President Nixon made riot renewal his major urban commitment. Early in 1969, he visited 7th Street, N. W., and let it be known that he expected the dirt to start flying in Shaw that September and in the other two areas by December. He also committed $30 million to help get the District started on the project. There was an air of excitement. Something was being done. Then it all fell apart. Gradually.

President Nixon's deadlines for action passed without any action. Ground was broken on the lone apartment building in Shaw in December 1969, 15 months behind schedule. At the ceremony, HUD Secretary George M. Romney pledged another $28.1 million for rebuilding. Urban-renewal plans for Shaw had been approved in early 1969. Plans for H and 14th Streets received HUD approval in early 1970.

But neither plans nor money—most of which is used to buy and assemble parcels for development—could get renewal moving.

The delays were especially frustrating since the riot areas were placed under the Neighborhood Development Program (NDP) created by the 1968 Housing Act. NDP was supposed to speed up the process. The traditional kind of renewal that took place in Southwest required completion of planning for the entire area before HUD would commit a cent. In NDP, smaller "action" areas are planned and funded on a year-by-year basis.

NDP wasn't working, but the experts blamed other factors for the delay. The inflation spiral of the late 1960s was ballooning construction costs far in excess of HUD ceilings. Nonprofit sponsors, usually well-meaning church groups, were taking an understandably long time to master the maze of government subsidy programs. Also, the odd-sized lots cleared from the riot rubble were difficult to market to developers interested in economies of scale.

The citizen participation issue plagued both the 14th and H Street programs. On H Street, the Model Cities Commissioners from that area vied for power with a coalition of citizen groups.

HUD required that they get together and form a Project Area Committee (PAC). In February 1972, the H Street PAC signed its first funding contract with RLA for $175,000 to hire a staff of 10.

On 14th Street, two separate groups received planning funds from RLA. Early in 1971, HUD required that the consultants working for the citizen groups contract directly with RLA. HUD also required that a PAC be created. The two consultants put their relatives on the payroll, and RLA in July 1971, revoked their $232,500 contract. By July 1972, a 14th Street PAC had yet to be certified by HUD, but elections were held June 24 to constitute the new committee. Meanwhile, the planning had come to a virtual halt. One project, a $3 million community health center, had been approved.

Some of the issues in urban renewal have come to a head in the changing relationship between MICCO and RLA. Some within RLA feel that MICCO represents primarily the political interests of its founder, D.C. delegate Walter E. Fauntroy, and the financial interests of his supporters rather than the people of Shaw.

The political issue served as a backdrop for recent disputes over two sites and in negotiations with RLA over a new contract. When MICCO's old contract expired in October 1971, the organization sought more money to hire staff to deal directly wtih developers. RLA wanted to restrict MICCO's activities to planning and to get away from past practices in which MICCO negotiated with developers. Instead, it wanted open competition for sites.

The political issue exploded into the open with charges by competing community groups of conflict of interest. The charges were directed at Fauntroy and some of his associates closely tied to MICCO who had various contracts in Shaw renewal.

RLA won on all counts. It voted to put the largest housing tract in Shaw out for competitive bidding after MICCO had already selected a developer that had offered to hire friends of Fauntroy. MICCO lost a second dispute over what to build on a 1.09-acre site along 7th Street. RLA forced Fauntroy to quit as president of MICCO by threatening not to refund the organization. On February 24, MICCO capitulated, approving a contract that Fauntroy contended destroyed the essence of citizen involvement.

In typical agency understatement, Melvin Mister said, "The board has been increasingly concerned about the whole issue of our relationship with community organizations."

The whole notion of competition for inner-city sites was novel. It was encouraged by a 1969 federal tax law which offered investors using limited-dividend corporations generous tax-depreciation credits in return for the use of their capital for subsidized housing.

The idea put forth by RLA was that it would employ "competitive negotiation," cranking in such intangibles as community involvement, minority hiring, and the like. The procedure signaled a move away from the inexperienced nonprofits and a new courting of large firms with established track records.

The first invitation to bid on 225 units of low- and moderate-income housing in the H Street corridor was issued in the summer of 1971. Applying the lessons of Shaw, the RLA issued strict conflict-of-interest guidelines for the PAC members who would recommend one of eight bidders. As it happened, these rules eliminated from voting half the PAC that belonged to an organization which was a co-bidder. The project went instead to a California-based limited-dividend group.

The stark fact about renewal of the riot corridors is that so little has been built. An important factor in the delay has been the lack of available dwellings for the relocation of residents and, tied closely to it, the lack of a clear definition of the target population that is to be the beneficiary of rebuilding.

The relocation issue began to surface in June 1970, when development plans for the second year of NDP were trimmed from $37.5 million to $30.4 million. The reason given for the cut was the lack of relocation housing.

In November 1970, the RLA staff contrasted the type of housing planned for the corridors with the needs of people there. The staff found a 2,696-unit surplus of moderate-income housing and a shortage of 725 low-income units. In other words, the plans fell far short of providing housing for the present residents and would, in effect, transform the character of the neighborhoods from low- to moderate-income. In fact, only 54 units of public housing are planned for Shaw, where 60 percent of the population of 33,000 qualifies for public housing. On H and 14th Streets, community groups have opposed any public housing in their planning.

In March 1971, RLA director Mister wrote city officials that the shortage of low-income housing needed for relocation was so acute that no new projects could be planned until housing already scheduled was built.

The basic problem is that neither community groups nor redevelopment officials have really defined their goals for renewal except in generalities and platitudes. Should Shaw rehouse all its poor? Should some be relocated elsewhere? What are the city's resources to relocate them outside their old neighborhood? How many would be willing to leave? How many want to stay?

Various studies have suggested the alternatives: rehouse the middle class first to create stability; build subsidized high rises with few large units for large families; build garden apartments and townhouses to accommodate the large families at lower rents.[4]

Another consideration is HUD's new site selection criteria. If strictly followed, these criteria would severely curtail inner-city construction of subsidized housing that would further concentrate low-income minority families. In other words, no more Northwest Ones.

At MICCO's sixth annual meeting on January 29, 1972, Terry C. Chisholm, director of HUD's D. C. area office, pleaded with the community group to

> deal with . . . tough questions. How much subsidized housing do you want in Shaw? Do you want merely low-income families housed in Shaw first, or only low-income families housed in Shaw? That's an important issue you have to tackle. Do you think the time has come to build some unsubsidized housing on parcels in Shaw? Nixon's commitment to the inner city still stands. However, it must be accomplished within new guidelines.

If anybody was listening, it was not readily apparent. MICCO was busy fighting the power game with RLA.

The New Town Escape

Urban renewal was put to a unique test in the proposal to build a new town at Fort Lincoln in Northeast Washington. So far it has not passed.

---

[4] Linton, Mields & Costin, OPPORTUNITIES AND CONSTRAINTS RELATED TO HOUSING PRODUCTION IN NDP AREAS (Washington: Linton, Mields & Costin, May 1971).

Fort Lincoln is the former home of the National Training School for Boys, a hilly site 335 acres large and mostly vacant. It is owned by the federal government and is now used as a Job Corps Center.

In August 1967, Lyndon Johnson had envisioned Fort Lincoln as an innovative way to use federal surplus land to ease the crushing problems of the inner city. It would be, in LBJ's words, "more than a housing project . . . the best of communities." Fort Lincoln would set a precedent for use of other federal surplus land in metropolitan areas across the country. It would be a monument to the urban-minded President from rural Texas. Some referred to it as "Fort Lyndon."

LBJ wanted to start a new town for 25,000 before the 1968 elections. The first authorized project was comprised of 400 subsidized housing units on 20 acres. A grant of $12.9 million was reserved and nearly $1 million more was allocated for planning.

The RLA hired nationally known urban expert Edward F. Logue to draw up a master plan. Logue's plan emerged in 1968. It discarded LBJ's emphasis on subsidized housing for what Logue called a socially, racially, economically, and functionally well-balanced community. The new town, in order to succeed, must go "first class," Logue insisted, with innovative schools, an internal minirail transportation system, and other amenities.

As with other Great Society programs, citizen involvement was to be of prime importance in Fort Lincoln. For two years, however, competing groups spent more time fighting for power than discussing the project. They united on one issue: they opposed the heavy low-income emphasis, leaving one building, a 120-unit public-housing project for the elderly, as the legacy of the initial effort.

The Nixon Administration had made a public commitment to rebuild the riot corridors. Fort Lincoln was seen as an LBJ project out of line with the new administration's priorities. In September 1970, HUD balked at funding the Fort Lincoln plan but authorized further study.

The RLA sounded out developers in 1970 and asked them to bid on the project. One developer would plan and build the entire project, a departure from traditional urban renewal. Eight major firms submitted bids.

A revived Mayor's Citizens Advisory Committee on Fort Lincoln narrowed them down to three. The two frontrunners were the Rouse Company, builder of Columbia, Maryland, and a joint venture led by Westinghouse. Rouse made the mistake of showing up with an all-white team. Westinghouse was more sophisticated and cynical: It reshuffled its all-white team at the last minute and put a black man nominally out front. The committee picked Westinghouse, and so did RLA.

The other half of the joint venture was Building Systems International, a Texas-based company affiliated with the French-Italian Balency System of industrialized housing. The Westinghouse-BSI planning effort was shrouded in secrecy—and with good reason, given community sensitivities. What emerged was, again, substantially different from the Logue plan that preceded it. To be "economically feasible" and to ensure integration, it would have to be even more middle-class than Logue's plan. The plan contrasted with the rhetoric of the Westinghouse-BSI brochure the previous fall. That had promised that Fort Lincoln would provide housing "desparately needed to replace old houses in slum areas." The brochure had also promised an industrialized housing factory, but instead of the 1,500 jobs promised, there would be about 150. Westinghouse ruled out Logue's internal minirail as too expensive but proposed to build a transit link to a nearby Metro station.

Just before Christmas 1971, a bombshell exploded in the papers. Westinghouse, with no federal assurances of funds for the transit line and other technological innovations, decided to drop out of the joint venture. BSI maintained the town could work without the features that Logue considered essential. It promised other advances in the social area, such as 75 percent home ownership and mixing of all income groups in the same building.

The total cost of Fort Lincoln was put at $245 million, with $203 million in private funds for land acquisition, housing, community facilities, offices, and shops. There was a GSA commitment to lease office space. And there would be additional funds from HUD, although nobody could say how much. President Nixon promised in February 1972, that the new town would ride his bicentennial gravy train as part of the Spirit of '76.

New Hopes, Old Fears

The 1968 riots had a major impact on Washington's old downtown retail core between the Capitol and the White House. After the riots, tourists stayed away from Washington, and the historic Willard Hotel at 14th Street and Pennsylvania Avenue shut its doors.

The area east of 14th Street grew increasingly seedy, with pornography shops proliferating and replacing more conventional stores. Meanwhile, the "new" downtown, west of 14th Street, grew without urban renewal. Block after block of new office buildings with few retail shops rose almost as far west as Washington Circle. At the same time, suburban shopping malls were sprouting and thriving.

The riots which "alienated" affluent whites from shopping in old downtown resulted in attracting a new clientele among lower and middle-income blacks. With the inner-city retail areas burned out, blacks went shopping downtown in large numbers for the first time. Business increased, and so did the number of black merchants. Despite the seedy outward appearance of much of the area, old downtown still contains many specialty shops and small businesses not found in the suburban malls or the antiseptic offices of new downtown. Much of the striking Victorian architecture remains in the squat buildings.

Why, then, urban renewal for downtown?

Because, basically, Washington's white power structure—the Board of Trade, the D. C. Realtors Association, the Convention and Visitors Bureau—has refused to accept the reality of a predominantly black city. These groups continue to nurture hopes of attracting the suburban shoppers back to the city, of making the downtown once again a place for the housewife from Wesley Heights.

In 1960, they banded together into a group called Downtown Progress. Meticulously secret about its activities, Downtown Progress has worked closely with the RLA. Its public list of directors has nurtured the belief among many small merchants downtown that Big Business wants to bulldoze them into oblivion to serve its own interests.

The proponents of renewal saw the whole picture differently. They saw the downtown dying with all the commercial development and taxes going to the suburbs. The new Presidential Building, at 12th Street and Pennsylvania Avenue, for example, had been unable to rent its ground floor retail space for two years. Much office space was vacant and bankers refused to discuss development loans for downtown. An image of crime and seediness was dooming the area, they said.

In the new Metro subway—with two major lines scheduled to cut through the downtown—they saw a golden opportunity to turn the situation around. They predicted that the activity generated by Metro would change the investment climate. Zoning incentives were also proposed to entice developers to include amenities, such as building setbacks from the street. There were also proposals for a public parking authority to attract off-peak shoppers with low short-term rates and discourage commuters with high all-day rates.

All these plans depended on congressional action. For 14 months, the Metro construction was held up by the highway lobby in Congress. Construction is now well underway, however. The parking lobby has effectively stalled the authority idea, even in a watered-down form, for the foreseeable future.

It was against this background that the National Capital Planning Commission and the city council formally declared the downtown an urban-renewal area in January 1969. Not just an urban-renewal area but an NDP area. By December 1972, RLA had spent $24 million buying property there for redevelopment.

The first-year plan called for purchase of sites mostly on 7th Street just below Shaw. The second-year plan focused on two proposed subway stops. Some of the 126 small businessmen facing displacement banded together into Businessmen Affected Severely by Yearly Action Plans, Inc. (BASYAP). They decided to fight urban renewal. Picking up the cry of the inner-city blacks, they complained that they had been left out of the planning process. BASYAP went to court in 1970 and succeeded in holding up property acquisition by RLA around the two subway stops for seven months, until July 1971.

The city council voiced concern for the fate of small businesses on June 25, 1970, when it approved the second-year plan with the strict proviso that the merchants be included in planning, that they not be displaced for 18 months, and that RLA come back by January 1971 with a more detailed plan for downtown.

A year later, the consultants hired by RLA offered a vision of a downtown with international specialty shops, towering office buildings with rooftop restaurants, auto-free pedestrian malls and covered arcades, and housing for the affluent. They concluded that downtown would never recapture its former role as the regional shopping center. Additional large department stores would be economically impractical. They predicted that even inner-city shoppers would eventually drift away to other redeveloped areas of the District. Downtown's future as a retail area, they said, lay in providing specialty shops that are lacking in the suburban Malls.[5]

The consultants called for 70 percent of the retail space at the subway stops to be rented by variety shops instead of the banks and airline offices that leased space in the new downtown. Eighteen percent would be for small shops and minority businessmen. At one of the subway stations the shops would have an international theme.

While RLA's consultants released their report, another consultants' report for the House Public Works Committee was recommending construction of a $100 million convention center-sports arena on a 25-acre downtown site. The idea was not inconsistent with RLA plans, although RLA later said it favored a smaller site. The problem was that the proposal threatened to displace 189 businesses, including a substantial part of Chinatown, displaced once before in the 1920s to make way for the Federal Triangle.

To small businessmen, like Mrs. Amelia Rifesnyder, in her late 70s and proprietor of a secondhand book shop, the noose was tightening. "The small businessmen are being shoved around," she told a reporter. "We're just thrown around like an old shoe." Urban renewal offered inadequate benefits for the Mrs. Rifesnyders to start all over again. Downtown Progress had proposed in 1970 that small businesses have their rents subsidized in new buildings for a few years, but so far nothing has come of it.

By the summer of 1971, the small businessmen had found an ally in a local architect who proposed that the old retail buildings be rehabilitated and that new office buildings be erected on stilts above them. The plan had the support of *The Washington Post* and the National Capital Planning Commission. It was strongly

---

[5] Okamoto-Liskamm/Development Research Associates, DESIGN AND DEVELOPMENT PROGRAM, DOWNTOWN WASHINGTON, D.C. (San Francisco: Okamoto-Liskamm/Development Research Associates, 1971).

opposed by RLA, which cited structural difficulties in the approach.[6] The city council, formerly sympathetic to the small merchants, was growing impatient by late 1971 with the lack of urban-renewal progress.

The face of downtown may be changing without urban renewal, however. In 1971, President Nixon reversed government policy that had encouraged location of federal offices in the District's suburbs. The General Services Administration was ordered to make every effort to stay inside the District.

Taking his cue from the President, one ambitious builder began buying up land both in and out of renewal "action" areas downtown and constructing buildings for GSA lease. Three were begun in 1971. The builder's representative also obtained approval from the city council to take out of renewal area a downtown square to allow the firm to build an office building.

Some questions about downtown urban renewal that remain unanswered were posed in a draft report prepared for a special city council commission studying redevelopment: "How much urban renewal is satisfactory? Is this going to be an intelligent, orderly facelifting, or a random, buckshot operation? . . . It is not entirely clear what is the ultimate objective of the program."

THE HOUSING PROGRAMS: NOBLE EXPERIMENTS THAT FAILED

Walk through the residential streets of Shaw and you will see old, dilapidated rowhouses that are inhabited next to ones that aren't. Throughout the District there are some 4,600 units vacant— most of them vandalized—and waiting to be renovated and there are 33,500 families poor enough to qualify for public housing, with another 17,000 families too poor even to afford public housing. Public housing accounts for 11,347 dwelling units in Washington—723 of them vacant and in need of repair before they can be occupied (Table 11). There are 5,000 families on the waiting list.

Some more statistics: According to the 1970 census, 180,000 people, or 24 percent of the D.C. population, live crowded more

---

[6] Redevelopment Land Agency, *Comments on the Air Rights Concept as Applied to the Downtown Urban Renewal Area 2d Year Action Sites*, October 1, 1971, mimeographed.

Table 11

PUBLIC HOUSING IN WASHINGTON, 1972

Type	Authorized	Actual
Conventional projects	9,361	9,295
Leased units	750	243
Turnkey projects (developer sells finished project to NCHA)	1,176	811
Buildings acquired and not rehabilitated	1,060	879
Buildings acquired and rehabilitated	728	119
TOTAL	13,075	11,347

Source: U.S. Department of Housing and Urban Development and National Capital Housing Authority.

than one to a room; 67,000 are jammmed more than 1.5 to a room. Forty-four percent of the children live more than one to a room, 7 percent more than 1.5 to a room. The 1970 census also showed an increase of 16,000 in the total number of housing units over the previous decade, but 3,700 fewer units of six bedrooms or more. The increase in housing supply had benefited small and medium-sized families, most of whom were already adequately housed, according to an analysis by the Washington Center for Metropolitan Studies.

The shortage in Washington's low-income housing is not a new problem. As mentioned above, at the end of the Civil War 30,000 freedmen flocked to Washington and were crowded into cheap alley dwellings. There was criticism of these dwellings from the start, but little action. In 1914, Congress outlawed their use after 1918, but the law was never enforced and was eventually ruled unconstitutional.

In 1934, Congress created the Alley Dwelling Authority (ADA) to rid the District of all such buildings in 10 years and to build low-rent housing for the former occupants. In the early 1940s, the ADA became the National Capital Housing Authority (NCHA).

"Bankrupt . . . From Every Point of View"

When James G. Banks, the present executive director of the NCHA, got his first job with the organization in 1945, the authority played a different game with different rules. Residents in Washington's then-segregated public housing were neither as black nor as disadvantaged as those of today. "There was more leeway to select tenants," Banks recalls. "You tended to pick the deserving poor, with good housekeeping habits and stable families."

In 1964, Mayor Walter E. Washington, then the NCHA executive director, explained the changes in the population and problems of public housing: "The problem essentially is that the increase in the income of our tenants did not match increases in the cost of operating services."

The problems that beset the NCHA by the late 1960s—maintenance, deficits, vandalism—were replicated in housing authorities across the country. Many poor blacks who migrated from the rural South to the cities were herded into large-scale public-housing projects in concentrated areas of the city without provisions to help them become upwardly mobile. More than half of Washington's public housing is located east of the Anacostia River; only one building, occupied by the elderly, is west of Rock Creek Park, the city's racial dividing line.

With mounting maintenance and other operating costs, the NCHA's financial picture plummeted. In 1966, per-unit monthly maintenance costs were $21.44; by 1970 they were $31.06. In 1966, the NCHA took in $60.95 a month per unit and had to spend only $57.14. In 1970, each unit ran an $18.19 monthly deficit, with the average operating expense at $83.45 and the average income at $65.29. For lack of funds, necessary maintenance was postponed and the properties deteriorated further.

"Residents who were accustomed to a higher grade of service became aware of the lowering standards and have become disgruntled," Banks acknowledged in February 1971. Relations between tenants and management were, he conceded, "strained and confused."

Conditions were aggrevated in the fall of 1969 when the NCHA sought to raise rents to cover rising operating costs. There were court suits and a tenant rent strike that lasted 9 months. In May 1970, the NCHA's financial picture was further affected by the so-called Brooke amendment to the 1969 housing act. The amendment lowered maximum rents to 25 percent of the tenant's income. NCHA would receive federal payments to make up the difference, but payments were delayed several months. Meanwhile, the rent increases went into effect for some families in July 1970.

The financial and administrative difficulties of the NCHA prompted HUD in the spring of 1970 to place a year-long freeze on new projects. The freeze resulted from an independent task-force report that concluded:

> The NCHA is in very serious trouble from every point of view. . . .
> To put it bluntly . . . NCHA is bankrupt. The staff, which includes
> many devoted and capable people, is a frustrated, indifferent bureauc-
> racy with little, if any, morale or spirit. There is no apparent sense
> of direction or force in administration.[7]

Despite promises of improvement, little had changed at the NCHA a year later. Vandalism continued at an alarming rate, amounting to $2.5 million in two years. Rent loss from the 600-odd vacant units amounted to $500,000 a year. The NCHA was spending another $430,000 annually just to keep the vacant units boarded up.

Apart from the discredited large-scale projects, the NCHA had been slow to use other less stigmatized scattered-site programs authorized for Washington in 1966. Of 350 units in sound buildings authorized for leasing by the NCHA and for subletting at public housing rents, only 221 had been secured. Of 204 rowhouses allocated to Washington for rehabilitation and rental to low-income tenants, only 119 had been completed. It was not that HUD hadn't provided the money or the programs for improvements. In fact, a $6.5 million modernization program had fallen far behind schedule because the NCHA proved simply incapable of spending the money.

Less than a year after the freeze began, some 40 HUD staffers spent nearly a month examining the NCHA.[8] Their findings were depressingly similar to the earlier report. Contrary to repeated District government assertions that the NCHA was not to blame for its troubles, the report termed "failure in executive leadership . . . the most damaging" of the authority's problems. The report attributed part of the NCHA's financial problems to the "spiraling cost of administration, principally administrative staff salaries," up 73.3 percent in five years.

---

[7] Frederic A. Fay, REPORT OF TASK FORCE ON CONDITIONS AND OPERATIONS OF THE NCHA (Washington: Redevelopment Land Agency, April 1970).

[8] HUD Task Force, *Summary Report, HUD-Comprehensive Coordinated Review of the NCHA,* January 18-February 12, 1971, mimeographed.

HUD offered more than criticism, however. This time it pledged $30.5 million in operating and maintenance subsidies over five years, mapped out a financial plan to erase the $3 million annual deficit, and authorized hiring of 92 additional maintenance and security workers to add to the NCHA's staff of 600.

Meanwhile, a resident advisory board had been formally recognized by Mayor Washington in September 1970. In early 1971, with the official encouragement, it began to solicit and screen applicants for the position of NCHA executive director. In May, however, Banks was suddenly and inexplicably chosen by the mayor over the tenant choices.

Banks, who also runs the Model Cities program, has emphasized the need for stable community development. He once said,

> I'm not given to slogans or programs you can't really control. I'm more interested in stabilizing the city. Our job is to provide decent housing and a good environment for all families. We think, however, that environmental factors and the stability of the neighborhood are of high priority.

To improve the NCHA's financial position and to add an element of middle-class "stability," Banks sought to give preference to applicants who needed help least. In 1971 he sought permission from HUD to give preference in public housing to male-headed families over other applicants on the waiting list. He has also asked that the maximum income limits be raised from $8,600 to $9,800 a year for a family of 10 or more.

Meanwhile, at the initiative of the District's progressive Corrections Department, convicts from Lorton refurbished 82 public-housing units between December 1970 and the spring of 1972. Rehabilitation efforts by private contractors have been moving along at a clip of some 40 units a week. Still, there were 723 vacancies as of January 31, 1972, more than existed a year before.

There has also been experimentation with private management for three years at two projects. Under a HUD grant, the private firm working closely with the tenants seems to be succeeding where the NCHA failed.

The fact remains, according to City Council Vice-Chairman Sterling Tucker, that there is little or no "sense of urgency" about providing additional family low-income units in Washington, especially not in the NCHA. Of the 570 new units opened in 1971,

348 were for the elderly. Only 54 units of "for-sale" public housing townhouses are programmed. And the urban renewal program is stalled for lack of relocation housing for the poor who would be displaced.

Promises, Promises

Project Rehab began without fanfare in 1969 to recoup thousands of vacant units in major cities across the country. Washington was invited by HUD to participate, and its application was accepted in February 1971. The application claimed that in March 1970, more than 6,000 vacant units were identified in Washington and also promised that vacant properties would be rehabilitated first to minimize displacement. RLA would be given responsibility for providing relocation counseling and services outside as well as inside urban-renewal areas.

In approving Washington's application, HUD authorized 1,000 units the first year and 1,500 the second, at an estimated construction cost of some $50 million. HUD also required that the city set up a private rehabilitation corporation within six months to operate the program.

A year and a half later, no such corporation had yet been created, although consultants were paid $45,000 to design one. Work had started on one major project, Brentwood Village, and two smaller ones. Tenants at the 738-unit Brentwood Village have received eviction notices, but no authority has assumed responsibility for relocation. A suit has been filed by the tenants to apply the benefits of the 1970 Uniform Relocation Act to Project Rehab. With the court suit in limbo, the eviction notices have not been executed and efforts are being made to find other units at Brentwood Village for the tenants. The ultimate fate of the tenants is uncertain, however.

The District government frequently cites Project Rehab as a major relocation resource for urban renewal, especially for large low- and moderate-income families. But most of the units in the program are occupied, creating a serious additional relocation problem. Project Rehab's bi-weekly report dated February 12, 1972, indicates in effect that only 391 new units would be added to the market by Project Rehab, not 2,500 as initially implied.

And despite promises that Project Rehab would provide badly

needed units for many large families, there is clear evidence that small units are being emphasized. Proposed are 3,231 efficiencies, one-, and two-bedroom units; 304 three-bedroom, 146 four-bedroom, and 24 five-bedroom units.

Sections 235 and 236

The 1968 Housing Act authorized two programs designed to aid low- and moderate-income families. Section 236 provided federal mortgage subsidies to developers of moderate-income apartments for families earning roughly from $6,000 to $12,200. Under the law, up to 40 percent of the units could be further subsidized under the rent-supplement program to aid families too poor for 236 rents but not poor enough for public housing. In practice, HUD has usually limited these units to 20 percent.

Section 235 was aimed at home ownership. Under this program, the government subsidized mortgage interest payments down to 1 percent, so that the homeowner would be assured of paying no more than 25 percent of his income for housing. Home buying, it was widely held, would instill pride of ownership in the poor who would then maintain their properties. Basically, a sound proposition. The problem, however, was that unscrupulous speculators and realtors, with the help of Federal Housing Administration appraisers, took advantage of the program. For years, FHA had refused to insure any inner-city properties; when the turnaround came, controls were missing.

Speculators would buy inner-city properties cheaply, then sell them at inflated prices—approved by FHA—to poor people. Often the properties for which FHA agreed to provide mortgage subsidies were in disrepair. For many of the poor, the American dream of home ownership became a waking nightmare.

A typical case was that of Ana A. Wabash, a night cleaning woman for GSA, a public-housing resident, and mother of four who aspired to home ownership through Section 235. She paid $50 down to buy a home for $14,000. With the interest subsidy, her mortgage payment would be $56. The problem was, according to the antipoverty lawyer who later represented her, the house was "unfit for people to live in." The realtor who sold Mrs. Wabash the home for $14,000 had acquired it for $7,000 a few weeks before.

In the first two years of Section 235, 937 FHA-insured mortgages totaling $15 million were approved in Washington. The House Banking and Currency Committee investigated Section 235 operations in 10 cities. A report issued in January 1971 concluded:

> The houses in almost every instance had numerous housing violations, many serious enough that the city could have required the owner to make repairs that would have cost hundreds of dollars. These violations, many of which obviously existed at the time of the purchase, include leaking roofs, obstructed and leaking plumbing, illegal electrical wiring and inadequate outlets, rooms classified as bedrooms which failed to meet the minimum requirement for sleeping one person, and inefficient and inoperative heating facilities.

In the wake of these disclosures, Romney suspended purchases of existing houses under Section 235 in February 1971. Several months later, the program was reinstated. In the District, a new policy was instituted in August 1971, requiring that all FHA- and Veterans Administration-insured houses costing under $35,000 pass city inspection before they are sold.

The controversy over Section 236 centers around the concentrated location rather than the quality of the projects. In its February 1971 study the Washington Center for Metropolitan Studies concluded, "HUD has sponsored and encouraged the perpetuation of racial and economic segregation by its continued practice of funding these projects." [9]

Reacting to such criticism and to federal court decisions, HUD on February 7, 1972, put into effect site selection criteria aimed at avoiding concentrations. If strictly followed, they will result in very little Section 236 housing being built anywhere. To attain the necessary "adequate" rating on location, projects cannot be situated in integrated neighborhoods, in suburban areas that already have some projects, or in suburban areas that don't have projects but at the same time aren't near jobs or transportation. As for the inner city, an overriding housing need that can't be met in the outer city can qualify a project there, but not if "the only reason the need cannot otherwise feasibly be met is that discrimination on the basis of race, color or national origin renders sites outside areas of minority concentration unavailable." A HUD "clarifica-

---

[9] Betty Adams, FEDERALLY ASSISTED LOW AND MODERATE COST HOUSING IN METROPOLITAN WASHINGTON (Washington: Washington Center for Metropolitan Studies, February 1971).

tion" last June made it possible for projects in renewal and Model Cities areas to receive the necessary "adequate" rating on location, which helps but does not insure their funding.

The regional "fair share" plan adopted by Washington's Council of Governments in January may help to qualify inner-city projects by providing alternative housing outside areas of racial concentration. But the plan is voluntary and far from self-fulfilling.

The impression that HUD was seeking to terminate Section 236 projects was reinforced two weeks after the guidelines were issued. A federal audit of Section 236 programs in 20 cities, including Washington, disclosed that exorbitant fees were driving up the costs of projects far beyond what they would cost in the private market. This meant that HUD was paying substantially more in mortgage subsidies to keep the rents at moderate-income levels. It also meant that tenants, and the taxpayers, were getting less value for the federal dollars invested. The dollars were going instead to high-priced architects and consultants, unnecessary insurance premiums, and unwarranted bonuses to developers.

"For the most part," the HUD report stated, "eligible tenants were provided housing of good quality." Nonetheless, across the country, Section 236 projects were being foreclosed and winding up in HUD hands at an alarming rate. The cycle of earlier FHA programs was being repeated. While no Section 236 projects in the District have defaulted, HUD owns, through foreclosure, 2,650 units in Washington, most of them in Southeast, the legacy of earlier FHA-insured projects that failed.

IS THE WHOLE THING WORTH IT?

> "The American Experience has proved that slum clearance and urban redevelopment have, if anything, accelerated the decline of the cities."
> —*Professor James Marston Fitch, Columbia University School of Architecture*

Federal largesse has been generously bestowed upon the District of Columubia's urban-renewal programs. Since 1949, government grants totaling $190.5 million have been made available. More than $300 million more has been spent in private monies for redevelopment. In the pursuit of renewal, 7,379 families have had to be relocated, and 1,206 businesses have been displaced. Of these businesses, 507 simply folded and 103 relocated outside the District. Given the investment of public funds and the upheaval caused in thousands of human lives, has it been worth it?

Not yet. So far, urban renewal has promised far more than it has delivered. Clearly, the prime beneficiaries of renewal have been the land speculators and legitimate property owners who sold to RLA, often at inflated prices far in excess of the assessed market value. Other beneficiaries are contractors and construction workers, including recently some blacks; mortgage bankers; lawyers; architects; and consultants.

Urban renewal has often resulted in the replacement of low-cost housing with high-cost housing, in the replacement of small, family-owned businesses with large chain stores. Too often urban renewal has meant a meat cleaver instead of a paring knife. And where the paring knife was used, as in the Neighborhood Development Program, the results have been equally disappointing. In traditional urban renewal, a whole neighborhood is razed and replaced, but at least, on paper, the residents get relocation benefits. In NDP, residents displaced by private action get no such benefits. And the uncertainty of which block will be included next gives landlords, in view of many critics of urban renewal, an additional excuse to abdicate responsibility for maintenance. Therefore, NDP accelerates deterioration of the neighborhoods it is supposed to renew.

Urban renewal, the RLA contends, has greatly improved the District's tax base. The increase has come at great cost to the taxpayers. For example, 2.33 acres in Shaw were bought by RLA for $1.5 million and are being sold to redevelopers for $56,700. The sites will contain 54 townhouses for public-housing families that the sponsors say will cost $24,125 each to build. But that figure is misleading. Add an estimated $100,000 more in site improvements for the units, $1.3 million for construction, and an estimated $1.2 million more in interest subsidies over the life of the mortgage. The total for 54 houses is $4.1 million, some $76,000 per unit. New upper-income townhouses in redeveloped Southwest and on Capitol Hill sell for $50,000.

Why not eliminate the rakeoffs and give direct cash grants to sponsors of low-income housing? That way what is built can be rented at rates the poor can afford and the taxpayer will have gotten his money's worth.

Urban renewal has traditionally been geared toward production, with environmental and service considerations getting low priority. Put another way, urban renewal has built housing but not communities. Even the residents of affluent Southwest complain that their area is sterile and lacks that intangible sense of "community." And residents of Northwest One complain that renewal has destroyed rather than rebuilt their community.

In our present enlightened state, everyone acknowledges these shortcomings. But as Sterling Tucker, the outspoken vice chairman of the D. C. city council, has said, "There's an awful lot to be embarrassed about, but no one seems too embarrassed. No one seems to have responsibility, and authority seems to be confused."

No one seems capable of shaking the system, in part, perhaps, because the planning and development process is fragmented and frought with overlap and duplication by different agencies often working against instead of with each other. The District desparately needs a central planning agency, or a superagency for planning and renewal, so that the total needs and resources of the city can be addressed. As it stands now, each urban-renewal area is planned in a vacuum. But there is no leadership in this schizophrenic federal city of divided jurisdictions and no elected local government.

With or without home rule in the District, it is now clear that "citizen participation" in redevelopment is not the panacea that many thought it three and four years ago. Clearly, citizen groups in the inner city may reflect political forces and pressures as much as government agencies.

The problems of the District will never be solved inside the city itself. There must be regional solutions to the problems that suburbanites are beginning to discover do not respect artificial boundaries. To this end, the District needs an urban-development corporation with metropolitan jurisdictions and powers, when necessary, to override local zoning ordinances and building codes. Delegate Fauntroy has proposed an urban-development corporation, but it is limited to the city. Such a corporation will not provide any long-range solutions.

In a metropolitan context, the housing programs should work better. With truly scattered sites, small-scale projects, and leased units in good buildings, low-income housing should blend into neighborhoods rather than intrude into them. There must be an aggressive pursuit of such programs, an aggressive pursuit which so far has been lacking.

The basic problems, however, are not specific programs, government red tape, or even lack of leadership. Such things are but symptoms. The problems are rooted deeply in the American psyche and in the American racism and inequitable distribution of wealth. As long as this country stresses profits over people, rich over poor, and white over black, the federal housing and renewal programs are doomed to failure.

RLA's Melvin Mister said in a speech to a group of housing and renewal officials on January 8, 1970,

> As the decade starts, I am optimistic that our new renewal approaches will be invaluable in meeting the challenges which face all of us involved in the exhilerating, albeit, at times very frustrating tasks, of rebuilding the Nation's Capital.

The record of the past and present, however, is clearly not one to inspire confidence in the future.

Chapter Ten

THE PAYOFF OF THE FEDERAL
SOCIAL DOLLAR

by Sar A. Levitan

A MATTER OF PERSPECTIVE

An assessment of federal social programs is largely a matter of perspective and values. From the bird's-eye view, the most salient feature is the increasing scale and cost of these efforts. The federal social dollar sustains a large and increasing portion of local budgets, and without it most large cities and many other units of government would be bankrupt or would be required to retrench with unpleasant consequences.

Federal aid is provided through a number of relatively well-defined categorical programs, directed to specifically perceived

259

needs and administered with various degrees of control to ensure that funds are spent in accordance with federal law. Though they cover a vast array of activities, the federally supported social programs and the allocations of funds among them are normally the product of legislative compromise, vested group pressures, and limited knowledge of performance. The assistance is addressed to the diverse problems faced by the citizenry in an increasingly complex society.

From the worm's-eye view, the picture is much more confusing. What appears as a fairly comprehensive and comprehensible system from above is often a confusing and incomplete maze from below. Each social program and each of its component parts can provide funds, but each requires a response to specific rules and regulations which are rarely coordinated with other programs. Dollars are passed down to the governors in some cases, to mayors or county officials in others, and to nonprofit or quasi-governmental groups at either the state or local level, or else funds are distributed directly to individuals. The federal spigots often turn off as quickly as they turn on, and there is sometimes little correlation between local needs and the availability of funds. What appears as a massive commitment of resources in the aggregate often ends up a small dribble when it finally comes down the pipeline to be applied to specific tasks; federal aid is rarely adequate to meet its intended goals.

There are also varying perspectives on the effectiveness of these social programs. Opponents have no shortage of horror stories: broken federal promises, strangling red tape, misdirected resources, indecision, and vacillation. Programs rarely achieve their grandiloquent aims, sometimes failing to even progress towards their presumed goals, and in a few cases their impact may even be counterproductive. There is little documented proof that most federal social expenditures have had a meaningful impact on human welfare, and much to indicate that the money could have been better spent in different ways. For the person who wants to find fault, there is no shortage of examples; and for those who are ideologically opposed to the further expansion of federal aid, there is no shortage of justifications.

On the other hand, a proponent might legitimately dismiss many of the charges leveled against the social programs and focus on the improvements they provide. Recognizing that many of these efforts are experimental and that resources have been extremely limited, the advocate of social programs resists attempts to measure performance against formal objectives that reflect rhetoric more than realistic goals. Focus on immediate problems often ignores progress and improvement. And even where problems exist, much good may still be accomplished which would not otherwise occur. While the federal presence might be deplored for its inflexibility or niggardliness, it might also be recognized as the only source of resources to help people or communities in trouble or to help in the realization of legitimate aspirations. Stressing the good that has been accomplished, and that much remains to be done, arguments for further expansion of federal aid appear persuasive.

It would be comforting to conclude that the federal social dollars are uniformly worthwhile, that they supplement local resources and provide the wherewithal to accomplish new and important goals. But the truth is not this simple, and it would be equally misleading to conclude that the federal social dollars have created chaos at the local level, have had little impact on the problems to which they are directed, and have demonstrated the intractability of people, problems, and institutions. The only way to sum up the experience with federal social programs is to recognize the variability which exists in such programs and the equivocality of the lessons which they provide.

A number of questions were posed at the outset, and these provide one way of looking at the experience with the federal social programs:

First, is the experience in the federal government's own backyard applicable to other large cities?

Second, how has the Great Society thrust towards an increased federal presence at the local level been altered under the Nixon Administration?

Third, is there a generally preferred mechanism for distributing federal aid?

Fourth, what are the contributions of the social programs to the solving of particular local problems?

Fifth, is the further expansion of federal social programs worthwhile?

There are no straightforward answers to such wide-ranging queries. Each reader can find support for his or her preconceptions. Yet some general, if tentative, lessons do emerge.

"IF YOU'VE SEEN ONE CENTRAL CITY, YOU'VE SEEN THEM ALL"

In examining the impact of the federal social dollar, it must be recognized that large cities differ in the extent of their problems, in how effectively they are dealt with by governmental social agencies, the magnitude of the assistance they receive, and the manner in which all these factors interact.

There is no doubt that the atypical governmental structure in the District of Columbia affects the experience with grants-in-aid, but the dependence of the city officialdom upon Congress can be exaggerated. As in other cities, the District officials, even if they are not elected, must be responsive to the wishes and views of the citizenry. If the press or community organizations make an issue of some aspect of grant-in-aid performance, the city government will react to protect its position and to preserve its grant-in-aid. For instance, the case of renewal in the District is often cited as an example of governmental insensitivity. Actually, policy has tacked quickly from the federal bulldozer approach in Southwest, to the attempted integration of Northwest One, to the slow community-control approach in Shaw. The problem is not insensitivity, as some allege, but the lack of awareness of the most effective approach or the consequences of certain courses of action and the need to try different approaches to diverse situations.

As for the District's lack of control over the allocation of funds, there is no doubt that it distorts the impact of grants-in-aid, but probably to a limited degree. Though the congressional appropriation subcommittees are not oblivious to funds that accrue to the District from various grants, the allocation of funds from these grants is not part of the budget approval process, and they come from different spigots as contrasted with the yearly direct federal contribution to the city's budget. The Congress frequently serves as a useful scapegoat, and its members are blamed for the inadequacy of aid to selected groups, much as state legislators are frequently charged by mayors for being insensitive to urban problems. It has been alleged that the representation on the committees has served to hold down welfare standards, but this is difficult to prove since the District's Aid-to-Families-With-Dependent-Children payment is between Maryland's and Virginia's, the two neighboring states.

The special status of the District as a state as well as a city, and as a "dependent" of the federal government, does make its experience atypical in at least one case, higher education. The public institutions in Washington are the creation of Congress and depend upon Congress in the same way that the state universities depend on their legislatures for funding. The analogy between Congress and state legislatures is not very realistic in this context, since congressmen have no political stake in the future of Washington. There are, however, some lessons which can be learned from the experience of private universities in Washington with research monies and student support funds.

Some of the other programs are also distorted a little by the District's status. For instance, the employment service in the city is a federal agency rather than an independent local body, and there is a regional manpower administration overseeing only the city's programs. While these arrangements may affect some specific matters, they generally do not alter participation in the grants. Washington has the same multiplicity of manpower programs as most other larger cities, and much the same problems.

The choice of the District as a demonstration site is frequently more rhetoric than reality. Any time a program is announced in the city, it is usually described as a "showcase" for the nation. As an example, President Nixon publicized the fact that massive renewal efforts would begin immediately in the areas burned out by the riots of 1968, but almost nothing had been accomplished four years later. Given the footdragging in the initiation of work incentives under welfare, and the lack of innovation in the use of Elementary and Secondary Education Act funds, it would be a mistake to picture the city as the vanguard of experimentation with social programs.

The special status of D.C. as the nation's capital cannot be ignored, though it affects performance under grants-in-aid only to a limited degree. The city gets more money because of its special status; it may be somewhat more conscious of legislative and administrative mandates; and local politics are less important than in some other cities. However, the problems with which it deals, the institutions which are chiefly involved, and the categorical grant programs which are utilized are basically the same. The litany of woes which underlies the District's social programs is a part of urban life, and there is no large city which does not have severe problems of poverty, malnutrition, inadequate housing, deteriorating schools, and crime. Likewise, the institutions are largely the same from city to city. Welfare agencies, school administrators, business organizations, community groups, the press, and government functionaries are the major actors in these matters. And federal assistance for social programs is a national rather than a local creation. Funding and allocation procedures, guidelines, and monitoring decisions are all made at the national level and apply to all cities alike. The District's experience with grants-in-aid is relevant, therefore, for other cities. To paraphrase a noted political figure: "if you've seen one central city, you've seen them all."

THE IMPORTANCE OF BIG BROTHER

To the degree that Washington is a typical case, the expansion and proliferation of federal social programs is staggering. The story is the same in most areas of social policy. In 1960, 2,000 children received free lunches in the District; in 1971, the number was 44,000. At the end of 1965, 3,500 persons were receiving food stamps, compared with more than 100,000 in 1972. The federally funded Federal City College and Washington Technical Institute, which together now serve some 10,000 students, were opened in 1968. The number of welfare recipients rose from 25,000 in 1966 to over 100,000 in 1972. Eleven separate manpower programs were established in the last decade. Housing programs grew in scale and number with the addition of private ownership and rent-subsidy approaches.

This growth and proliferation has had profound effects. The thrust towards new governmental responsibility has largely been provided by federal programs. Left to their own devices, most large cities, such as Washington, can barely scrape up enough funds to provide their traditional services. The federal aid enables D.C. and other cities to undertake new functions, including efforts to improve the employment prospects of the unskilled and unemployed, to deliver health services to low-income families, to provide food subsidies to those unable to afford an adequate diet, to build or restore homes for the ill-housed, to open opportunities for a higher education for those unable to afford enrollment in private colleges, and to encourage community organization. Once these responsibilities are assumed, the impetus for further expansion is self-generating. Experimental measures give rise to awareness of unfulfilled aspirations that in turn create pressure for the expansion of any particular service to all those in need. Then, a substantial clientele is established which can lobby for improved benefits. This "foot-in-the-door" process is exhibited over and over again in all the areas of social programs; once the first step is made, there is no retreat.

Self-generated demands for expanded and more costly services have put pressure on local governments. While grant-in-aid programs have expanded dramatically, local expenditures also have had to grow rapidly. In 1964, the District's revenues were roughly $225 million, or more than three fourths of all expenditures, while grants-in-aid were $25 million, or less than 10 percent. By 1972, the grants-in-aid had risen to $210 million, roughly a fifth of the budget. Though accounting for only three fifths of the budget, local revenues had nearly trebled, nevertheless, to $630 million. This is probably typical of the experience of other cities: While the proportion of the budget subsidized by federal funds has risen, federal funding has generated increasing burdens for the cities.

Local revenue sources are inelastic compared with federal revenue sources, and the rising burden of social programs has strained the resources of most localities as it has those of the District. Added reliance on "soaking the rich" is no solution because the rising progressive personal income tax creates an additional incentive to escape the city. Therefore, the share of budget growth financed by grants-in-aid is likely to continue in the foreseeable future. These subsidies increasingly help determine the priorities of city programs. Where federal programs are merely frosting, the existence of nationally established and enforced guidelines is not important; but when such programs account for a major share of the budget, they deeply affect the government and the type of services the city offers to its residents. These developments accentuate the issue of whether centralized decision making can effectively cope with local problems.

All these developments are reflected in the recent history of grants-in-aid in the District. The Nixon Administration came into office promising decentralization of decision-making authority. But the tide of federal grants loosed by the Great Society programs continued unabated and even accelerated. Welfare rolls, for instance, doubled between 1970 and 1972 despite the President's announced efforts to cut back relief rolls through "workfare" programs. In health, food, basic education, manpower, and housing, federal subsidy dollars expanded even faster than they had in the past. This merely illustrates the force of unfilled needs and vested interest groups created by the Great Society social legislation. It is apparently impossible to backtrack on social commitments, and it is even difficult to tighten the reins.

Local control over grants-in-aid also has become an issue more and more in recent years. There has been an effort to reorganize the programs and decentralize controls. The Emergency Employment Act, which provided $3.6 million to the District in fiscal 1972 for the hiring of unemployed workers in the public sector, left a relatively great deal of control in the city's hands. The housing interest-subsidy programs were an attempt to substitute private-industry involvement for the public-housing approach. The experiment with contract health services was an effort to withdraw aid from the hands of the health establishments so that each person would receive the care best suited to his or her needs. Despite these steps, however, the trend towards further centralization was hardly abated. Welfare, the major growth area, is increasingly federally controlled, as are most of the manpower programs. To correct deficiencies in the Elementary and Secondary Education Act, the feds have also begun to exercise greater oversight, as they also have done in the food program. Despite the rhetoric of decentralization, the fact remains that he who pays the piper calls the tune. As grants-in-aid programs continue to expand, government at the local level will become more and more a response to federal initiatives.

IS THE GRANT-IN-AID APPROACH WORKABLE?

The congressional mills continue to churn out new social programs, and the grants-in-aid share of the local budget is continuing to increase. It is vital, therefore, to determine whether the grants-in-aid approach is workable or whether some form of revenue sharing would be more effective. Recent experience in the District and elsewhere strongly indicates that decentralization is a difficult process to effect administratively, and a massive legislative restructuring is needed to shift substantially the focus of decision making.

The alleged weaknesses of centralized programs include unnecessary red tape and both gaps and overlaps in services at the local level because of the lack of coordination of related efforts and the failure to adapt to local needs and institutions. On the other hand, the centralized approach offers some degree of federal control over local actions where these may be contrary to national priorities; it permits comparison of different approaches and the more rapid replication of those which prove successful; and it ensures the maximum utilization of limited expertise.

The reality from the worm's-eye view, however, is not as neat as these arguments would suggest. For instance, arguments have been made for comprehensive reform of the manpower effort because of the complexity of the system which has evolved over the last decade and the duplication and waste this involves. Yet, in Washington there appears to be little overlap, as each program has carved out a particular clientele and approach. Likewise, several federally funded community organizations exist, but each is controlled by a different segment of the resident community.

If the era of "maximum feasible participation" has taught anything, it is that no single person or group speaks for all the interest groups in the central city. A pluralistic society requires diverse institutions. There is, for example, a clear need for multiplicity of housing programs to reach different clienteles; to provide different kinds of subsidy; and to provide for rehabilitation, rental construction, leasing, or home ownership. And different groups may be best suited to furnish the different approaches.

The programs to provide for these varied needs may be complex, but they are not incomprehensible, and the bureaucrats who must operate the programs quickly learn the ins and outs. The multiplicity of programs permits a variety of groups to get a piece of the action and to make their contributions to the total effort rather than fight over their share of a single pie.

Nonetheless, lack of coordination frequently results in poor services and frustrations for prospective clients. It would be a full-time job for a public assistance recipient to take advantage of all the available welfare subsidies and services. In part, this is due to the fact that the money comes through a number of separate spigots, and there is little incentive to coordinate. But this is not the only reason for problems. In any complex social system, whether centralized or decentralized, there will be coordination problems. These may serve functional purposes, such a differentiating among clienteles. And even under the grant-in-aid approach, it is possible to solve many of the problems at the local level merely by better organization. In Washington many of the problems of coordinating food stamps and welfare arose because the city did not adequately staff and organize the food-stamp program, not because there were two separate categorical programs. Additionally, it is possible to ensure greater coordination at the national level by reducing the number of categorical programs or funding coordinating agencies; this does not necessarily involve greater decentralization.

The degree of federal control and monitoring varies markedly from program to program. Under the Elementary and Secondary Education Act, the District school bureaucracies expended the federal grants pretty much as they saw fit, and it was only after several years of operations that there was any attempt to insure accountability. It is surprising to find that federal bureaucrats exercised so little control, even though they could follow the course of District programs by a site visit or newspaper accounts; the freedom of action given to other cities can only be guessed.

It is also important to realize that fewer and fewer cities can ignore the needs of the recipients of federal social programs. When welfare recipients or the poor were a powerless minority, mayors could afford cavalierly to subvert federal intents; now, they have little reason or latitude to do this on a large scale, since the disadvantaged are becoming a major force in the largest cities.

As a blanket policy, then, it is difficult to argue for or against any large-scale restructuring of the grant-in-aid approach. Despite its shortcomings, the present system is not unworkable and can be improved. Revenue sharing has some advantages on a limited basis, especially to provide glue money for participation in diverse grant-in-aid programs. It is not likely, however, to substantially alter the current thrust in intergovernmental relations towards an increased federal presence.

SOLVING SOCIAL PROBLEMS

The Great Society social efforts have been continued by the Nixon Administration, and these sustained efforts have made substantive contributions to life in the District. Without federal grants-in-aid, Washington and other cities would likely have no manpower programs to help those who have difficulty in competing in the labor market; their housing and urban renewal efforts would be almost nil; feeding the hungry would be left, as in the past, to private welfare organizations lacking adequate resources; providing income support to so many of the poor would not be feasible; low-income individuals would have to depend on their limited resources in the medical marketplace; institutions of higher education would be in financial straits and many would go out of business; and the capacity of city schools to provide even the current low quality of education would be threatened.

Whatever the faults of these social programs, there can be no doubt that they help individuals and contribute toward the alleviation of local problems. In the District, most of the 7,000 students at the Federal City College and the 3,000 at Washington Technical Institute would not have been able to pursue post-secondary education without federal aid, and there is doubt whether most private universities could continue without assistance. The 100,000 persons on food stamps are undoubtedly eating better because of this assistance, and the growth in the number of recipients attests that the clients themselves value this aid. It is difficult to denigrate the fact that the 44,000 youths who receive free lunches get at least one balanced meal a day. The 125,000 patients annually who receive $49 million in Medicaid benefits are obviously better off than if they were left to their own resources to obtain medical help. The 12,000 youths who are hired in the summer under the Neighborhood Youth Corps owe their jobs to federal largesse, and the 14,000 other trainees in federal programs may benefit from otherwise unavailable manpower services. As the city moves toward greater self-determination, many of the indigenous leaders are nurtured in federally funded community organizations, and community participation is now taken for granted in almost all programs. Though there is litttle evidence that public schools have improved their performance with federal aid, they would be in bad shape if they had to give up the teachers, equipment, and instructional materials financed with federal dollars. Even the much maligned housing programs do some good; there are nearly 11,000 households living in public housing at less than market costs, and whatever the problems of the program, 5,000 families are on the waiting list, believing that they can improve their position by getting into these units.

The fact that federal funds are helping to provide for basic needs, such as food, shelter, health care, education, and community organization, does not mean that the grant-in-aid programs have solved any social problems. On the other hand, their failure to accomplish any substantial solutions does not deny that they are making a positive contribution to human welfare. In seeking once-and-for-all, comprehensive solutions, critics are often likely to forget the good that is being done.

There is not a single social program that has adequate resources to meet all the needs to which it is addressed. Even a program which is highly effective in meeting human needs can be criticized for reaching only a small proportion of potential beneficiaries. In Washington, the welfare, food, and higher education programs are criticized most for being inadequate in scale and scope, not for being ineffective. Public education and health can be criticized for not doing enough with the resources which are provided, but this does not deny that there is some worth in what is being accomplished. Other programs, such as urban renewal, are criticized because, in achieving their purposes, they have had undesired and unexpected side effects; however, this does not mean that on balance the tradeoff has not been worthwhile. Overall, any program can be criticized for failure to follow legislative goals to the letter or else for failing to adapt to local conditions, for serving some groups rather than others with limited funds, for operating without complete effectiveness, for assisting only a portion of those in need, or for costing too much. And every program is usually criticized on at least one of these grounds.

Given the limited resources which plague all efforts, the legitimate question should not be whether they solve identified social problems but whether they contribute to a solution. In all cases the answer is unequivocally positive, though in some the contribution is small per dollar of resources committed, while in others it is large.

WHAT IS THE VALUE OF HUMAN WELFARE?

While critics of social welfare programs admit, when pressed, that such programs do much good, they may still argue against further expansion on the ground of "cost-effectiveness"— *i.e.,* that the payoff in terms of improved welfare per dollar of expenditures is not high enough to justify any greater expense. This concept is vague since it is impossible to measure units of welfare or their cost, but more basically because there is no standard against which to compare the payoff.

For instance, it has been one of the fundamental tenets of the Great Society programs that efforts should be made to measure and improve program performance. In most areas, policymakers have shifted back and forth trying to get the furthest distance on limited resources. In fact, one of the criticisms of many of these programs, especially housing and manpower programs, is that they have been too quick to abandon ongoing efforts in favor of untried alternatives promising higher payoffs. In some other areas, such as welfare, reforms which will improve performance may be overdue. But to assert that there are cost-effective alternatives to present social programs does not argue against expansion. If such alternatives exist, they can be and probably are being tried.

It may also be true that the payoff in some areas of social policy is higher than in others. Scarce resources obviously should be allocated where they will do the most good. Those who criticize the Great Society programs as a whole because of the lack of cost-effectiveness have failed to offer comparably scaled programs and strategies which will have a better payoff. On the contrary, they generally criticize any further tinkering with new approaches or efforts at improvement as a hopeless waste of time. In other words, they are comparing the programs with an ideal rather than a reality.

To one camp of critics, drawn largely from the discouraged engineers of the Great Society, the inability to *solve* social problems, *i.e.,* the lack of total effectiveness, is the essential fault. Some have attacked the welfare, food-stamp, housing-subsidy, medical-aid, and education-assistance programs as failures because they have not eliminated all manifestations of poverty. Certainly, if every poor person's income were raised substantially above the poverty threshold, there would be no need for the various programs; and this may be the only really effective way of solving many problems. But, because it would also be many times more costly than present efforts, there is no assurance of increased cost-effectiveness. Card-carrying liberal critics tend to recognize that a basic restructuring of society is needed if the problems are to be solved. Disillusioned with the slow progress made by existing programs, they criticize the social programs for not doing enough according to a "cost-effectiveness" standard that assumes ultimate effectiveness through unlimited costs.

Other critics of the Great Society programs, usually those identi-fied as traditional conservatives, are more concerned with the pro-grams' cost relative to doing nothing rather than their effectiveness relative to some larger goal. If dollars are not spent on social pro-grams, they can alternately be spent on defense, roads, environ-mental control, or consumer goods. It is difficult to argue that these are cost-effective ways of dealing with the social problems addressed by social programs, since there is some effect at no cost. Housing and nutrition standards improve with economic growth, and the number of poor falls with rising incomes; in other words, there is a "trickle down" effect. But these long-run trends are of little help to those presently in need, and they will occur with or without social expenditures. If it is admitted, as it must be, that the Great Society programs do *some* net good, then those who would rather trust prevailing social and economic forces are simply unwilling to pay the going price for an incremental improvement in human welfare. This should not be disguised by the claim that social programs do not improve human welfare.

Unfortunately, those disillusioned with the success of social pro-grams in achieving more ambitious goals are now joining ideo-logical ranks with those who are dissatisfied because they consider the current goals and the costs of achieving them too high. It is paradoxical that those who would favor a much greater share of the nation's wealth in the hands of society's less fortunate members have joined with those resisting any change in the current balance. To date, this "unholy" alliance has not checked the growth of social welfare programs. If this occurs, however, it would simply be an admission that we are unwilling to pay the price of improving social welfare, and that our society falls short of aspiring to greatness.

ABBREVIATIONS

The saga of federal grants-in-aid necessarily makes frequent reference to a plethora of agencies, organizations, and programs typically boiled down to an alphabet soup of abbreviations and acronyms. Those below are referred to in this volume and each is also indexed under its full name.

ADA, Alley Dwelling Authority
AFDC, Aid to Families With Dependent Children
ARA, Area Redevelopment Act

BASYAP, Business Affected Severely by Yearly Action Plans, Inc.

CAA, community action agency
CAP, Community Action Program
CEP, Concentrated Employment Program
CIC, Near Northeast Community Involvement Center
CW-S, College Work-Study

DCTC, D.C. Teachers College

EOG, Educational Opportunity Grants
ESEA, Elementary and Secondary Education Act

FAP, Family Assistance Plan
FCC, Federal City College
FHA, U.S. Federal Housing Administration

GAO, U.S. General Accounting Office
GHA, Group Health Association
GSA, U.S. General Services Administration
GSL, Guaranteed Student Loans

HEW, U.S. Department of Health, Education, and Welfare
HMO, health maintenance organization
HUD, U.S. Department of Housing and Urban Development

JOBS, Job Opportunities in the Business Sector

LEAA, U.S. Law Enforcement Assistance Administration

MDTA, Manpower Development and Training Act
MICCO, Model Inner City Community Organization

NAB, National Alliance of Businessmen
NCHA, National Capital Housing Authority
NDC, neighborhood development center
NDEA, National Defense Education Act
NDP, Neighborhood Development Program
NDSL, National Defense Student Loans
NYC, Neighborhood Youth Corps

OEO, U.S. Office of Economic Opportunity
OIC, Opportunities Industrialization Center

PAC, project area committee
PEP, Public Employment Program
PIC, Peoples Involvement Corporation
PSC, Public Service Careers

RLA, D.C. Redevelopment Land Agency

UPO, United Planning Organization

WIN, Work Incentive program
WMATA, Washington Metropolitan Area Transit Authority
WTI, Washington Technical Institute

NAME INDEX

A

Adams, Betty, 254
Alexis, Carlton, 189
Aubin, Henry, 181-183, 187

B

Banks, James G., 207, 224, 248-249, 251
Barry, Marion, 107, 108, 117
Binswanger, Robert B., 46, 48, 49
Bode, Barbara, 170
Bouchard, André, 222
Branton, Wiley, 207
Brooke, Edward W., 25, 249
Brooks, Mildred, 150, 161
Brown, Clara, 234
Bundy, McGeorge, 47
Burns, Thomas J., 45
Bush, Norman, 161
Butts, James, 206

C

Califano, Joseph, 139
Canevello, Victor, 171
Chase, Francis S., 54
Chisholm, Terry C., 241
Clark, Evelyn M., 185
Cohen, Wilbur J., 192
Collins, T. Byron, S.J., 74, 75
Cooper, Mildred, 44
Copen, Melvin, 162, 163
Cornely, Paul B., 183
Corning, Hobart, 166-167
Cox, Tricia Nixon, 172

D

Dabney, Velvin, 215
Daniels, Watha, 223
Davis, Benjamin O., 25
Davis, Mrs. John F., 167
Dennard, Cleveland, 63
Drake, James, 148, 163

Duncan, John, 202
DuPont, Robert L., 193, 195

E

Earl, Louise, 155
Edstrom, Eve, 166

F

Fantini, Mario, 47
Fauntroy, Walter E., 221-223, 239, 257
Fay, Frederic A., 250
Feinberg, Lawrence, 25
Fitch, James Marston, 255
Flax, Michael J., 18, 19

G

Gardner, John, 192
Gorman, Mike, 192
Grant, Murray, 184
Green, Constance McLaughlin, 201

H

Hailes, Edward A., 96
Hansen, Carl F., 26, 37
Hardin, Clifford, 160
Harris, Marjorie, 156
Henley, Benjamin, 36, 37
Hobson, Julius, 26, 207
Hollis, Frank 210
Howard, Charles, 213
Huff, Lillian, 170

J

James, Betty, 206
Javits, Jacob, 154, 157
Josephson, Diana, 224

K

Kelley, Isabelle, 158
Kennedy, Edward M., 156, 185
Kennedy, Robert F., 152
King, Martin Luther, Jr., 14, 22, 237

275

TOPICAL INDEX

277